DEPT. H

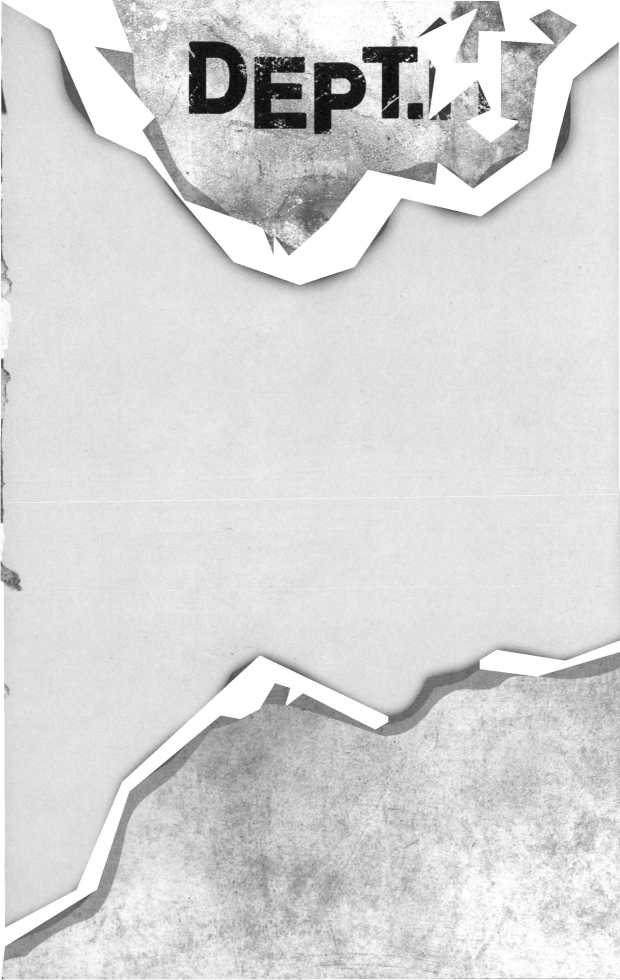

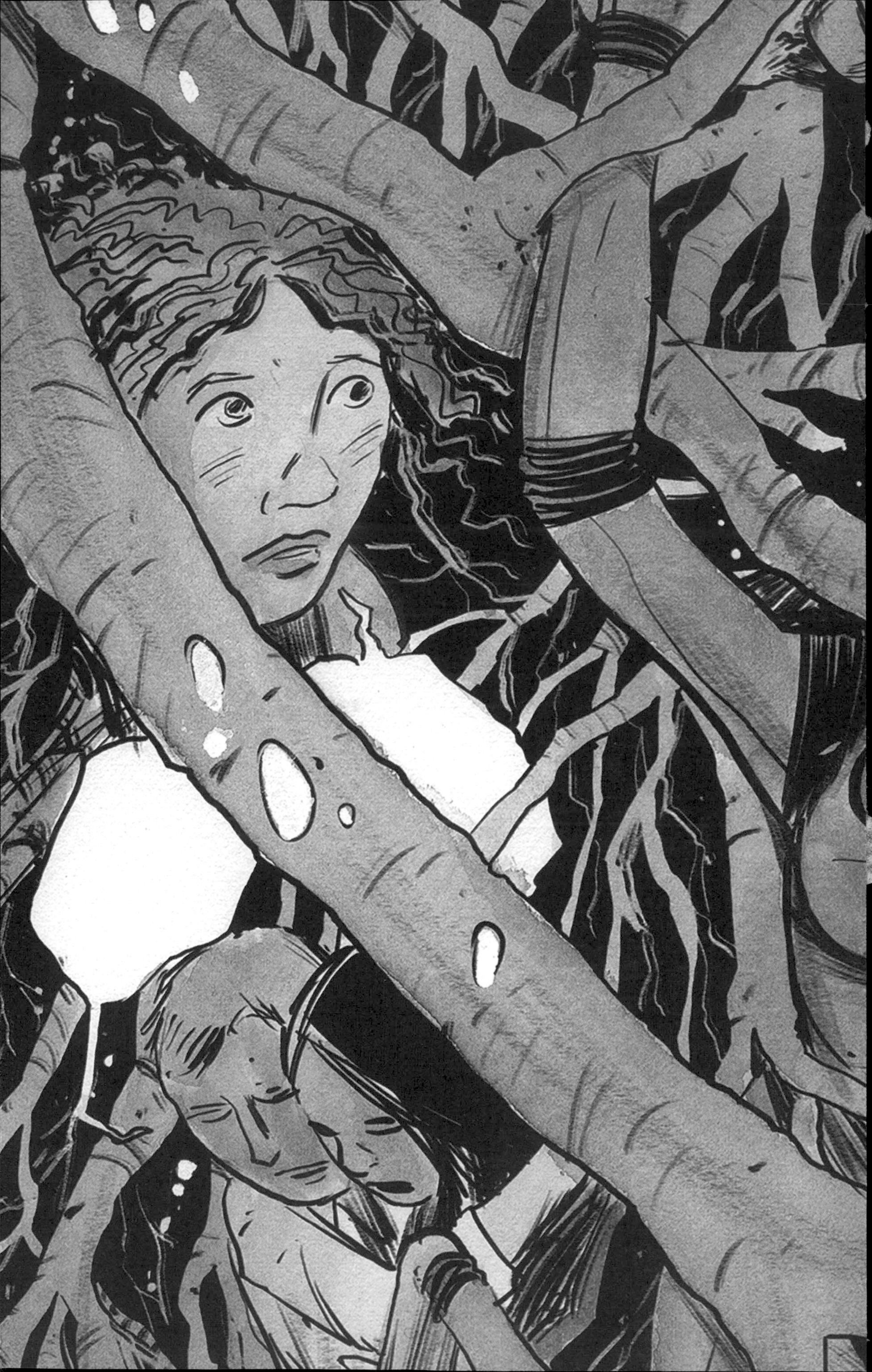

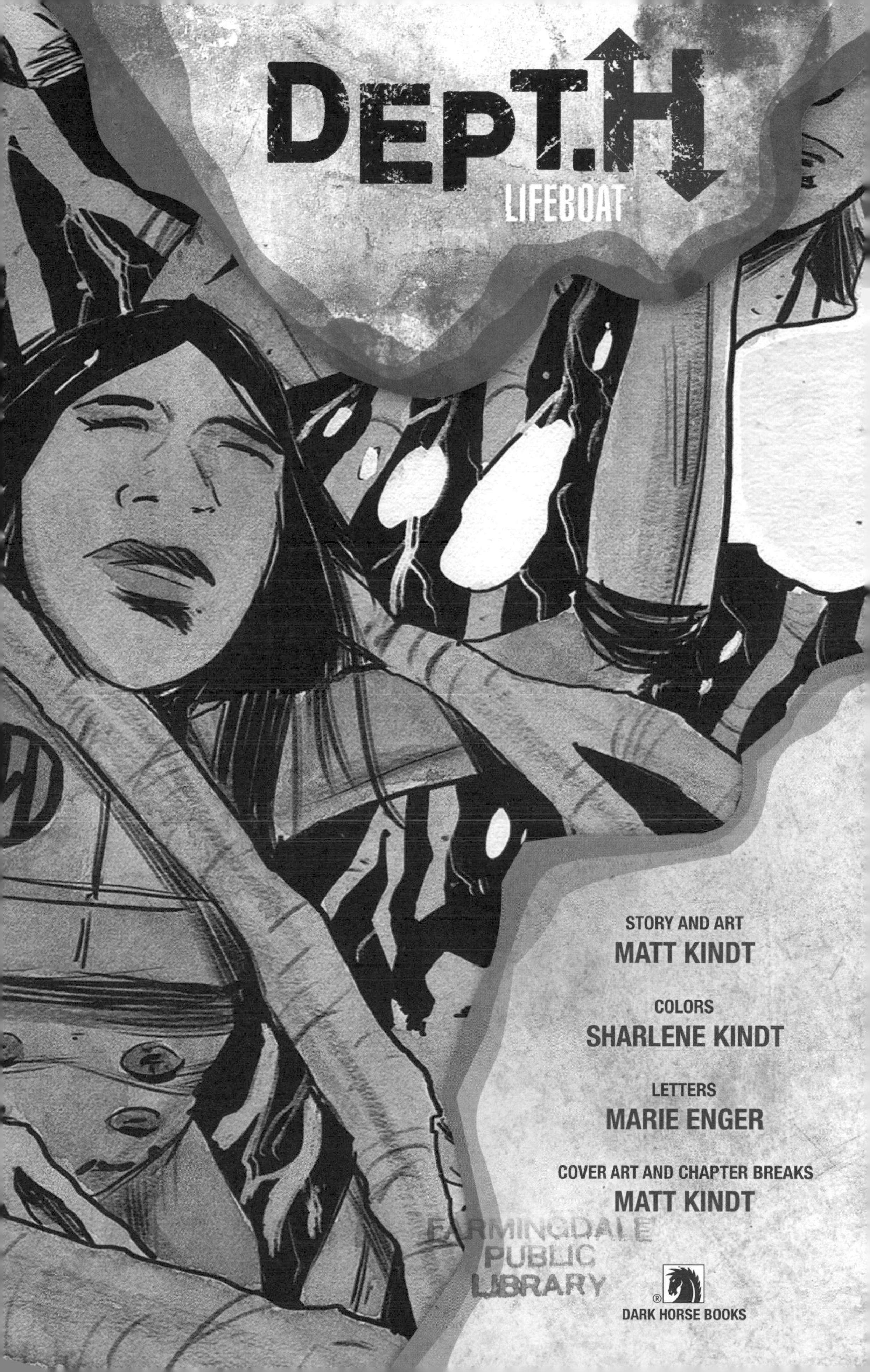

DEPT.H

LIFEBOAT

STORY AND ART
MATT KINDT

COLORS
SHARLENE KINDT

LETTERS
MARIE ENGER

COVER ART AND CHAPTER BREAKS
MATT KINDT

DARK HORSE BOOKS

PRESIDENT AND PUBLISHER
MIKE RICHARDSON

EDITOR
DANIEL CHABON

ASSOCIATE EDITOR
CARDNER CLARK

ASSISTANT EDITOR
BRETT ISRAEL

DESIGNER
ETHAN KIMBERLING

DIGITAL ART TECHNICIAN
ALLYSON HALLER

Published by Dark Horse Books
A division of Dark Horse Comics, Inc.
10956 SE Main Street
Milwaukie, OR 97222

First edition: July 2018
ISBN 978-1-61655-992-2

10 9 8 7 6 5 4 3 2 1
Printed in China

Comic Shop Locator Service: comicshoplocator.com

DEPT. H VOLUME 4: LIFEBOAT

This volume collects the Dark Horse Comics series *Dept. H* issues #19–#24.

Names: Kindt, Matt, author, artist. | Kindt, Sharlene, colourist. | Enger, Marie, letterer.
Title: Dept. H / story and art, Matt Kindt ; colors, Sharlene Kindt ; letters, Marie Enger ; cover art and chapter breaks Matt Kindt.
Other titles: Department H
Description: First edition. | Milwaukie, OR : Dark Horse Books, 2017-2018. | v. 1. "This volume collects the Dark Horse Comics series Dept. H #1-6" | v. 2. "This volume collects the Dark Horse Comics series Dept. H #7-12" | v. 3. "This volume collects the Dark Horse Comics series Dept. H #13-#18" | v. 3. "This volume collects the Dark Horse Comics series Dept. H #19-#24" Contents: v. 1. Murder six miles deep -- v. 2. After the flood -- v. 3. Decompressed -- v. 4. Lifeboat.
Identifiers: LCCN 2016034697| ISBN 9781616559892 (v. 1 : hardback) | ISBN 9781616559908 (v. 2 : hardback) | ISBN 9781616559915 (v. 3 : hardback) | ISBN 9781616559922 (v. 4 : hardback)
Subjects: LCSH: Graphic novels. | BISAC: COMICS & GRAPHIC NOVELS / Crime & Mystery.
Classification: LCC PN6727.K54 D47 2017 | DDC 741.5/973--dc23
LC record available at https://lccn.loc.gov/2016034697

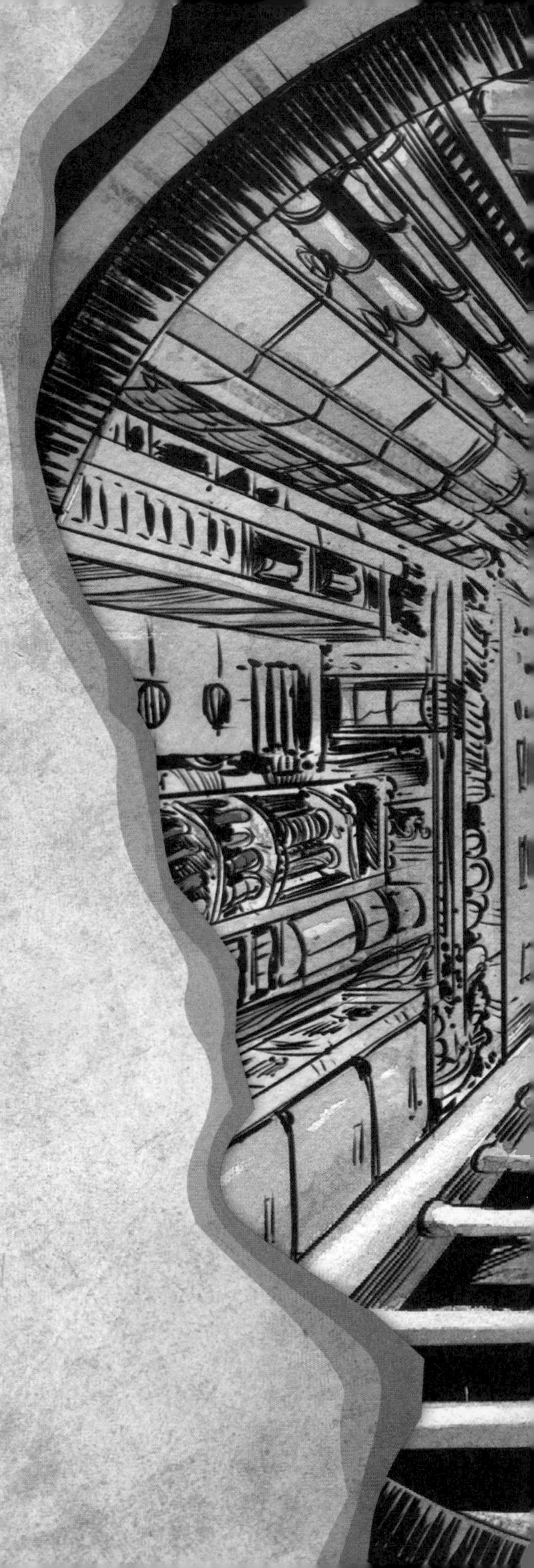

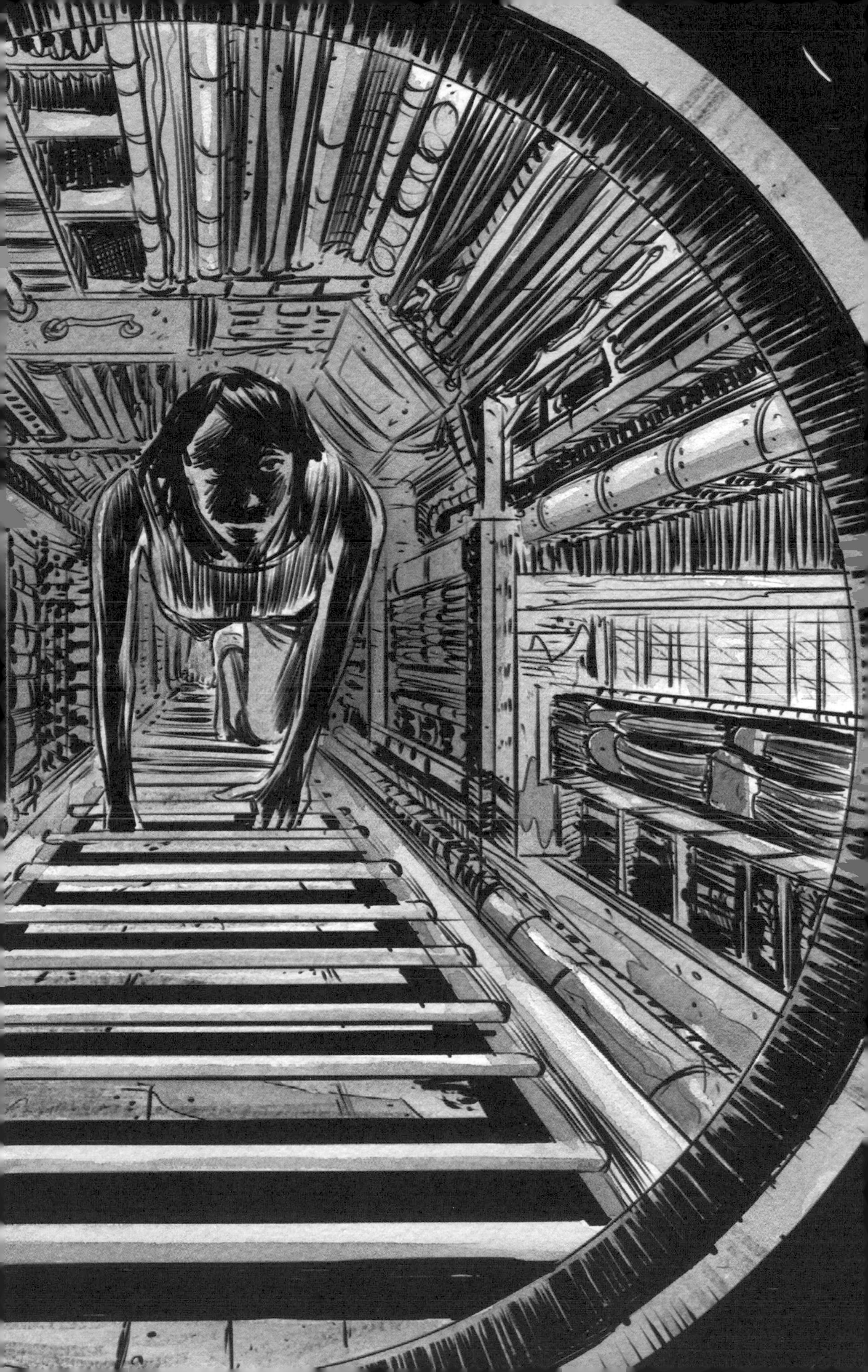

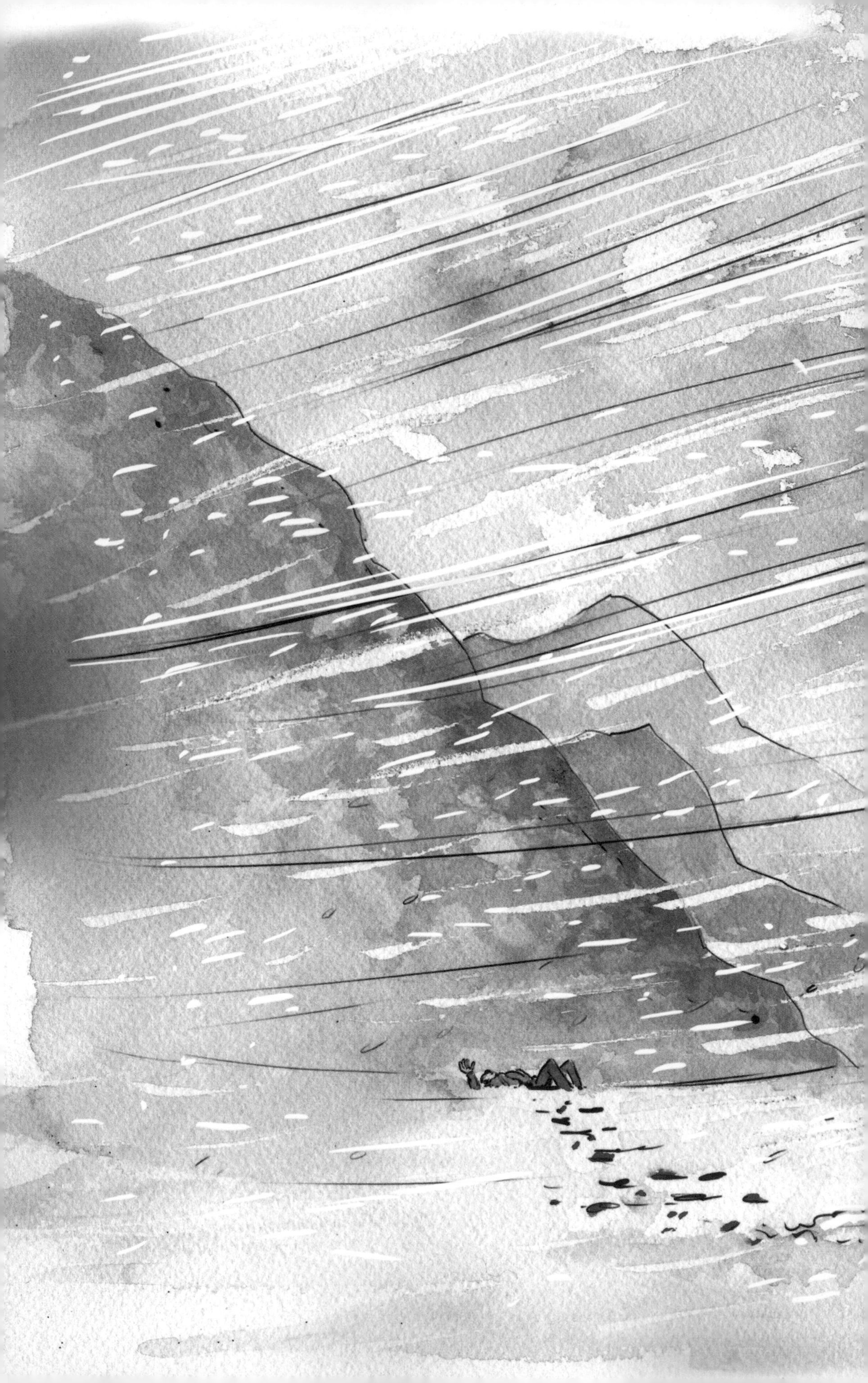

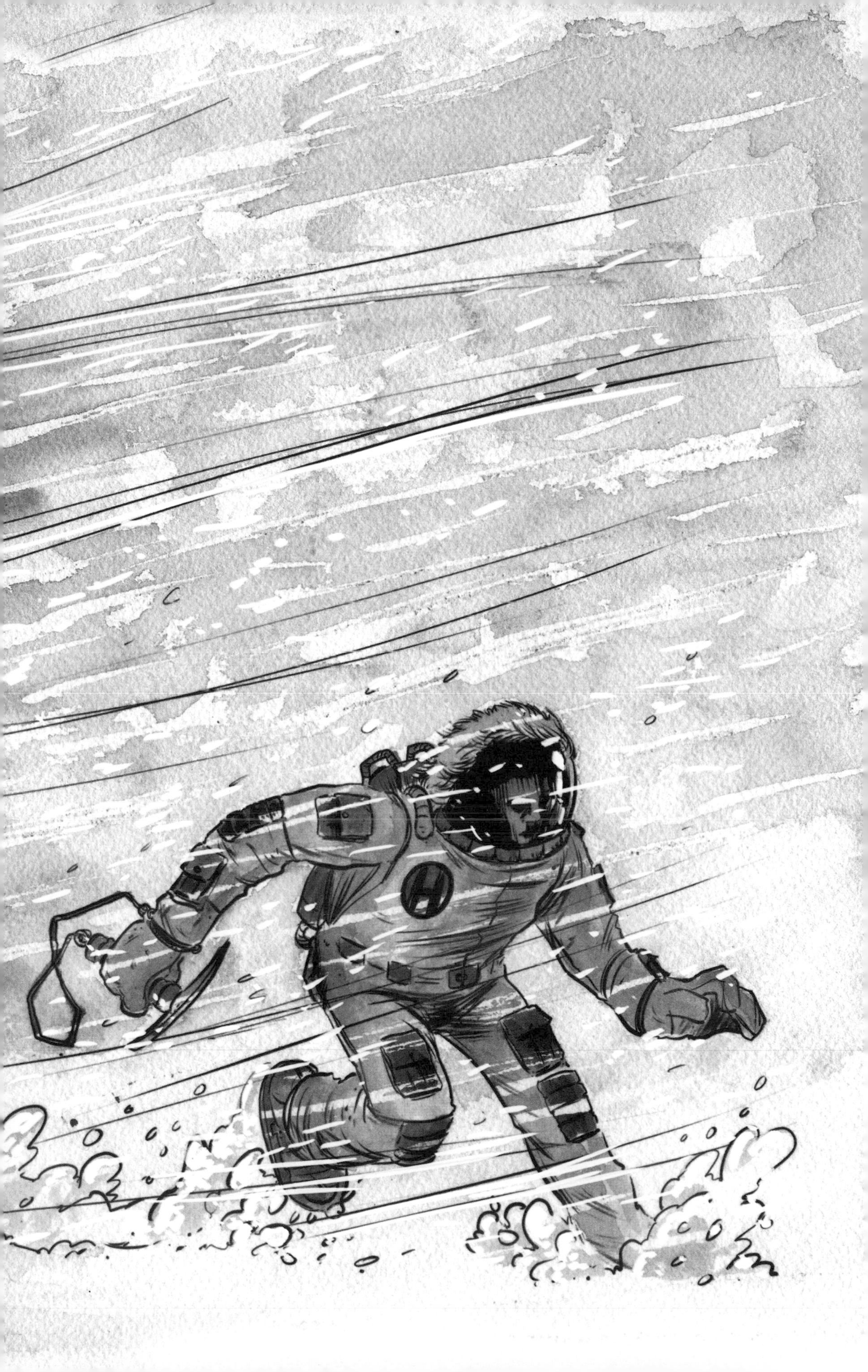

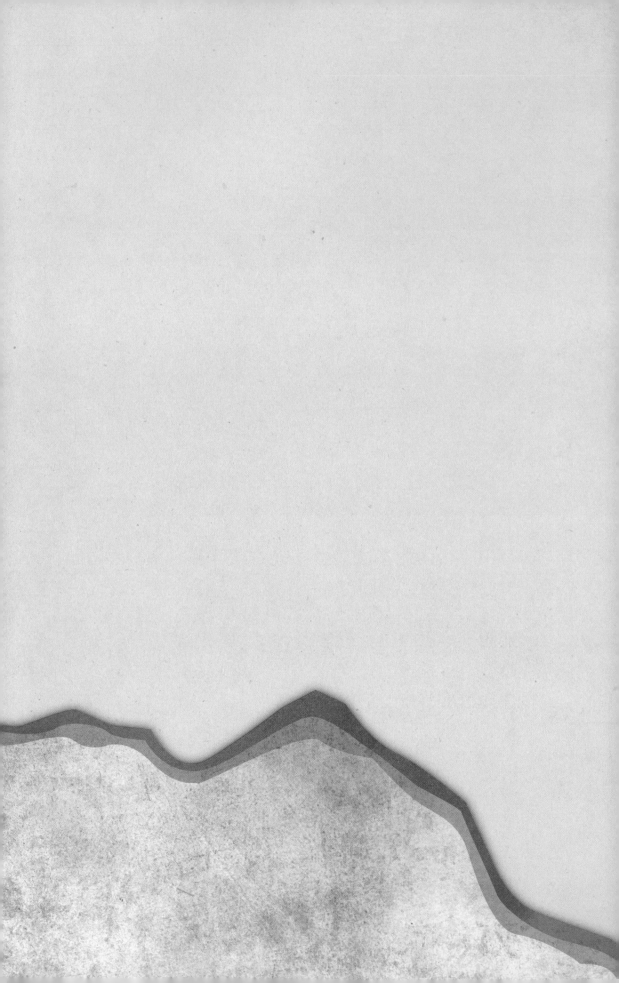

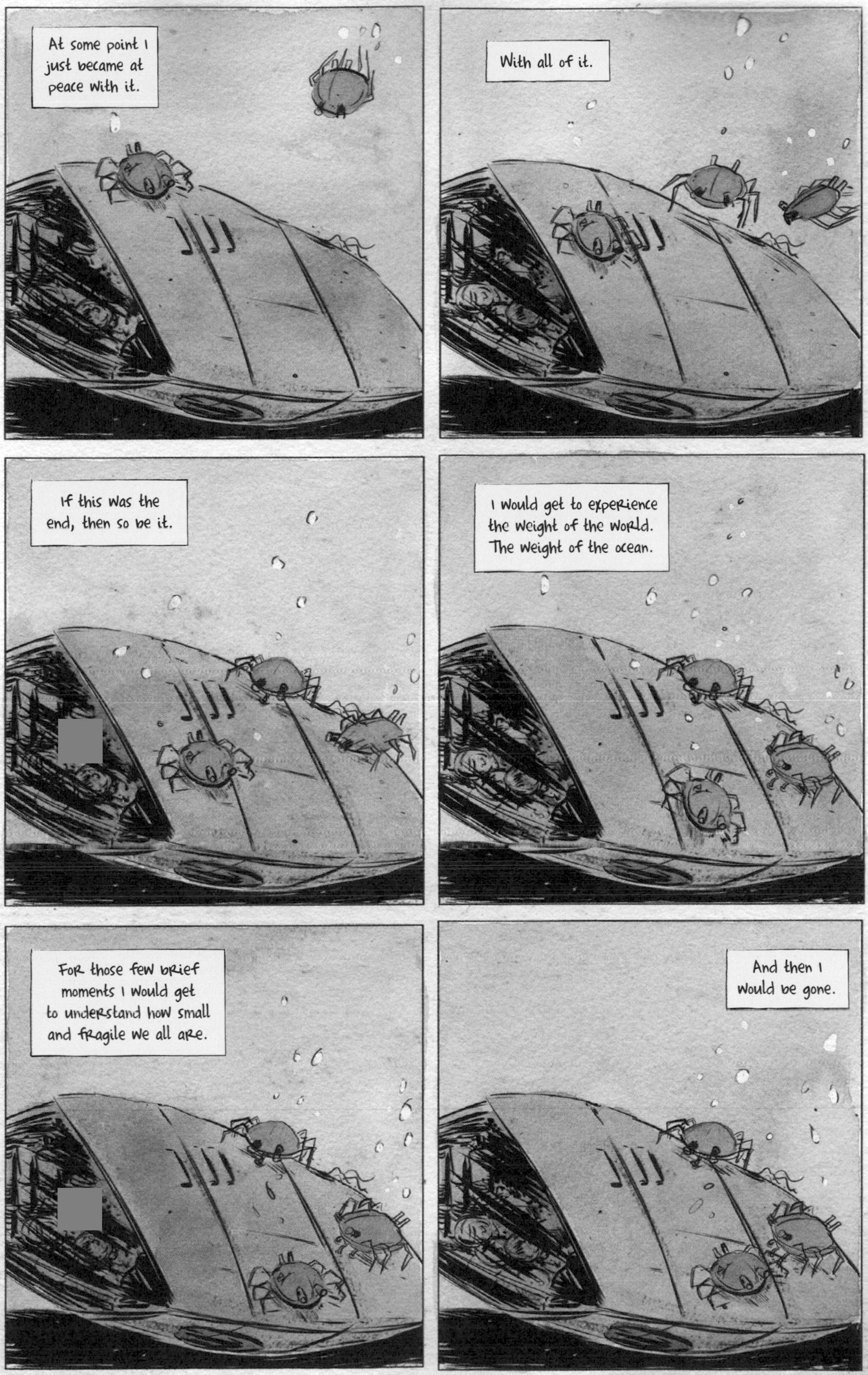
At some point I just became at peace with it.
With all of it.
If this was the end, then so be it.
I would get to experience the weight of the world. The weight of the ocean.
For those few brief moments I would get to understand how small and fragile we all are.
And then I would be gone.

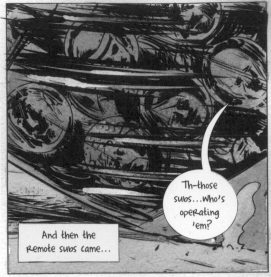

And then the remote subs came...

Th-those subs...Who's operating 'em?

Someone on the surface... watching out for us...

They're plugging in...using themselves as temporary battery packs...

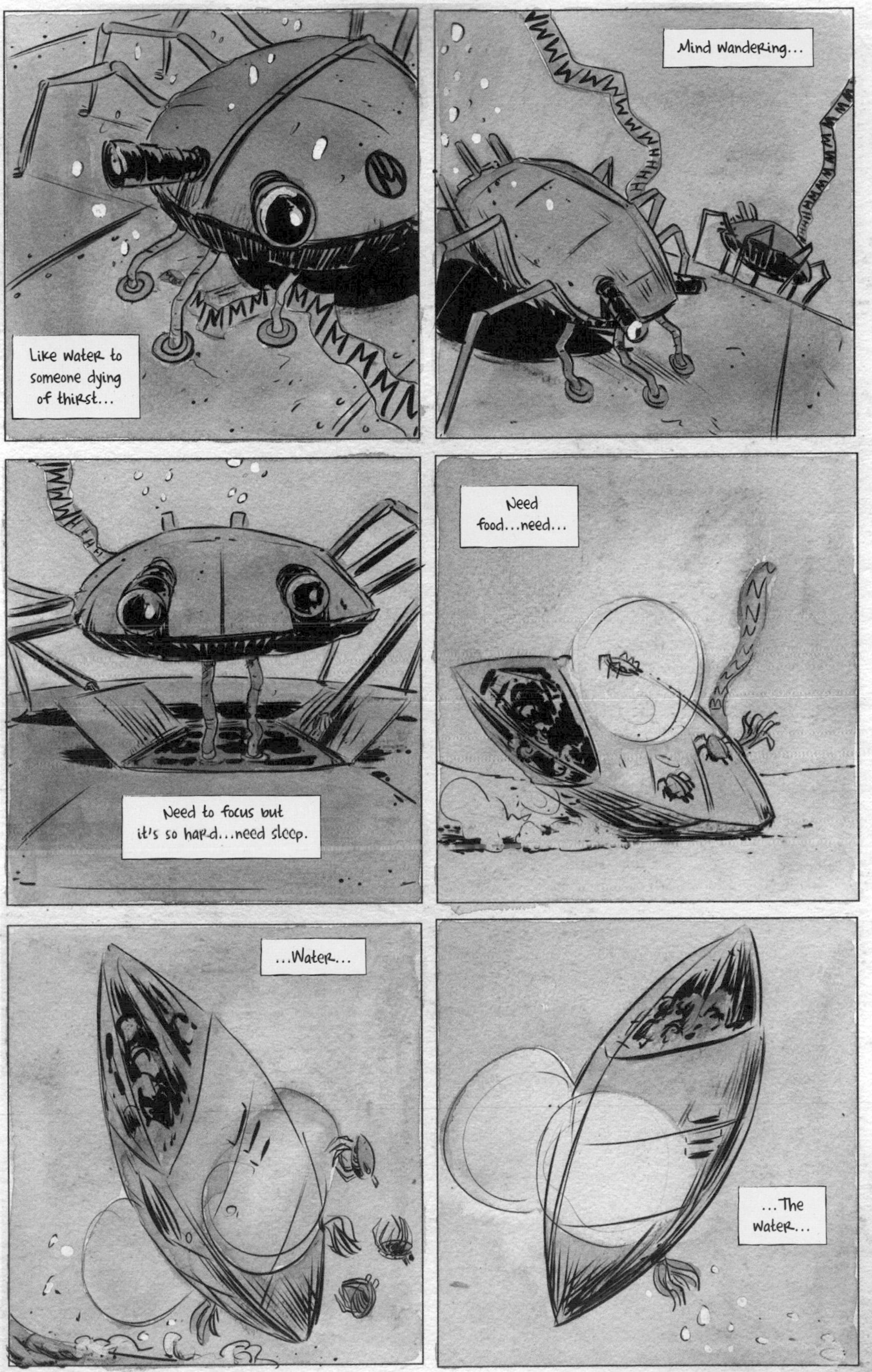
Like water to someone dying of thirst...
Mind wandering...
Need to focus but it's so hard...need sleep.
Need food...need...
...Water...
...The water...

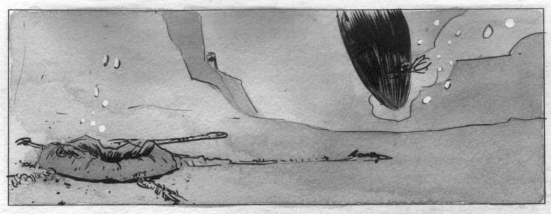

Next stop. Sub station X.

Let's hope it's still intact. You think that's where Aaron headed?

Depends on what kind of suit he patched together. He won't get far, I know that much.

Hopefully 'e doesn't sabotage anything. That station—'eets our only hope...

"We chain 'eet off from there to tha next and tha next. We only make it if all tha stations are still in operation. Gonna take forevah just to re-pressurize at each stop."

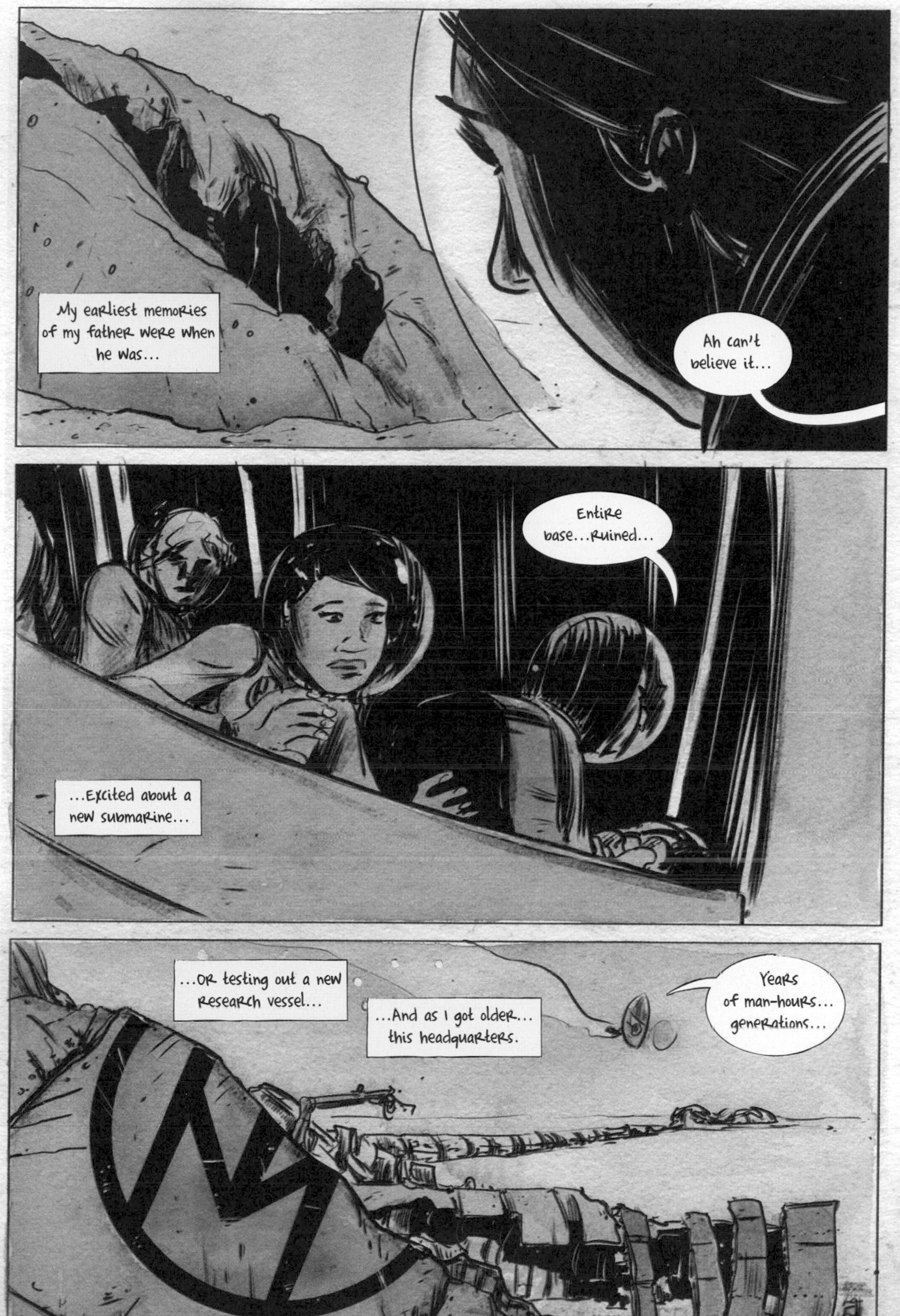
My earliest memories of my father were when he was...
Ah can't believe it...
Entire base...ruined...
...Excited about a new submarine...
...Or testing out a new research vessel...
...And as I got older... this headquarters.
Years of man-hours... generations...

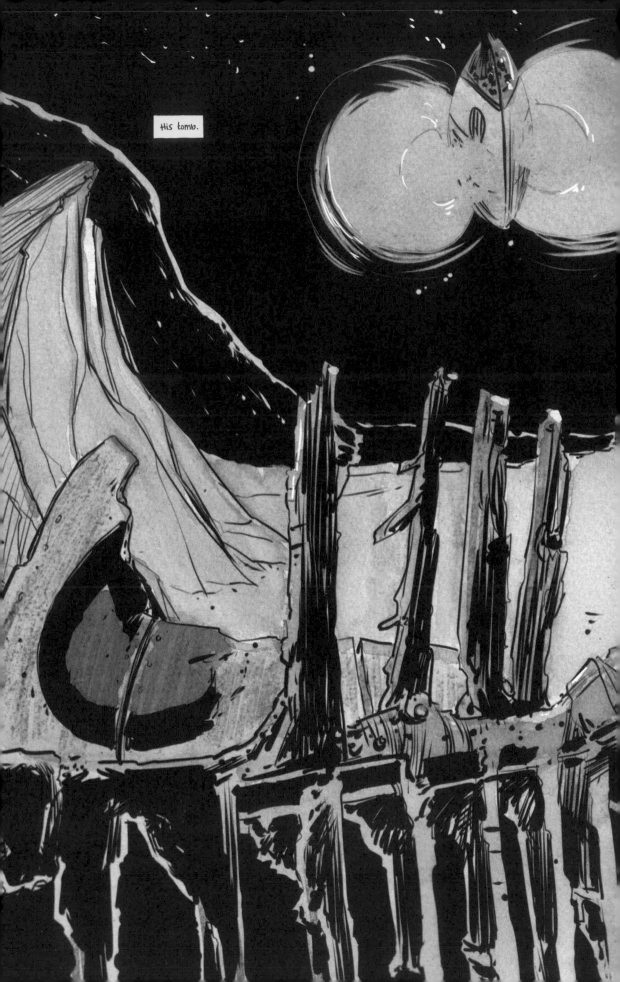

His tomb.

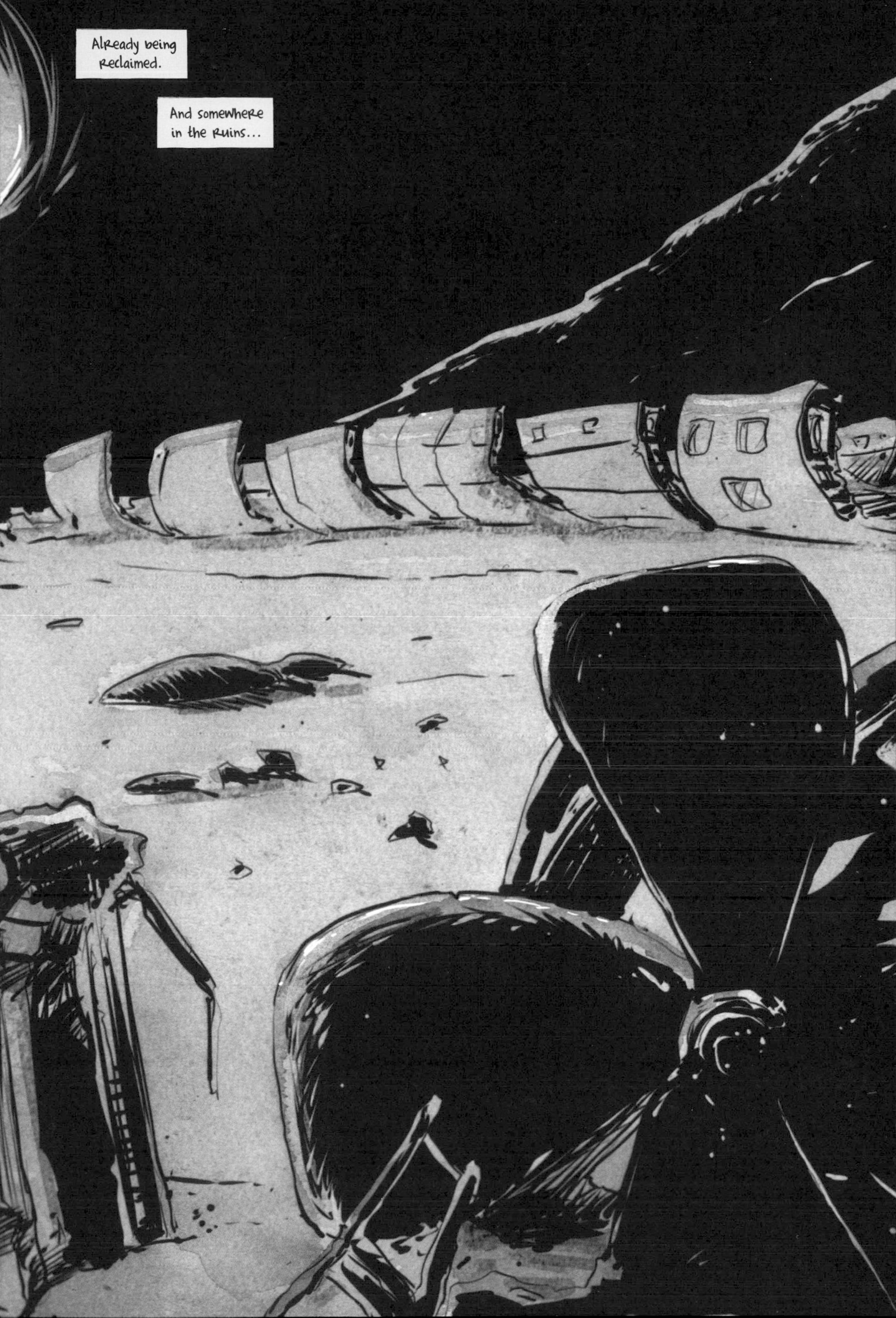
Already being reclaimed.
And somewhere in the ruins...

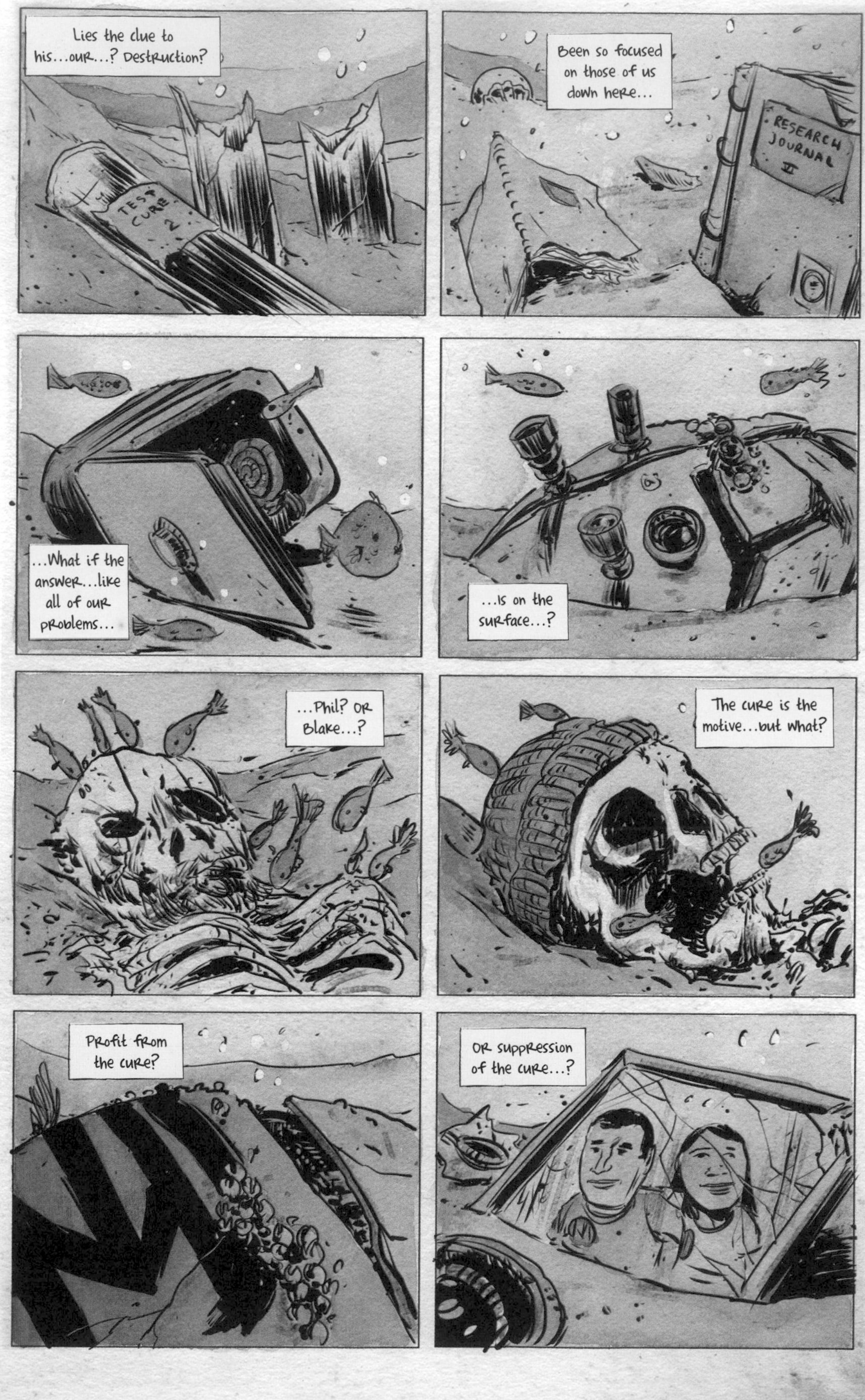
Lies the clue to his...our...? Destruction?
TEST CURE 2
Been so focused on those of us down here...
RESEARCH JOURNAL II
...What if the answer...like all of our problems...
...is on the surface...?
...Phil? Or Blake...?
The cure is the motive...but what?
Profit from the cure?
Or suppression of the cure...?

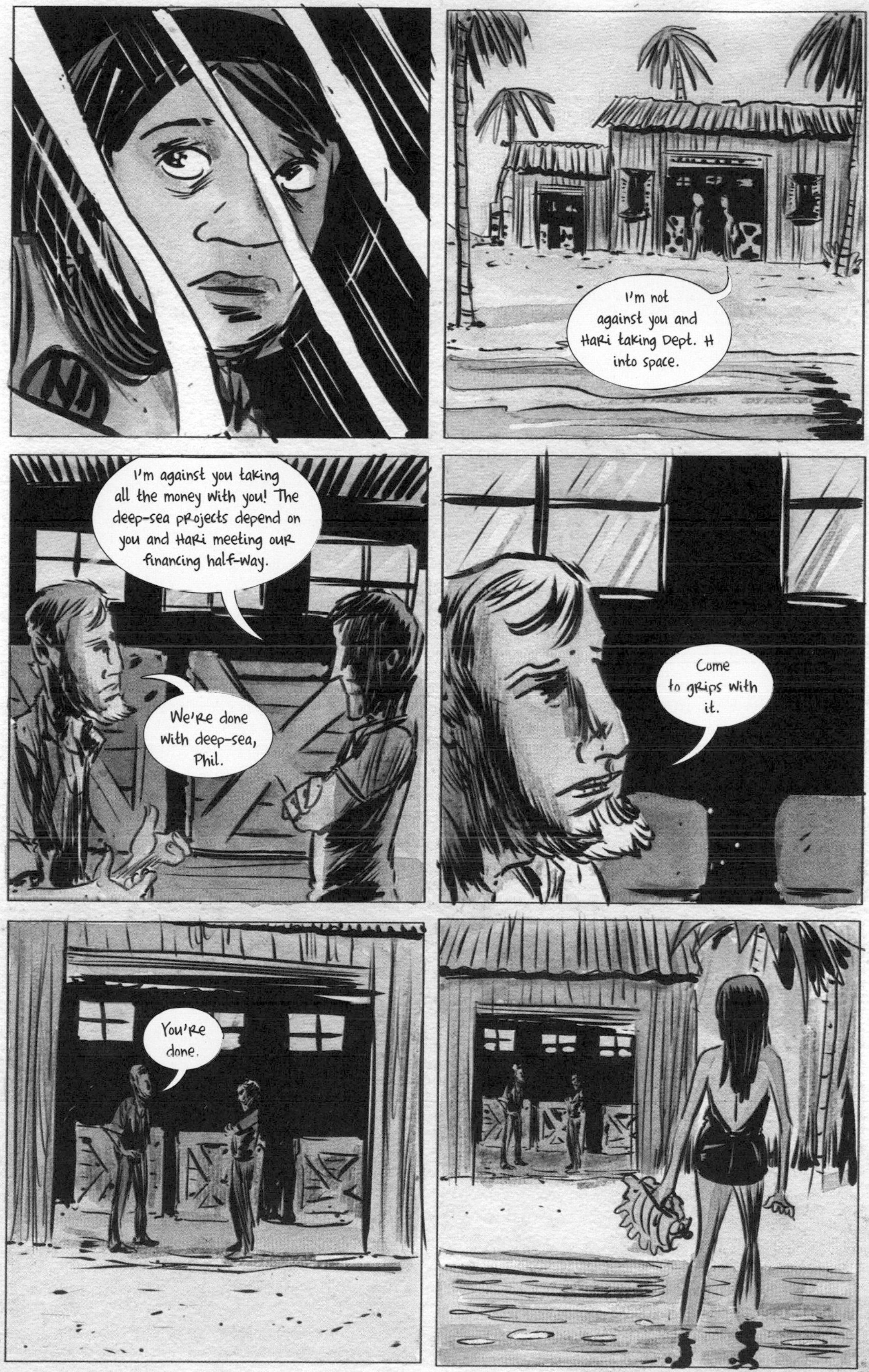
I'm not against you and Hari taking Dept. H into space.
I'm against you taking all the money with you! The deep-sea projects depend on you and Hari meeting our financing half-way.
We're done with deep-sea, Phil.
Come to grips with it.
You're done.

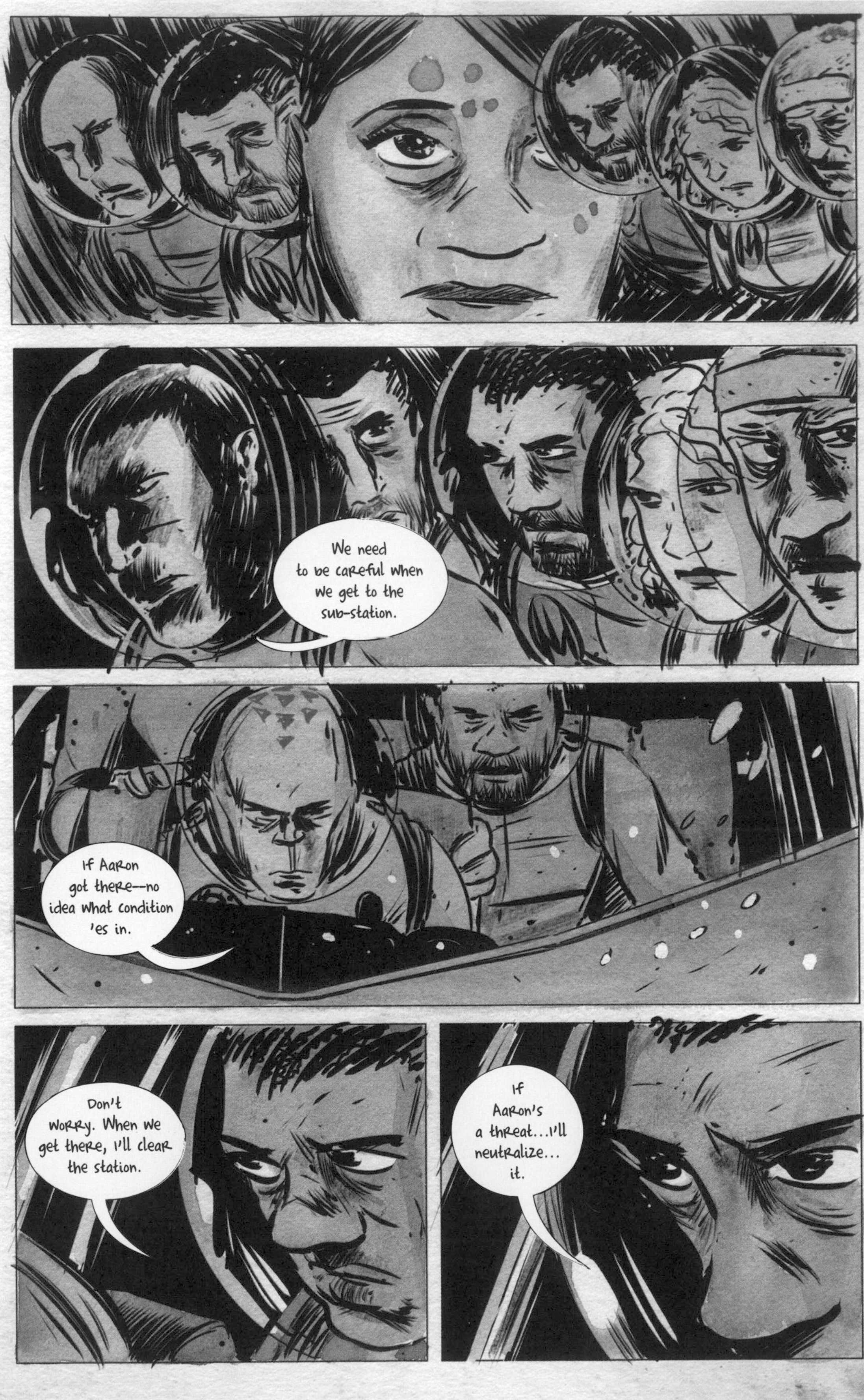
We need to be careful when we get to the sub-station.
If Aaron got there--no idea what condition 'es in.
Don't worry. When we get there, I'll clear the station.
If Aaron's a threat...I'll neutralize... it.

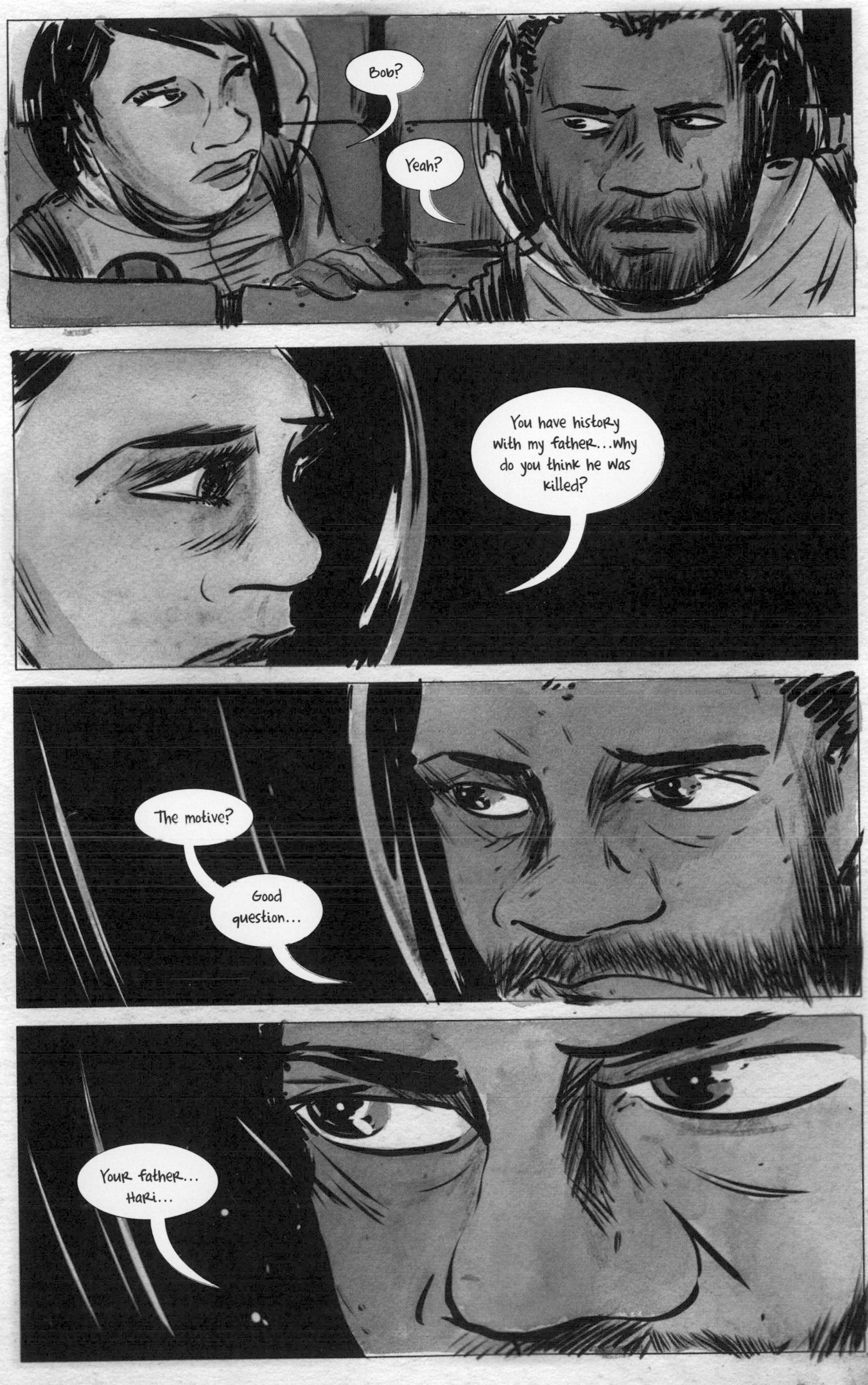

Bob?
Yeah?
You have history with my father...Why do you think he was killed?
The motive?
Good question...
Your father... Hari...

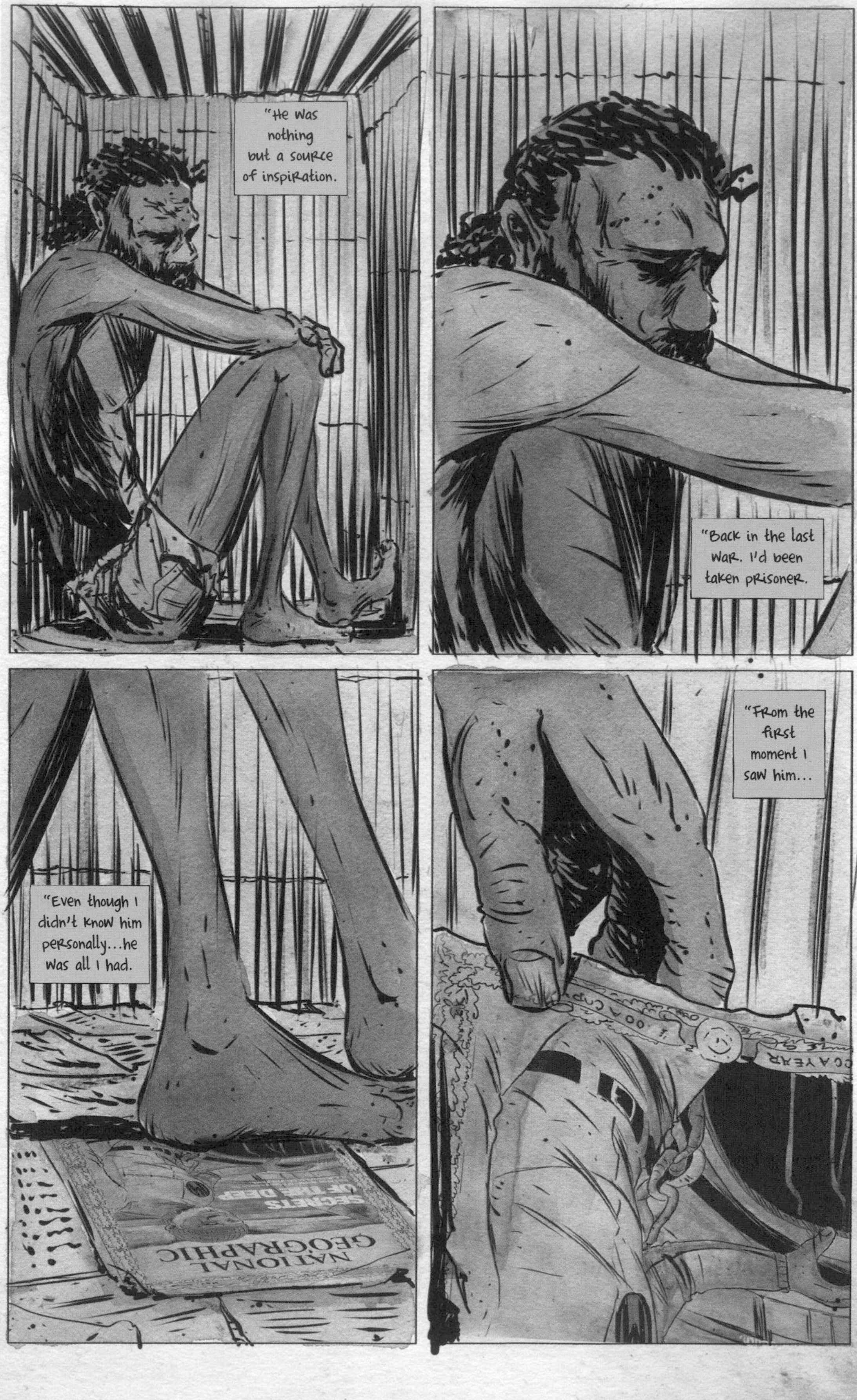
"He was nothing but a source of inspiration.
"Back in the last war. I'd been taken prisoner.
"Even though I didn't know him personally...he was all I had.
NATIONAL GEOGRAPHIC
SECRETS OF THE DEEP
"From the first moment I saw him...

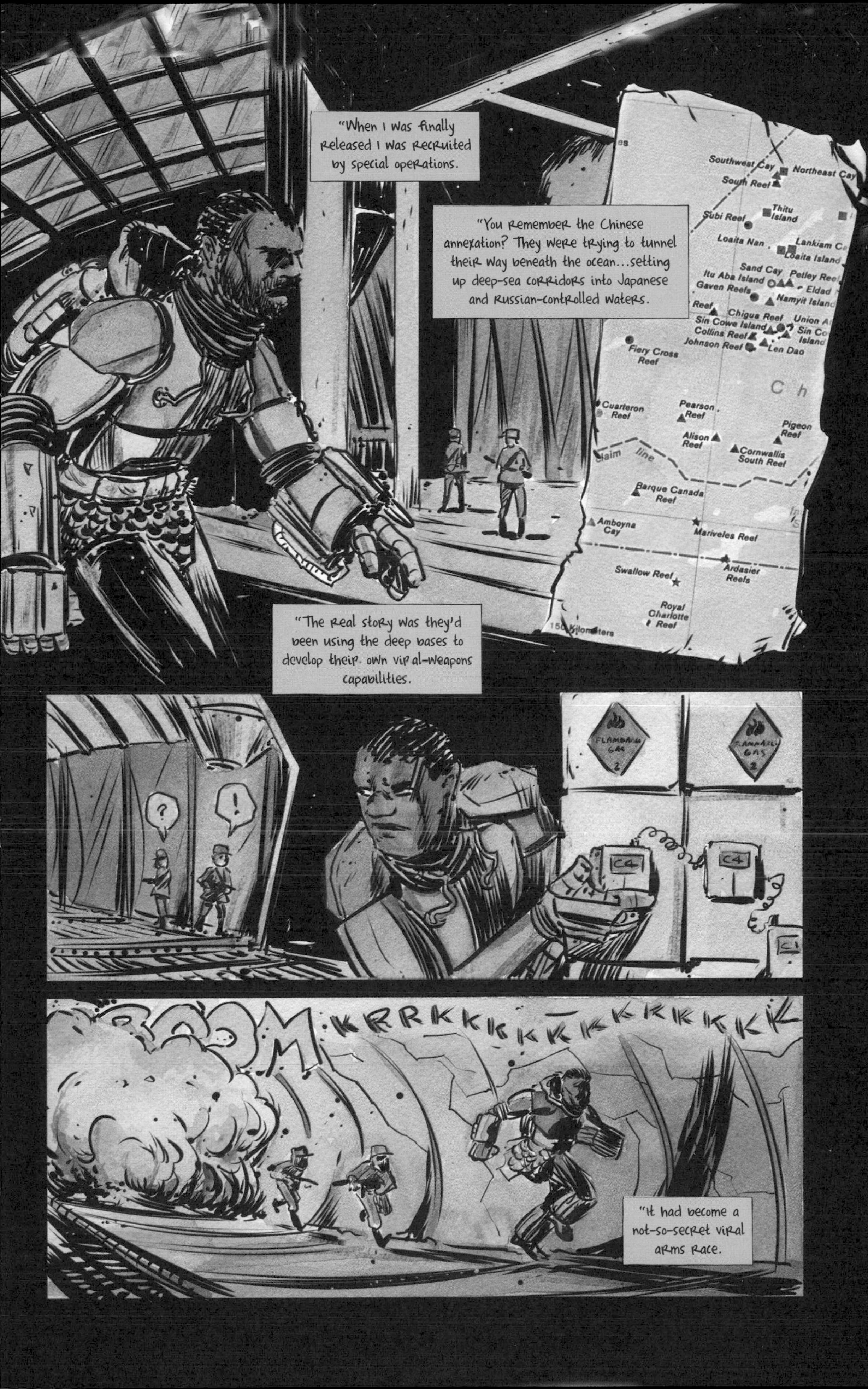
"When I was finally released I was recruited by special operations.
"You remember the Chinese annexation? They were trying to tunnel their way beneath the ocean...setting up deep-sea corridors into Japanese and Russian-controlled waters.
Southwest Cay
Northeast Cay
South Reef
Thitu Island
Subi Reef
Loaita Nan
Lankiam Cay
Loaita Island
Sand Cay
Petley Reef
Itu Aba Island
Eldad
Gaven Reefs
Namyit Island
Chigua Reef
Sin Cowe Island
Union
Collins Reef
Sin Cowe Island
Johnson Reef
Len Dao
Fiery Cross Reef
Cuarteron Reef
Pearson Reef
Alison Reef
Pigeon Reef
Cornwallis South Reef
claim line
Barque Canada Reef
Amboyna Cay
Mariveles Reef
Swallow Reef
Ardasier Reefs
Royal Charlotte Reef
150 Kilometers
"The real story was they'd been using the deep bases to develop their own viral-weapons capabilities.
?
!
C4
C4
BOOM
KRRKKKKKKKKKKKKKKKK
"It had become a not-so-secret viral arms race.

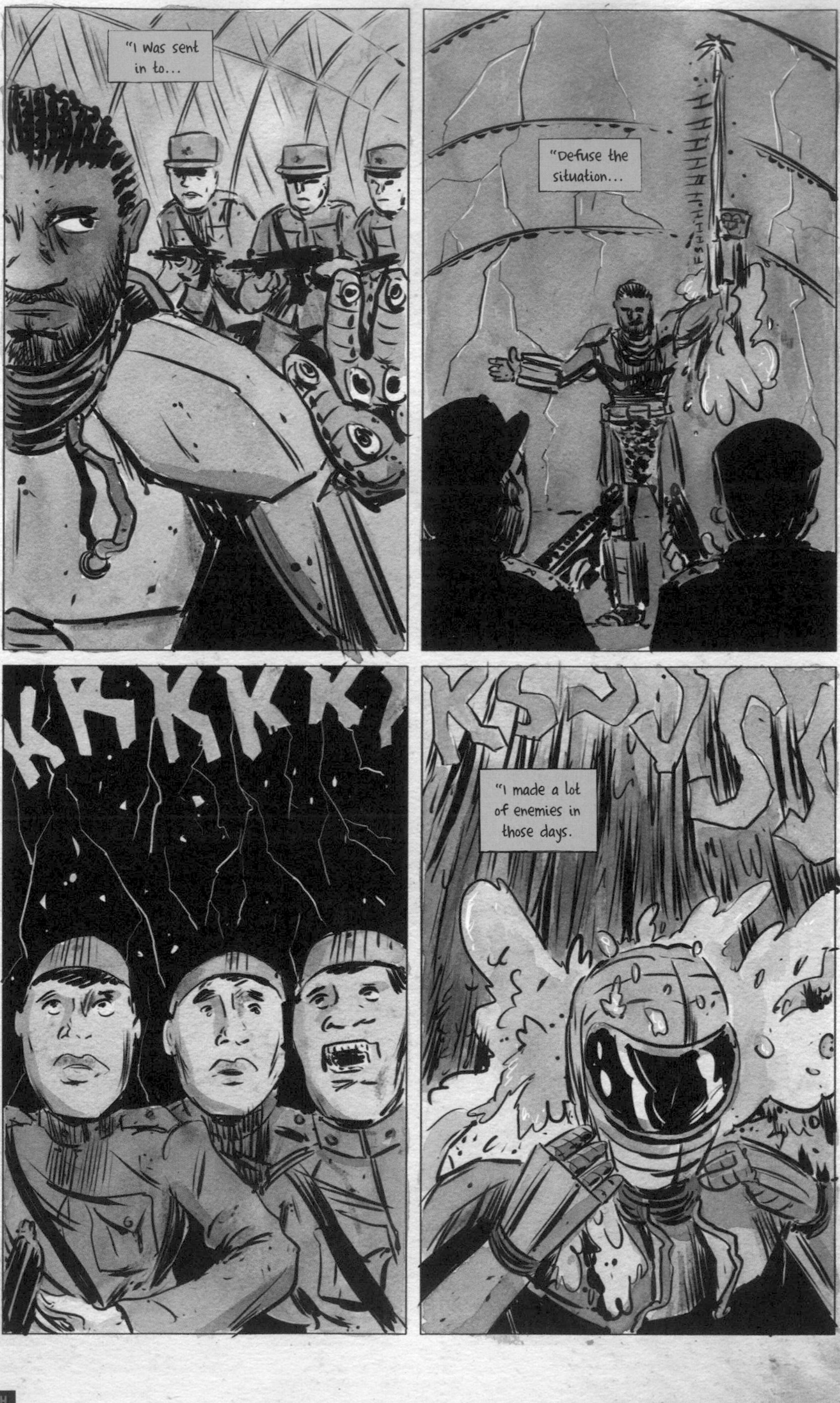
"I was sent in to...
"Defuse the situation...
"I made a lot of enemies in those days.

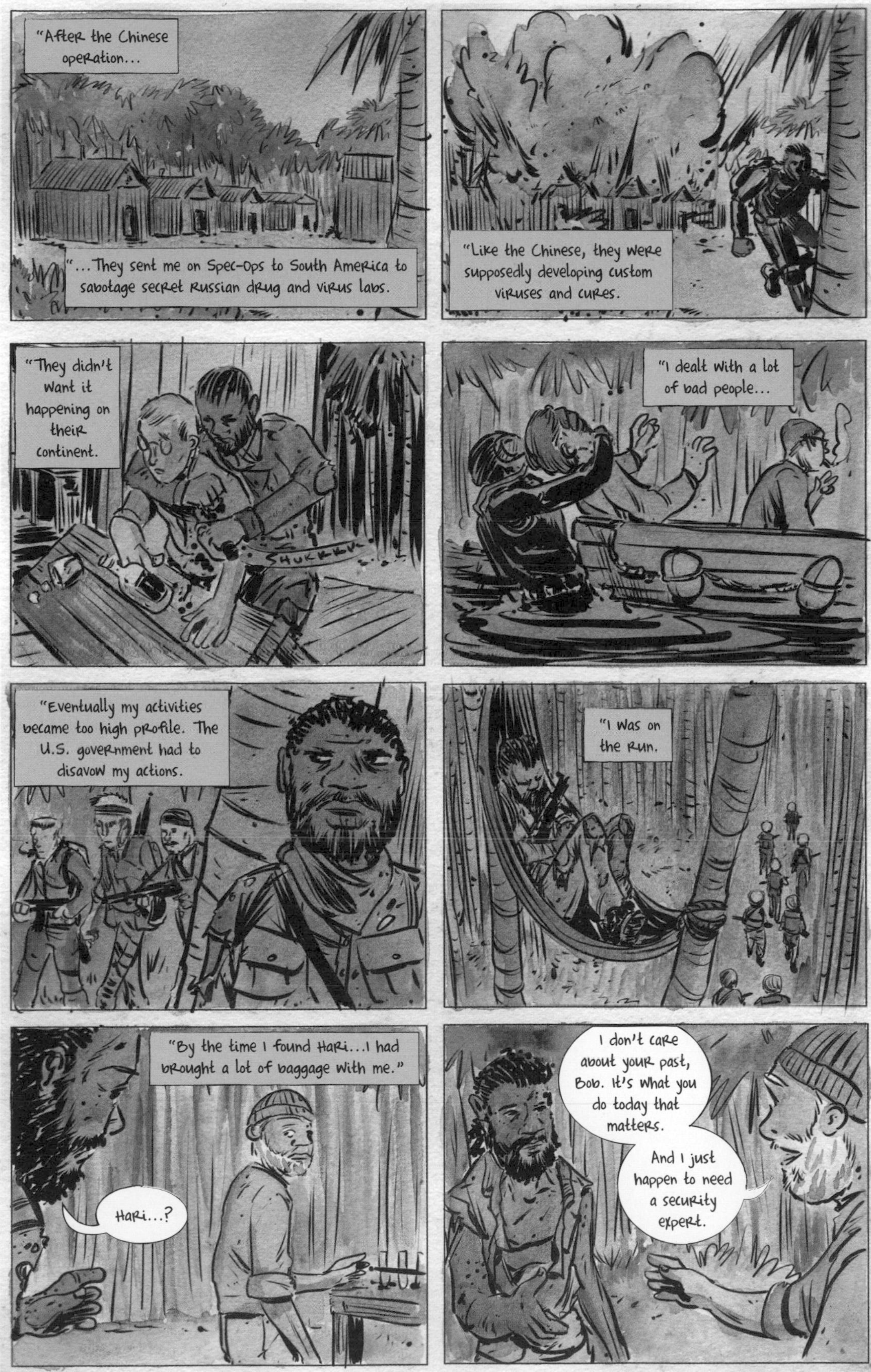
"After the Chinese operation...
"...They sent me on Spec-Ops to South America to sabotage secret Russian drug and virus labs.
"Like the Chinese, they were supposedly developing custom viruses and cures.
"They didn't want it happening on their continent.
SHUKKKK
"I dealt with a lot of bad people...
"Eventually my activities became too high profile. The U.S. government had to disavow my actions.
"I was on the run.
"By the time I found Hari...I had brought a lot of baggage with me."
Hari...?
I don't care about your past, Bob. It's what you do today that matters.
And I just happen to need a security expert.

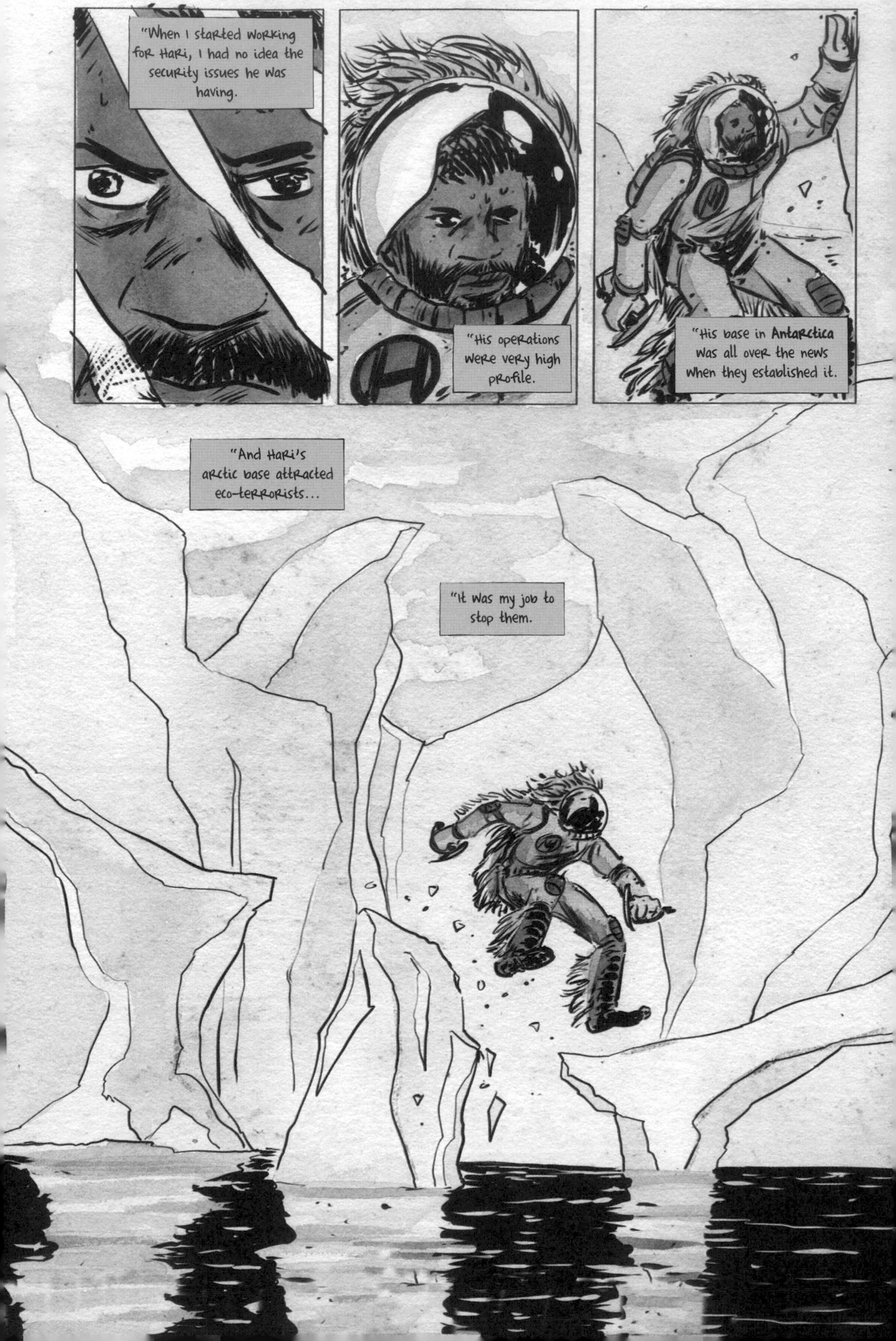
"When I started working for Hari, I had no idea the security issues he was having.
"His operations were very high profile.
"His base in Antarctica was all over the news when they established it.
"And Hari's arctic base attracted eco-terrorists...
"It was my job to stop them.

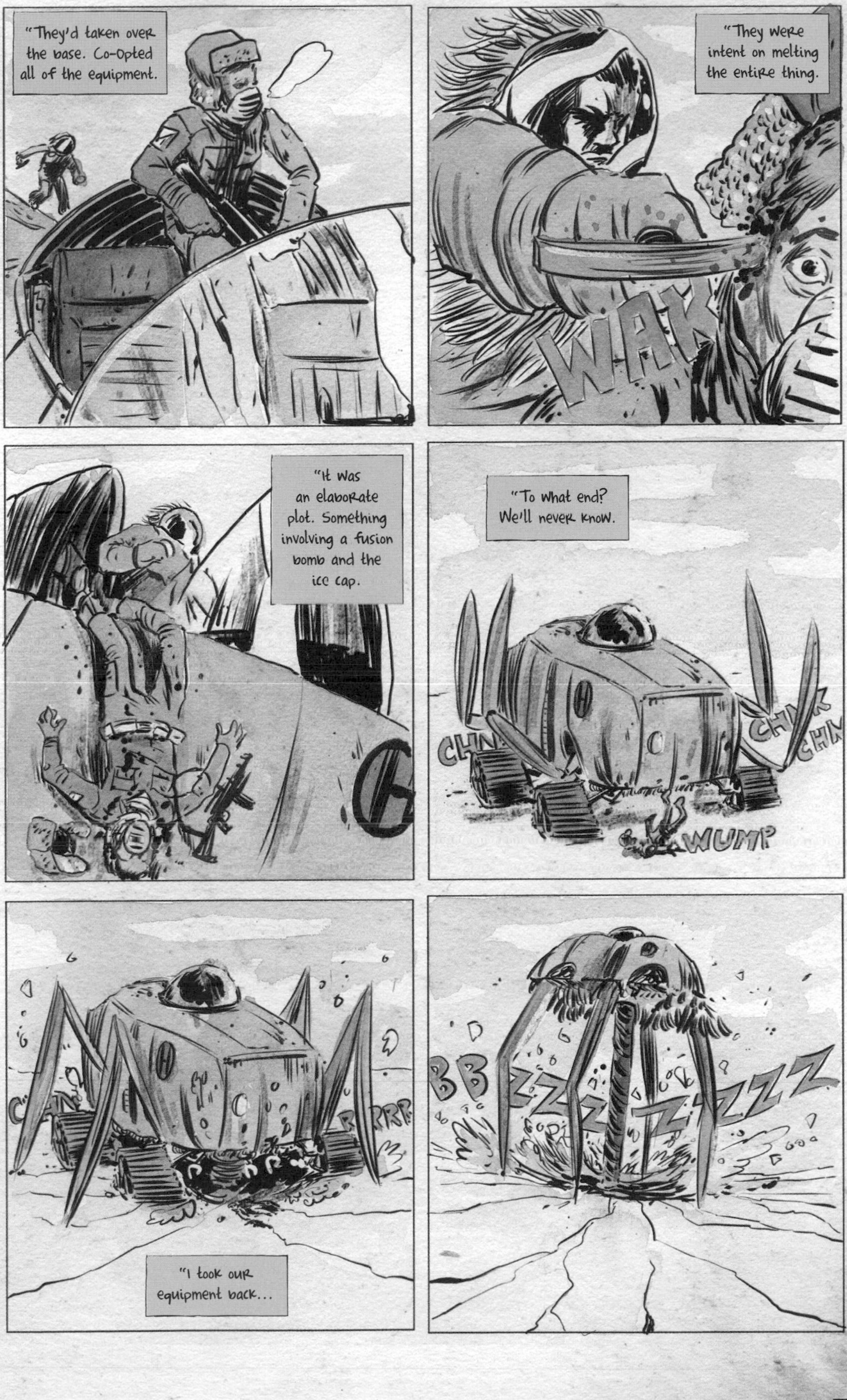
"They'd taken over the base. Co-Opted all of the equipment.
"They were intent on melting the entire thing.
WAK
"It was an elaborate plot. Something involving a fusion bomb and the ice cap.
"To what end? We'll never know.
WUMP
"I took our equipment back...

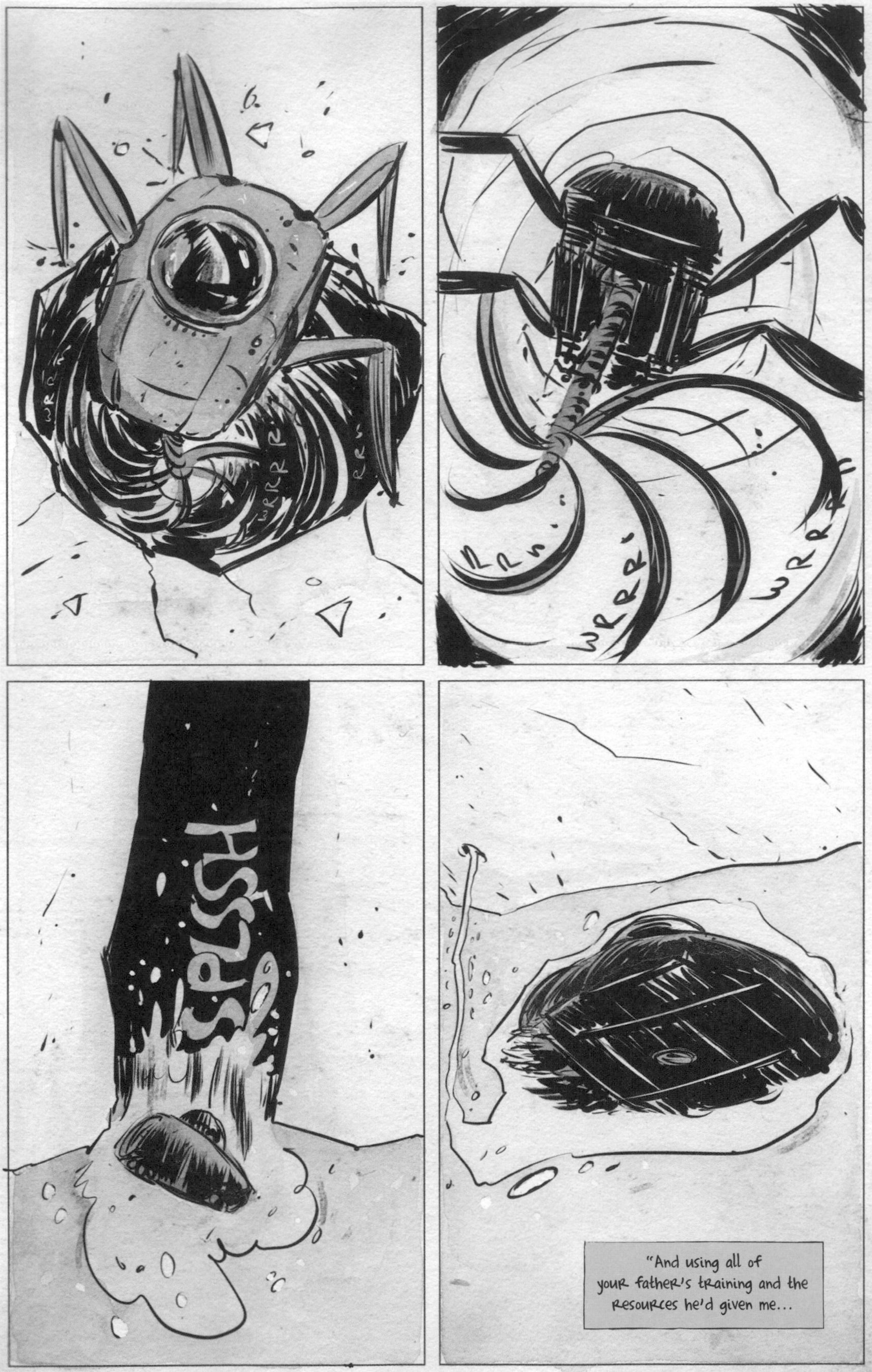
WRRR
WRRR
RRR
WRRR
WRRR
WRRR
SPLSSH
"And using all of your father's training and the resources he'd given me...

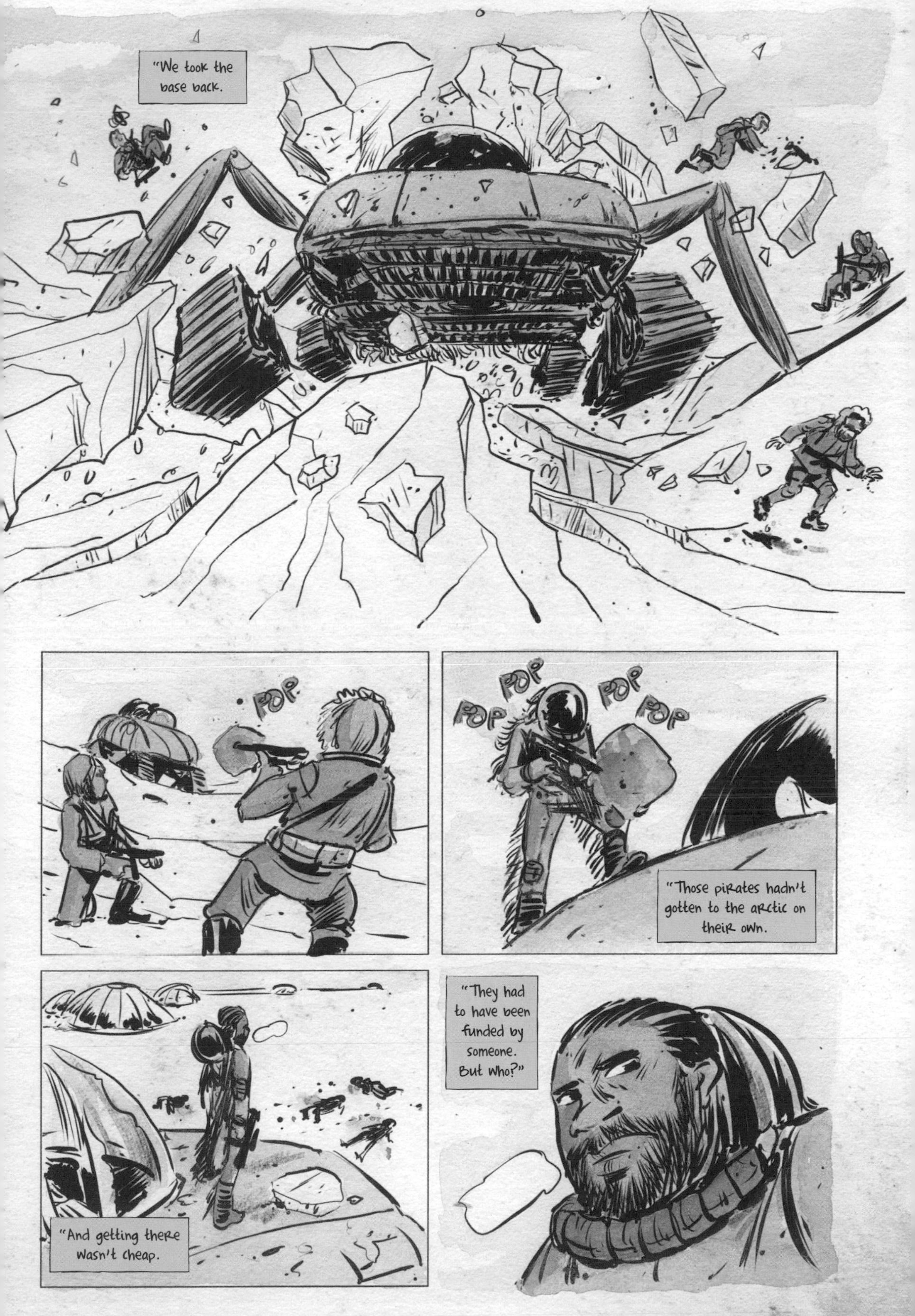
"We took the base back.
POP
POP POP
POP POP
"Those pirates hadn't gotten to the arctic on their own.
"And getting there wasn't cheap.
"They had to have been funded by someone. But who?"

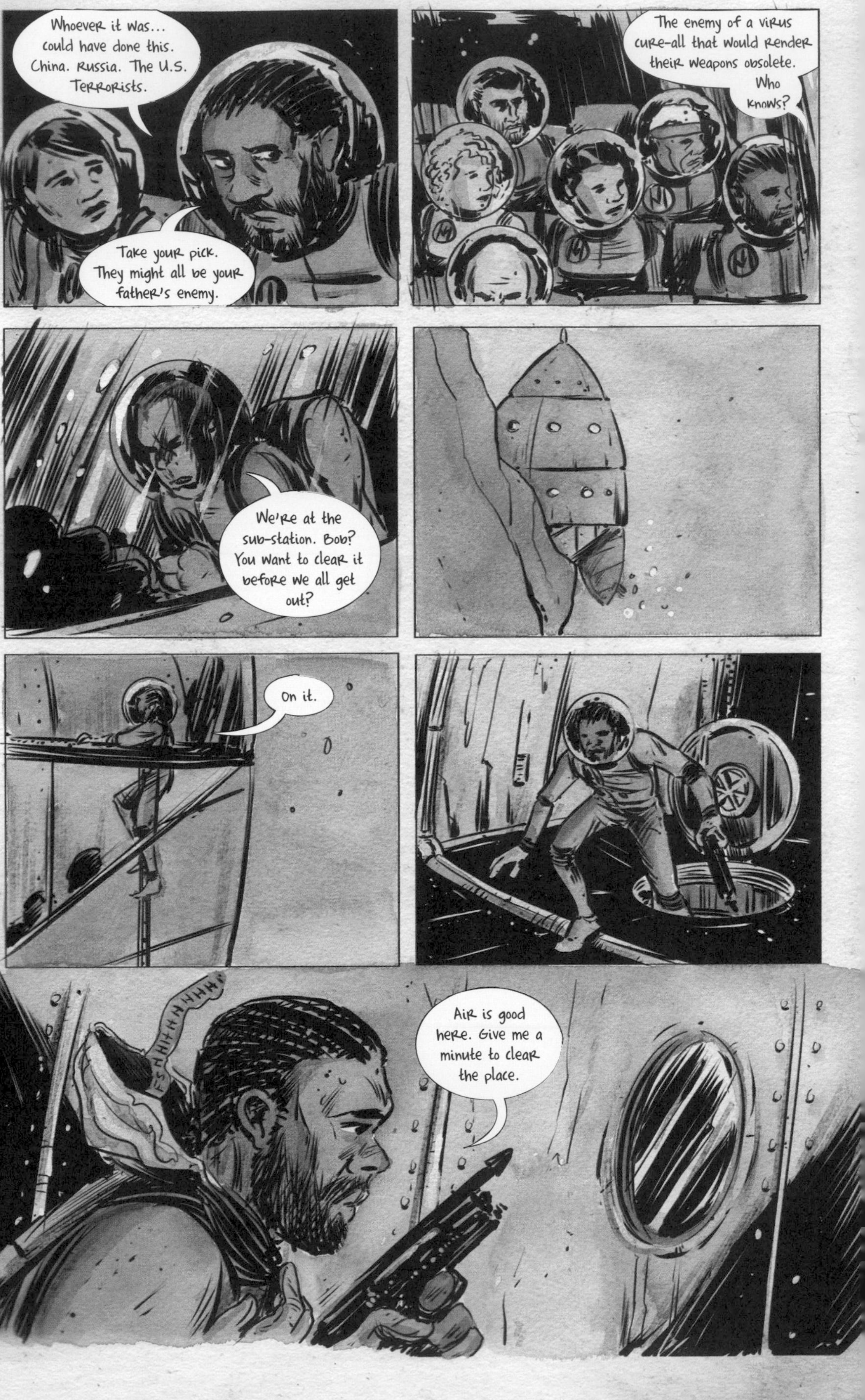
Whoever it was... could have done this. China. Russia. The U.S. Terrorists.
Take your pick. They might all be your father's enemy.
The enemy of a virus cure-all that would render their weapons obsolete. Who knows?
We're at the sub-station. Bob? You want to clear it before we all get out?
On it.
Air is good here. Give me a minute to clear the place.

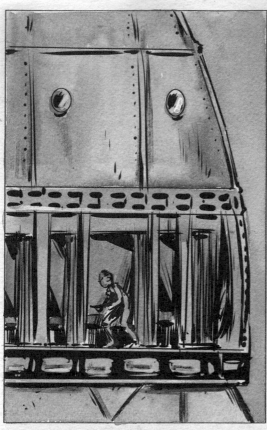

Aaron?

It's clear.

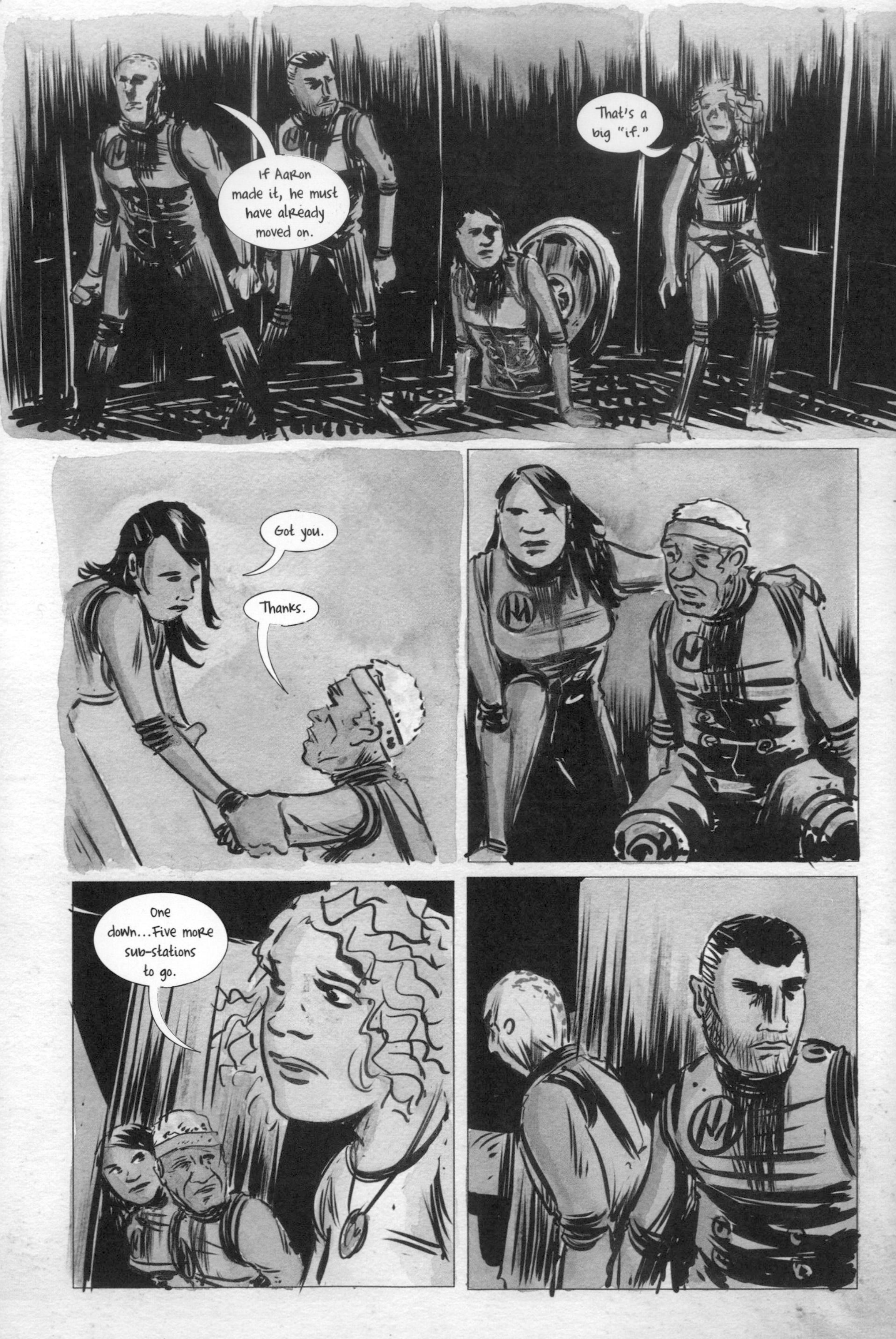
If Aaron made it, he must have already moved on.
That's a big "if."
Got you.
Thanks.
One down... Five more sub-stations to go.

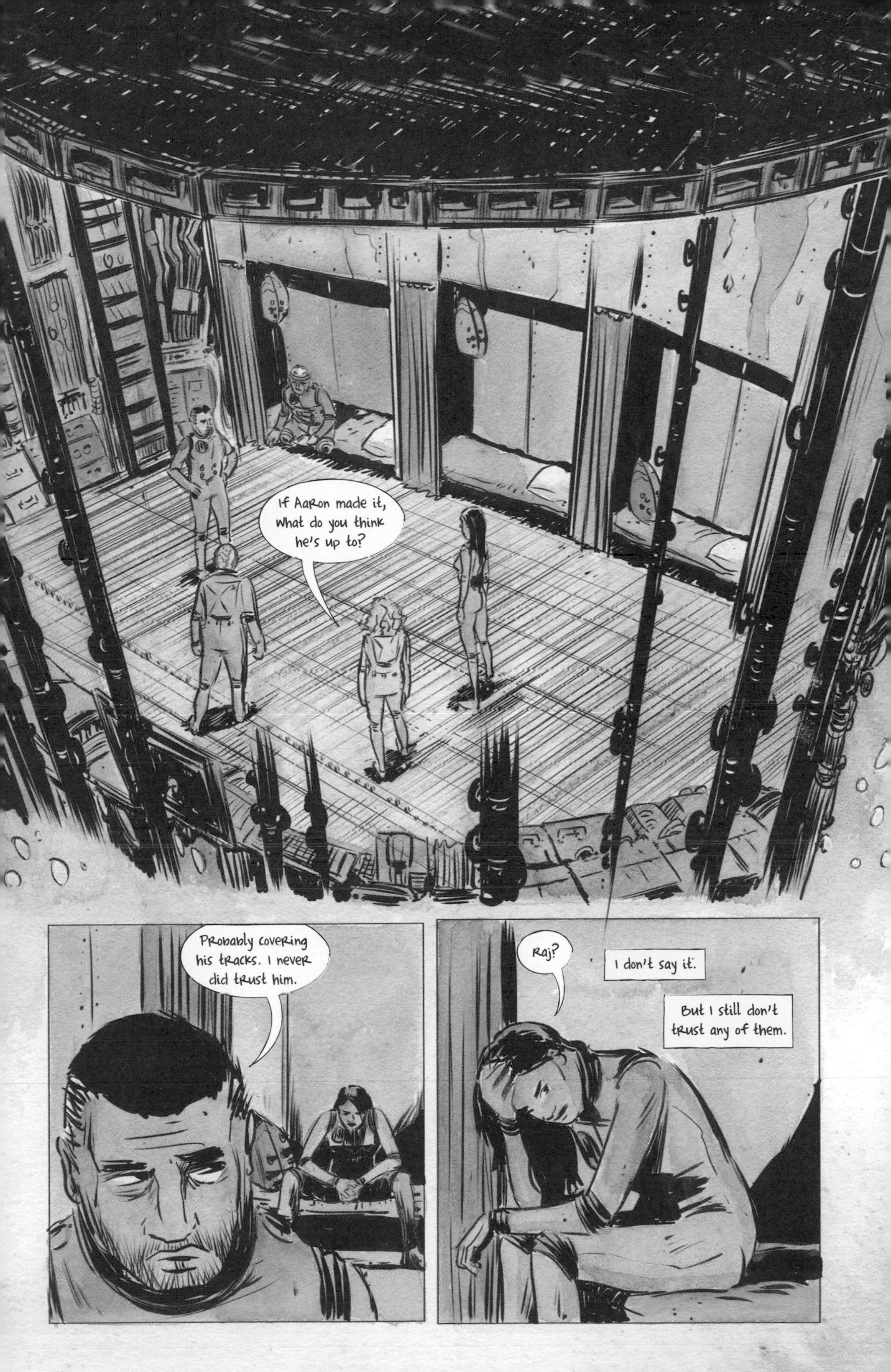
If Aaron made it, What do you think he's up to?
Probably covering his tracks. I never did trust him.
Raj?
I don't say it.
But I still don't trust any of them.

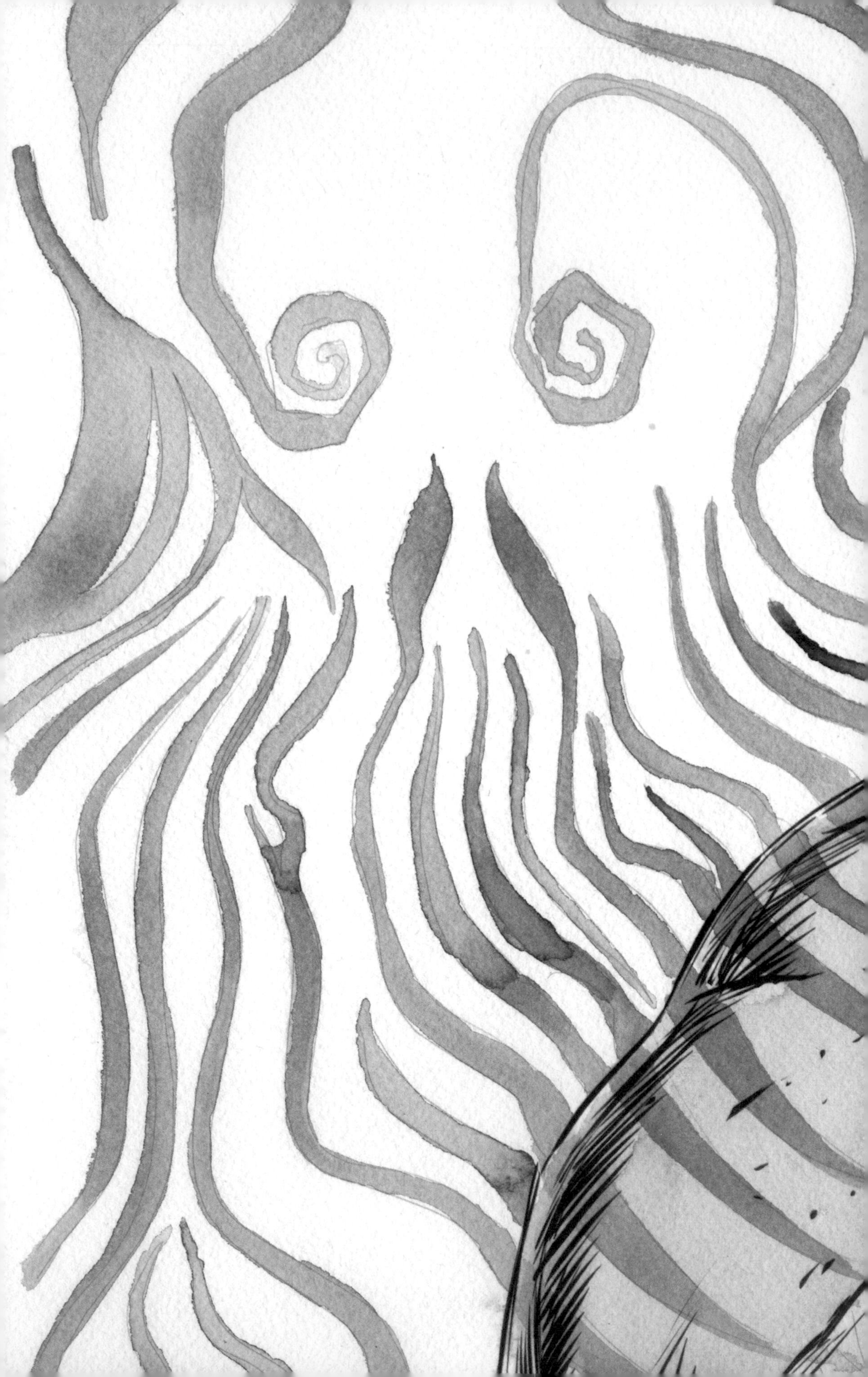

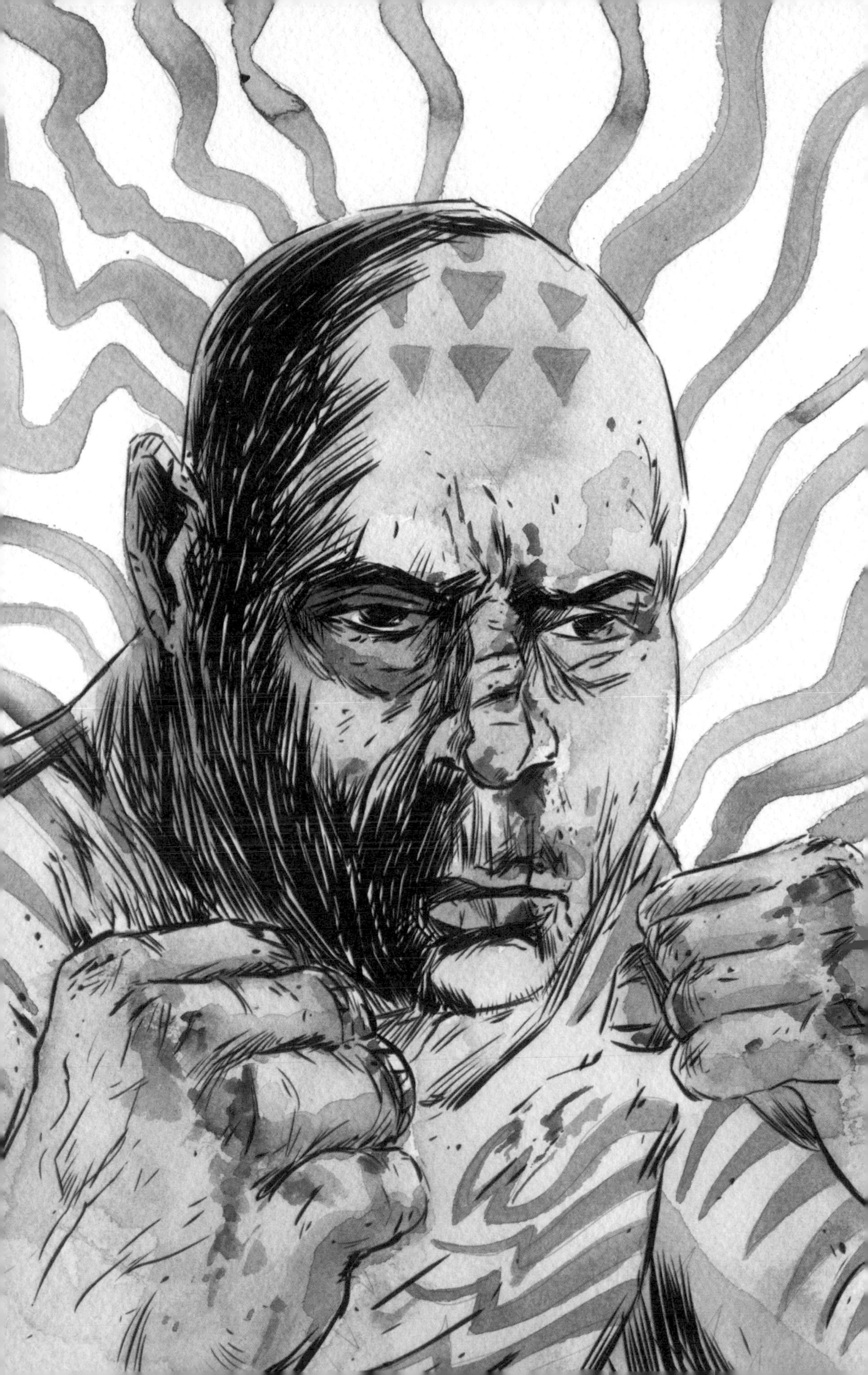

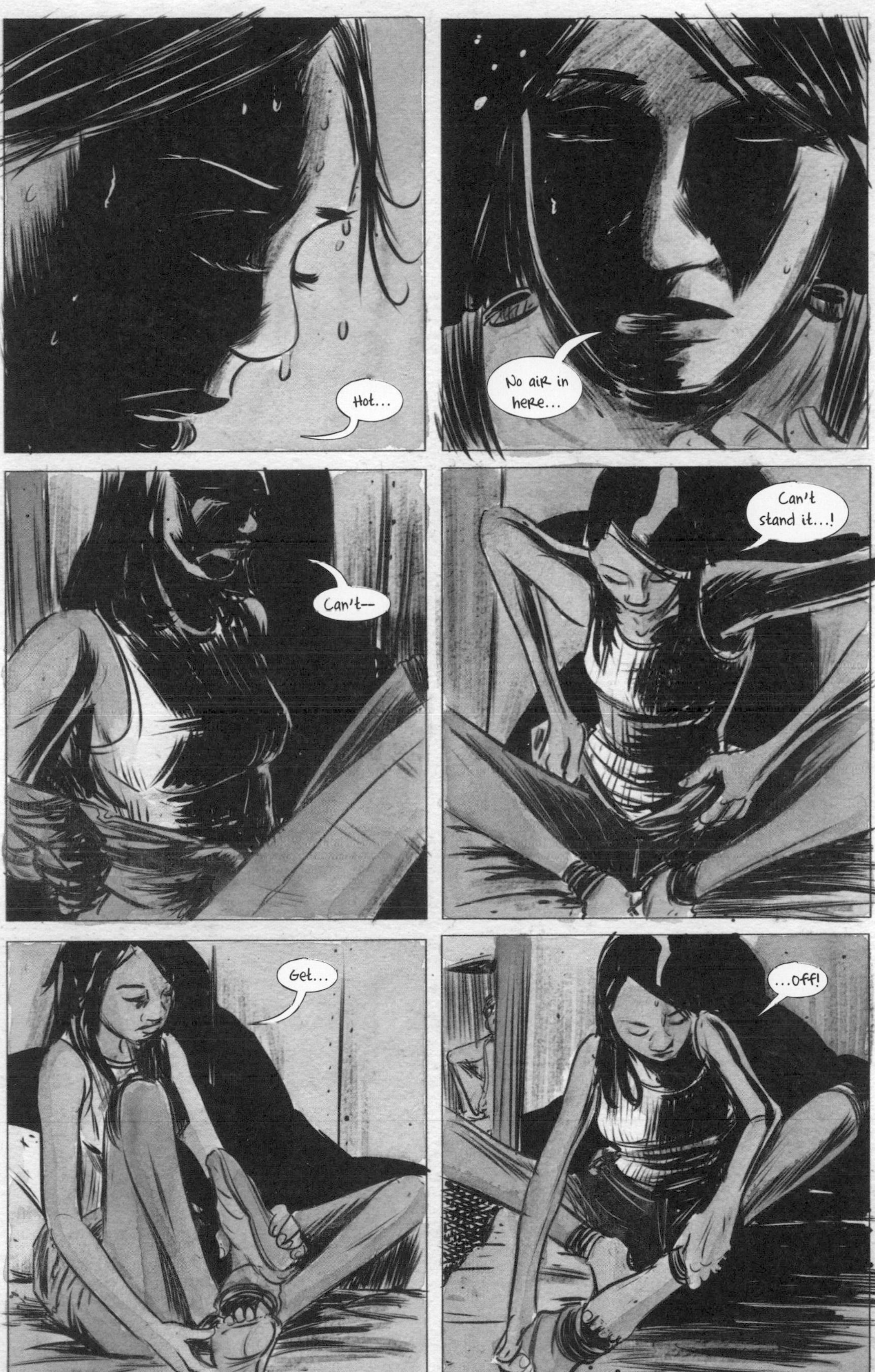
Hot...
No air in here...
Can't--
Can't stand it...!
Get...
...Off!

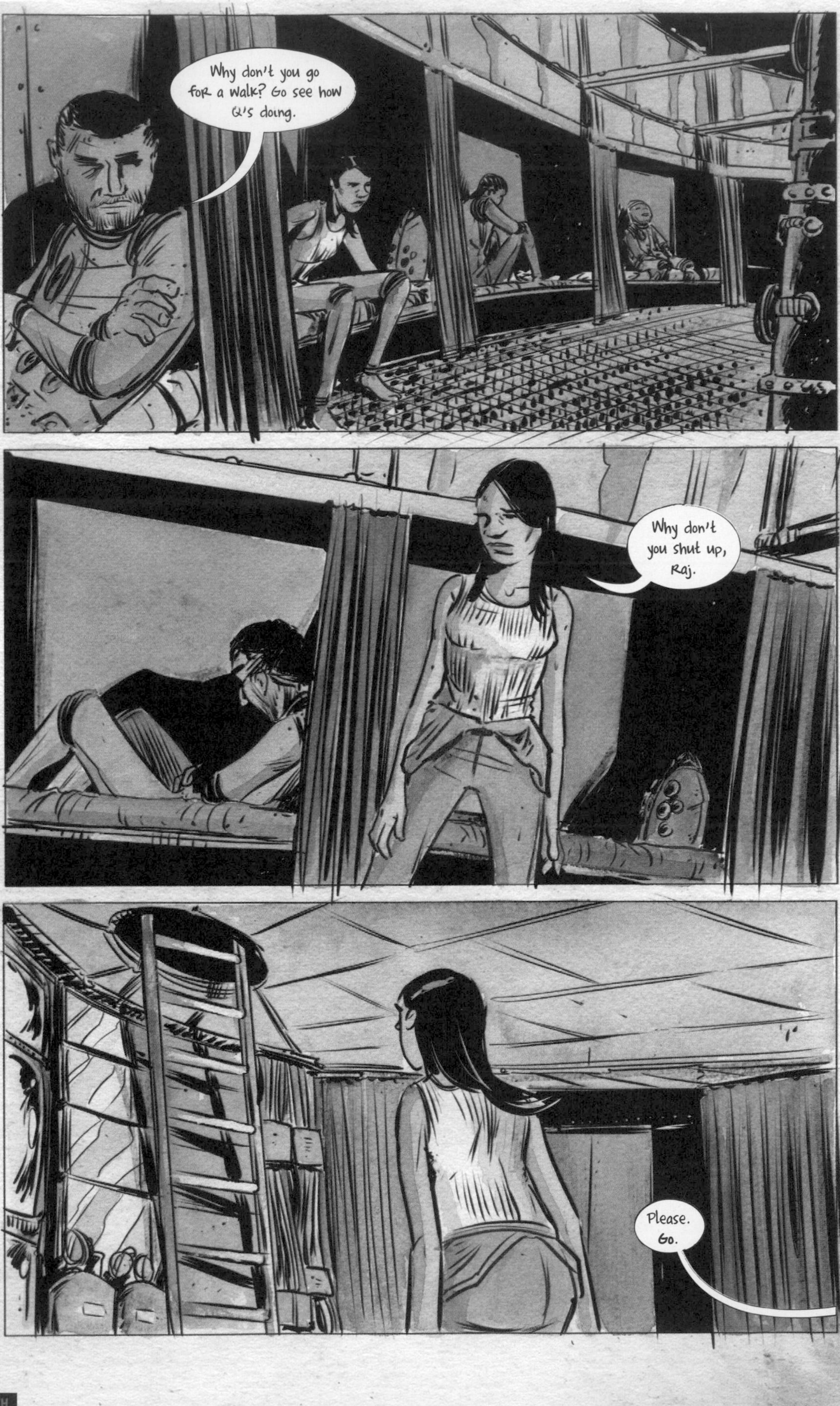
Why don't you go for a walk? Go see how Q's doing.
Why don't you shut up, Raj.
Please. Go.

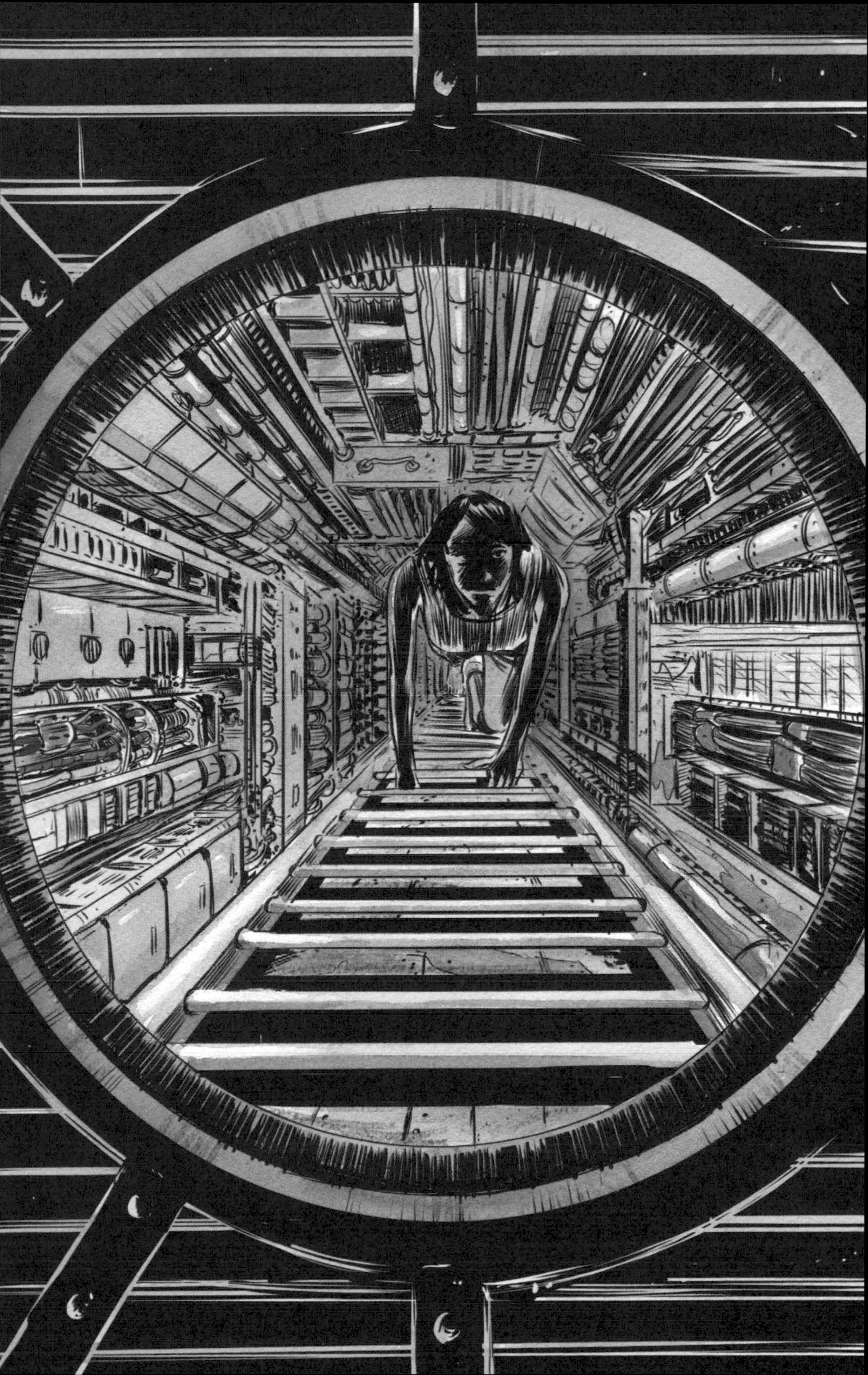

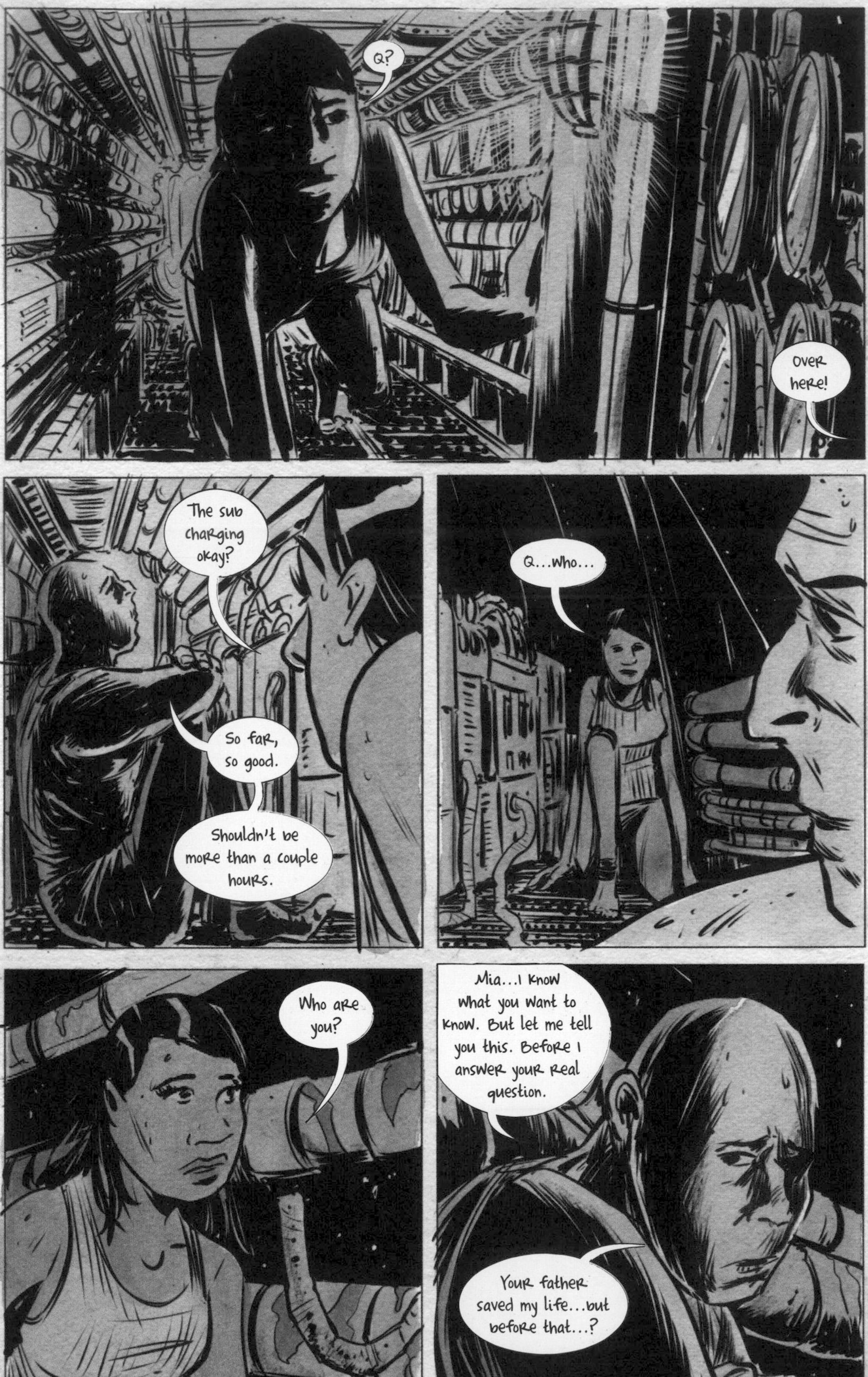
Q?
Over here!
The sub charging okay?
So far, so good.
Shouldn't be more than a couple hours.
Q...Who...
Who are you?
Mia...I know what you want to know. But let me tell you this. Before I answer your real question.
Your father saved my life...but before that...?

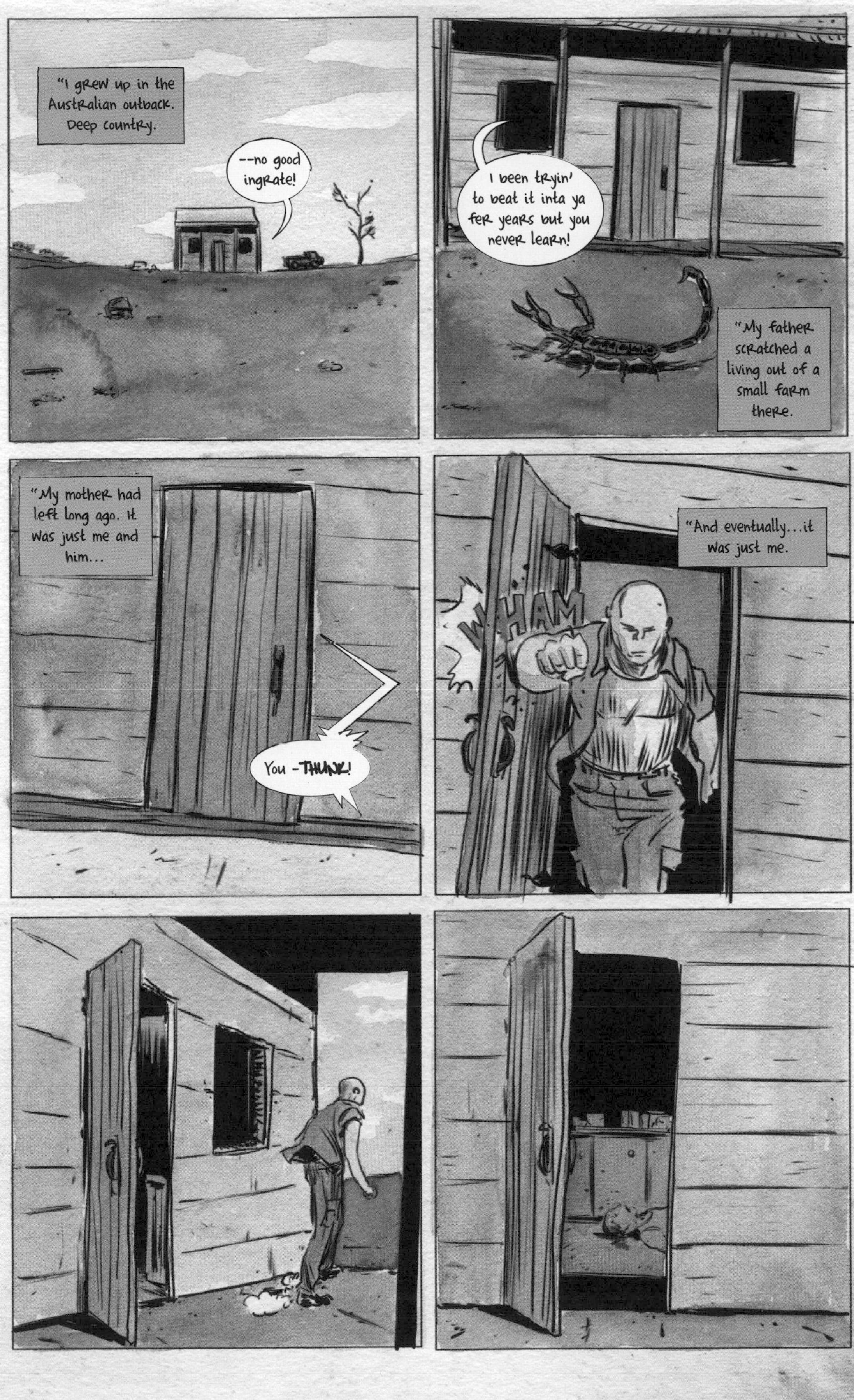
"I grew up in the Australian outback. Deep country.
--no good ingrate!
I been tryin' to beat it inta ya fer years but you never learn!
"My father scratched a living out of a small farm there.
"My mother had left long ago. It was just me and him...
You -THUNK!
"And eventually...it was just me.
WHAM

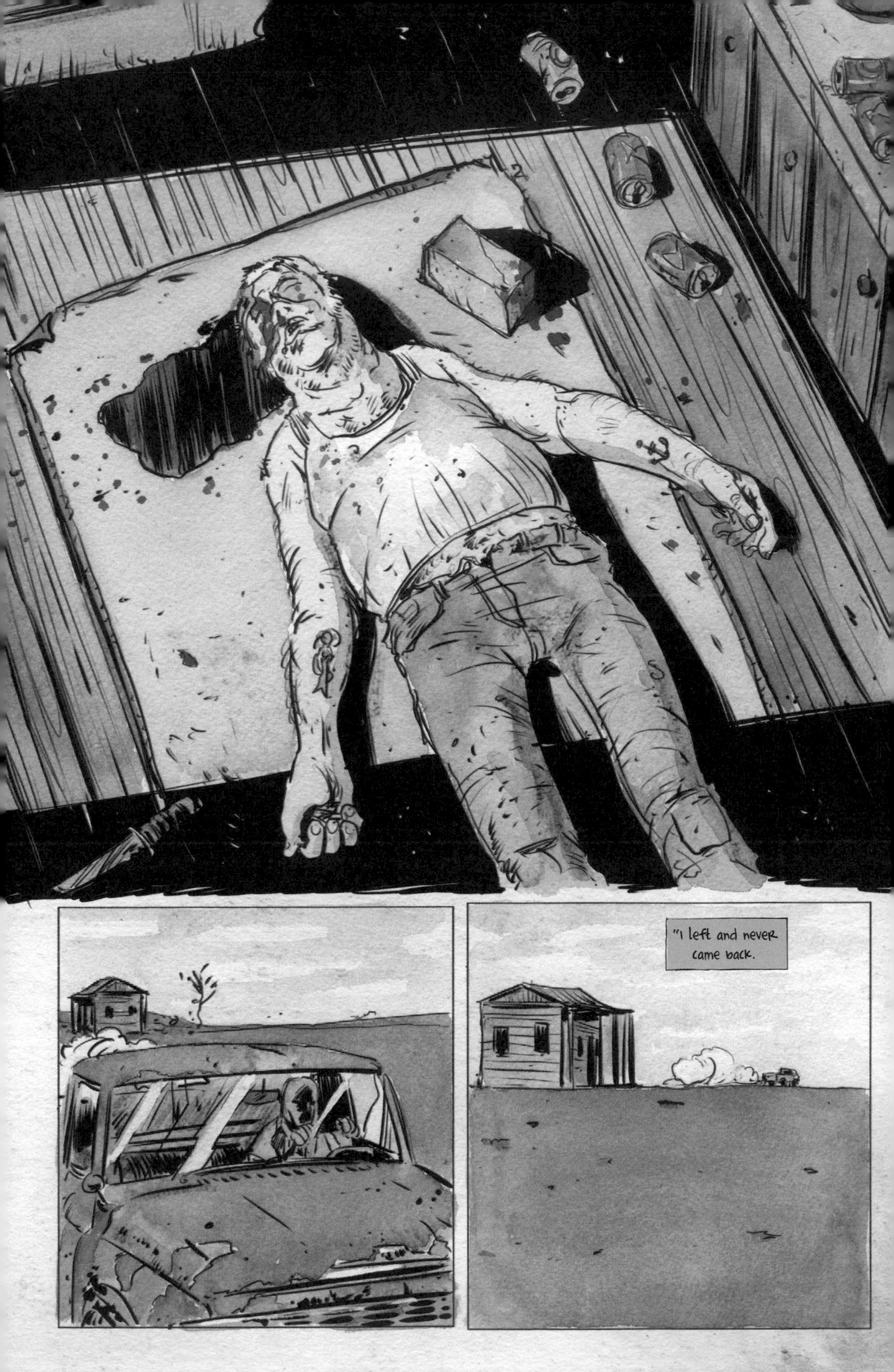
"I left and never
came back.

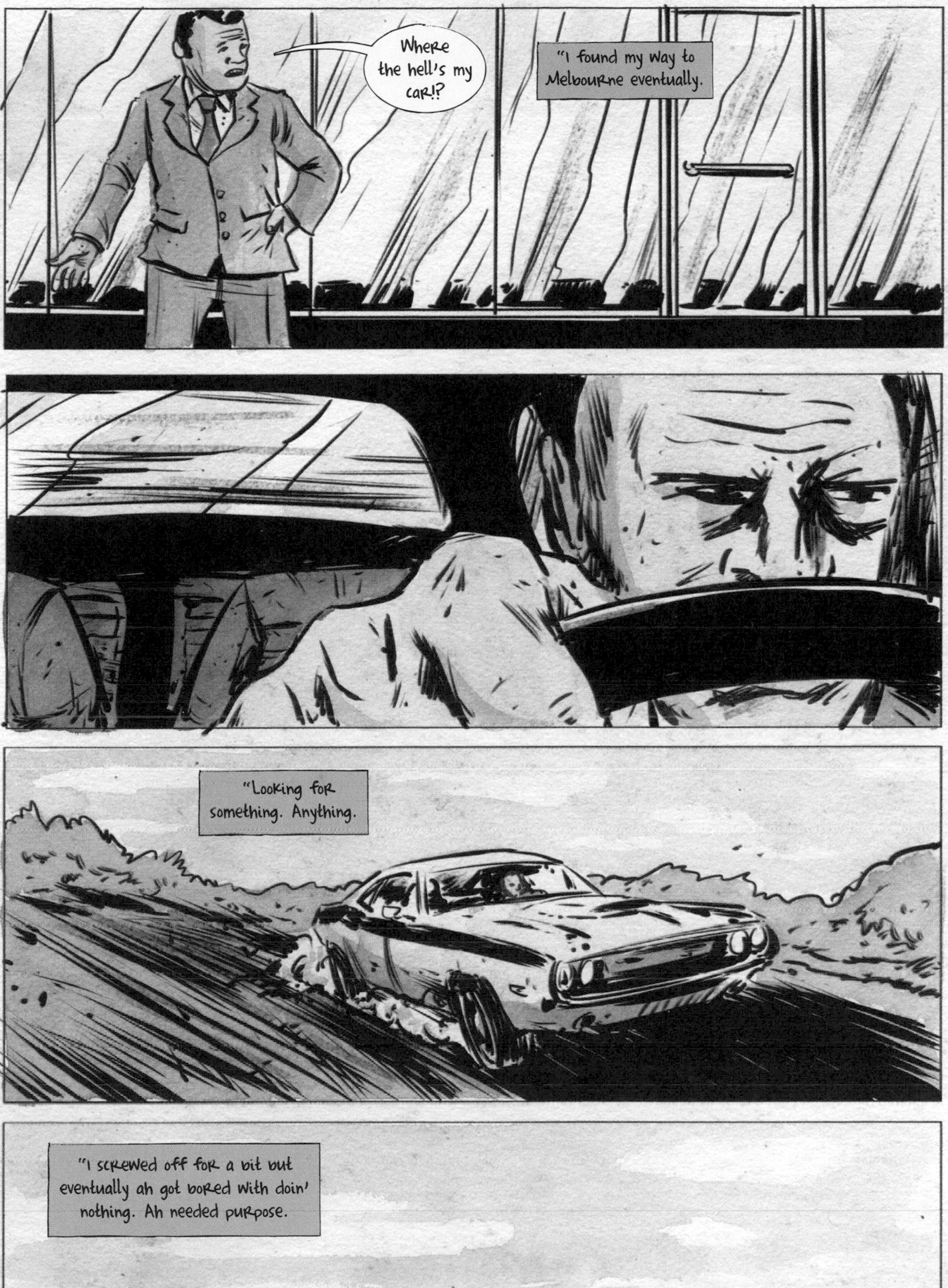
Where the hell's my car!?
"I found my way to Melbourne eventually.
"Looking for something. Anything.
"I screwed off for a bit but eventually ah got bored with doin' nothing. Ah needed purpose.

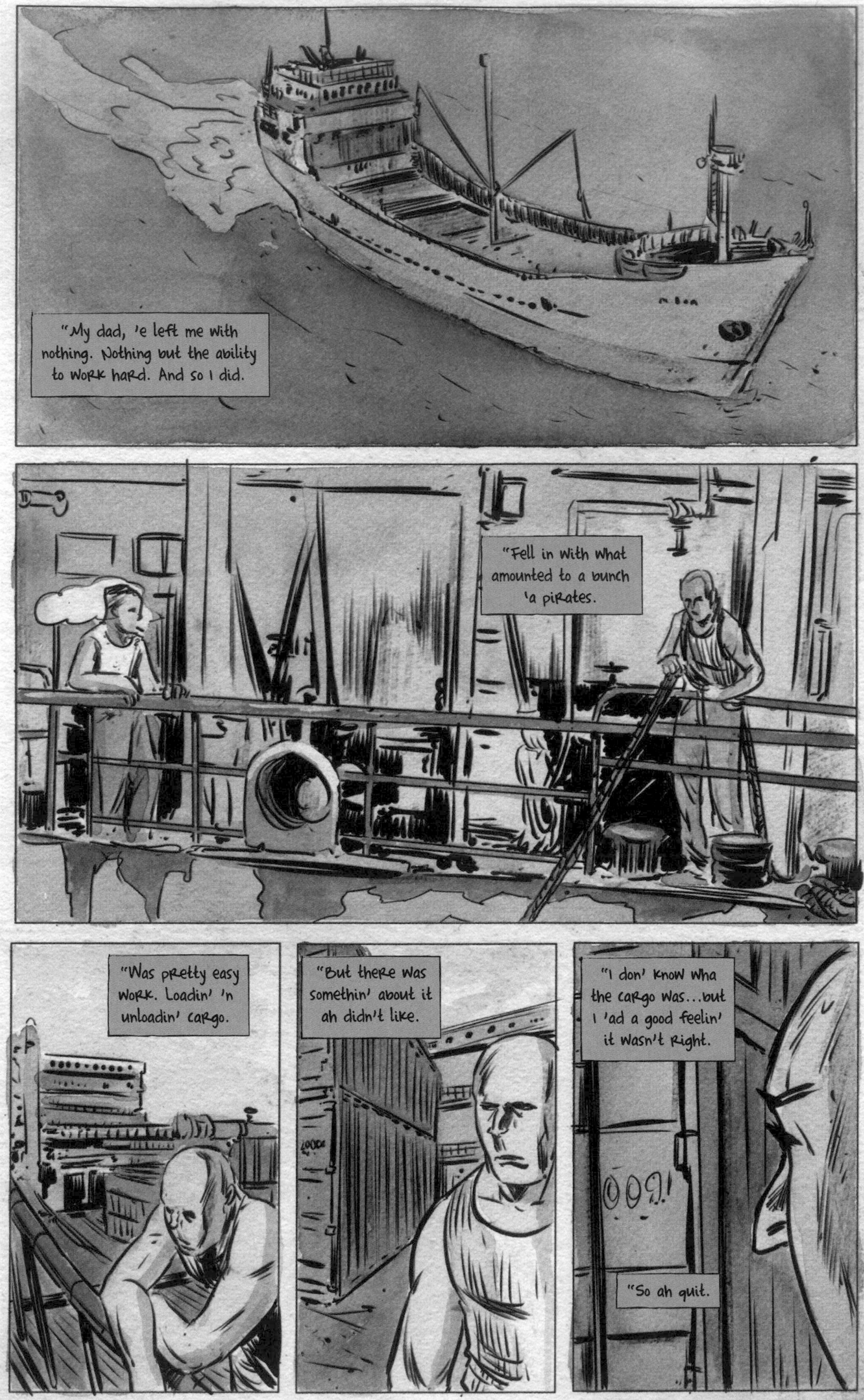
"My dad, 'e left me with nothing. Nothing but the ability to work hard. And so I did.
"Fell in with what amounted to a bunch 'a pirates.
"Was pretty easy work. Loadin' 'n unloadin' cargo.
"But there was somethin' about it ah didn't like.
"I don' know wha the cargo was...but I 'ad a good feelin' it wasn't right.
"So ah quit.

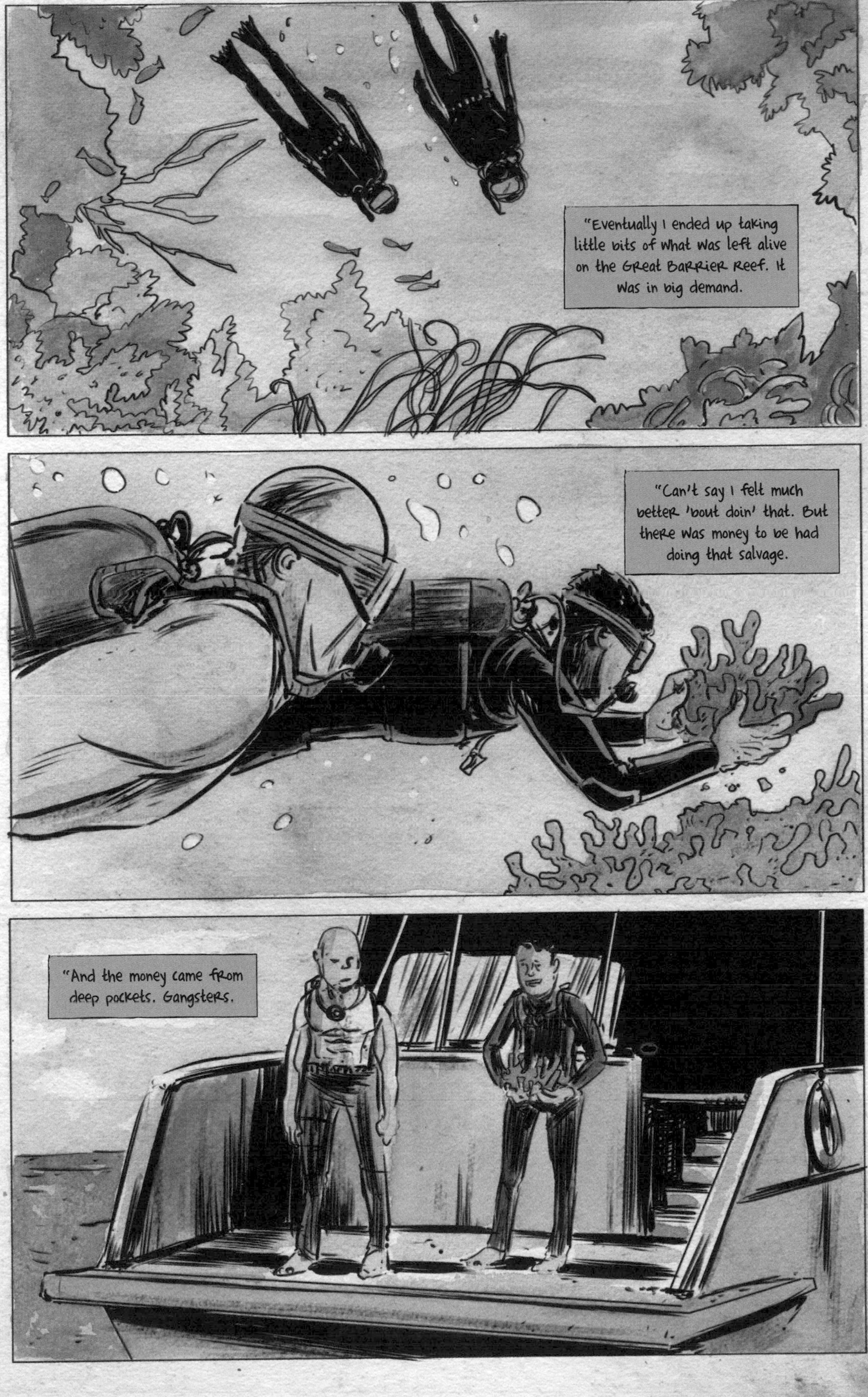
"Eventually I ended up taking little bits of what was left alive on the Great Barrier Reef. It was in big demand.
"Can't say I felt much better 'bout doin' that. But there was money to be had doing that salvage.
"And the money came from deep pockets. Gangsters.

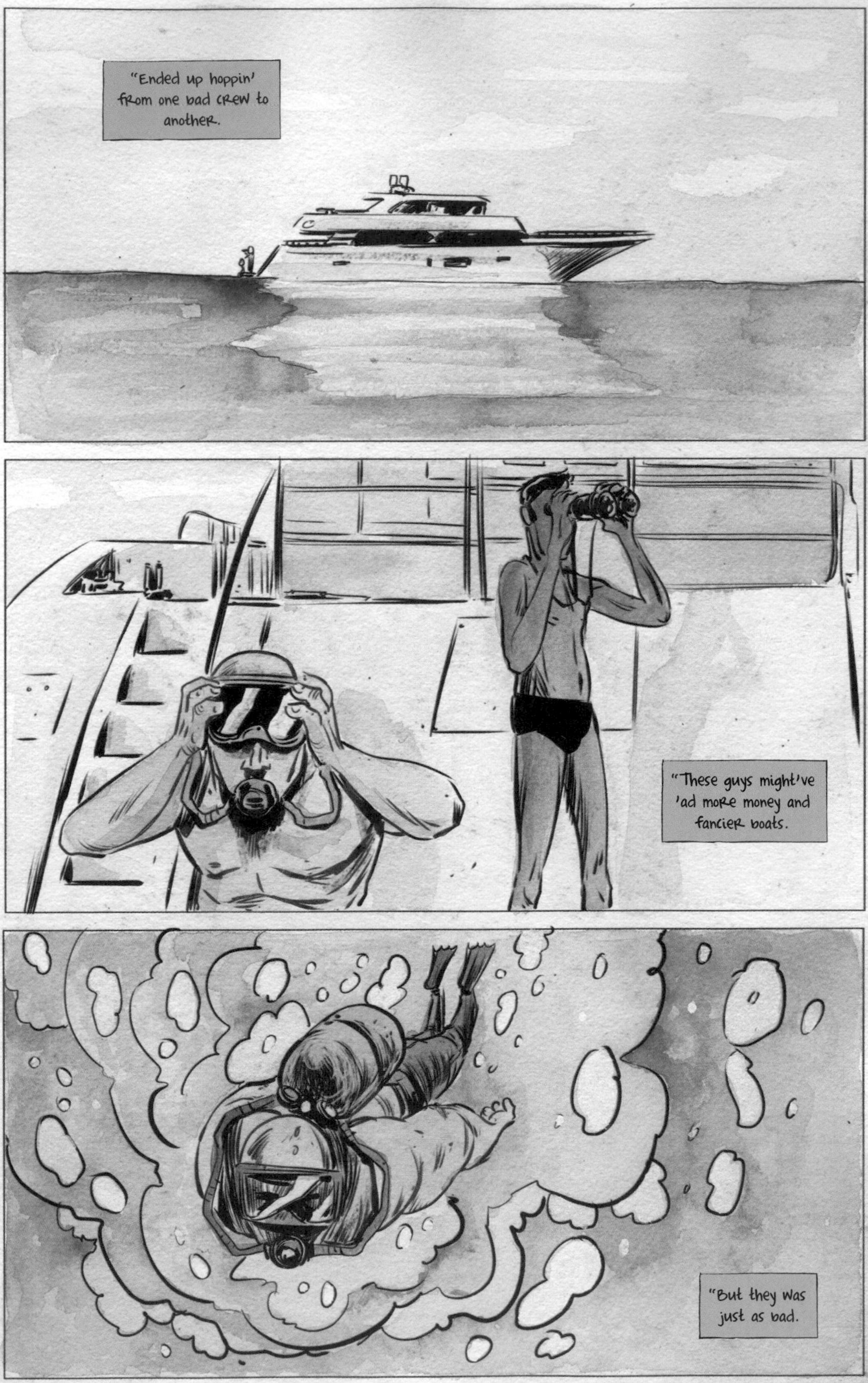
"Ended up hoppin' from one bad crew to another.
"These guys might've 'ad more money and fancier boats.
"But they was just as bad.

"Once a month they'd send me down to salvage a box or crate for 'em.

"Again, I 'ad no idea what they were dealin' in and I didn't ask questions.

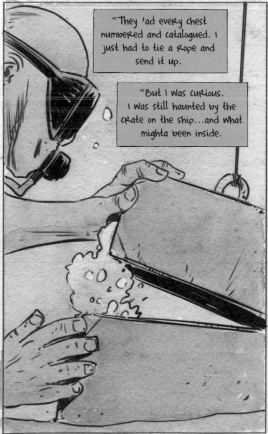

"They 'ad every chest numbered and catalogued. I just had to tie a rope and send it up.

"But I was curious. I was still haunted by the crate on the ship...and what mighta been inside.

"I had to know. Gold or drugs. No problem.

"But what they was dealin' in...

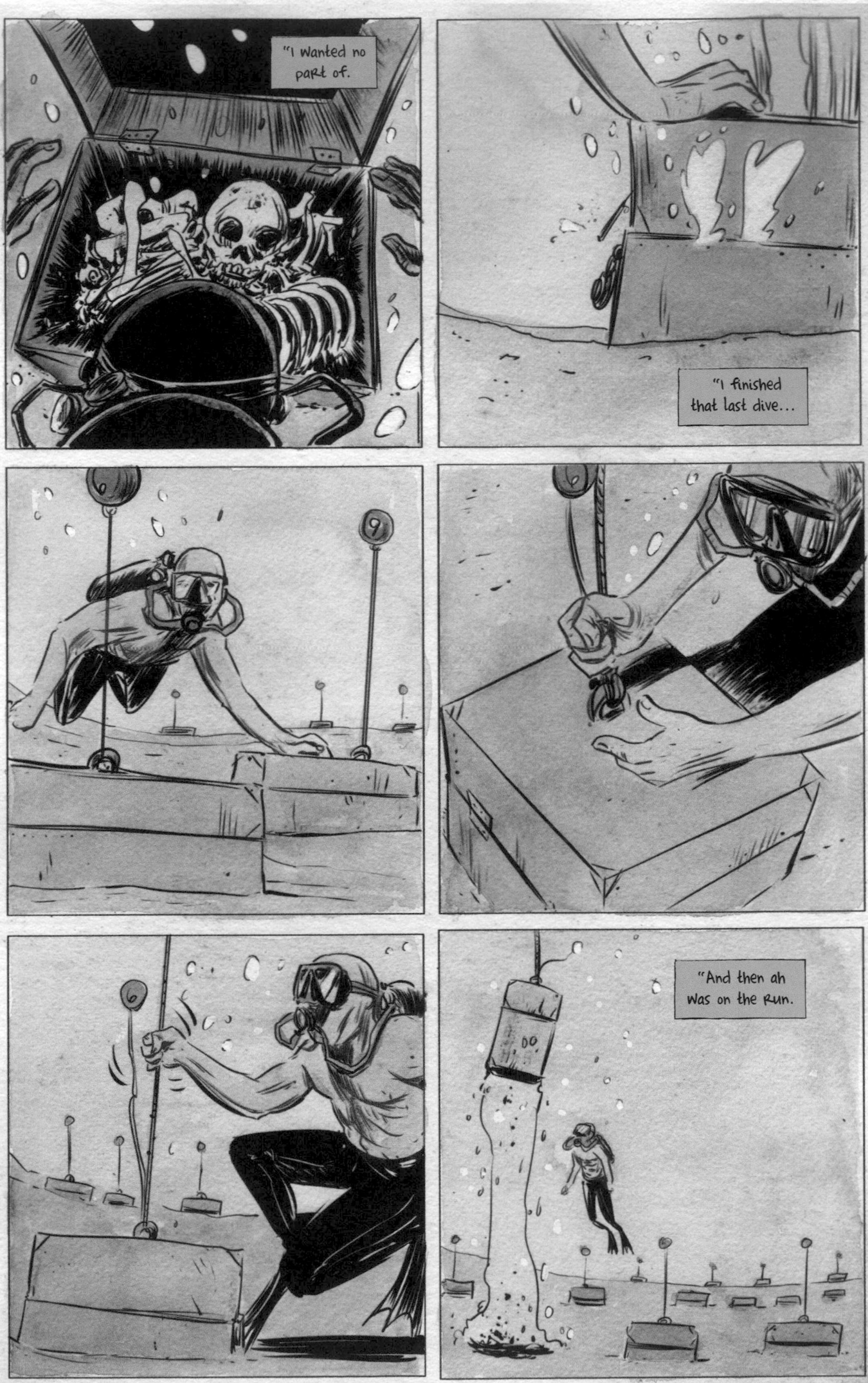
"I wanted no part of.
"I finished that last dive...
"And then ah was on the run.

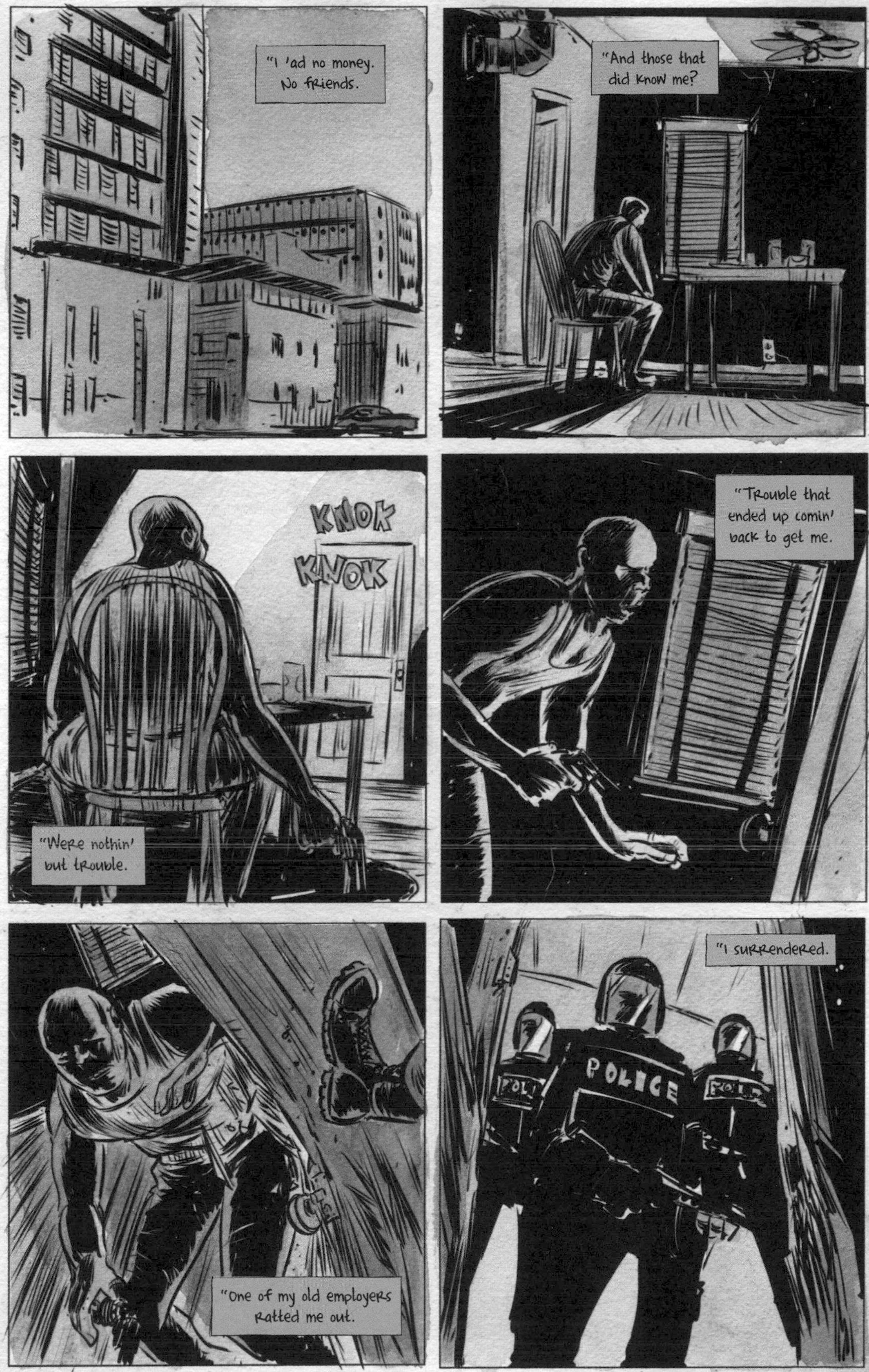

"I 'ad no money. No friends.
"And those that did know me?
KNOK
KNOK
"Were nothin' but trouble.
"Trouble that ended up comin' back to get me.
"One of my old employers ratted me out.
"I surrendered.
POLICE

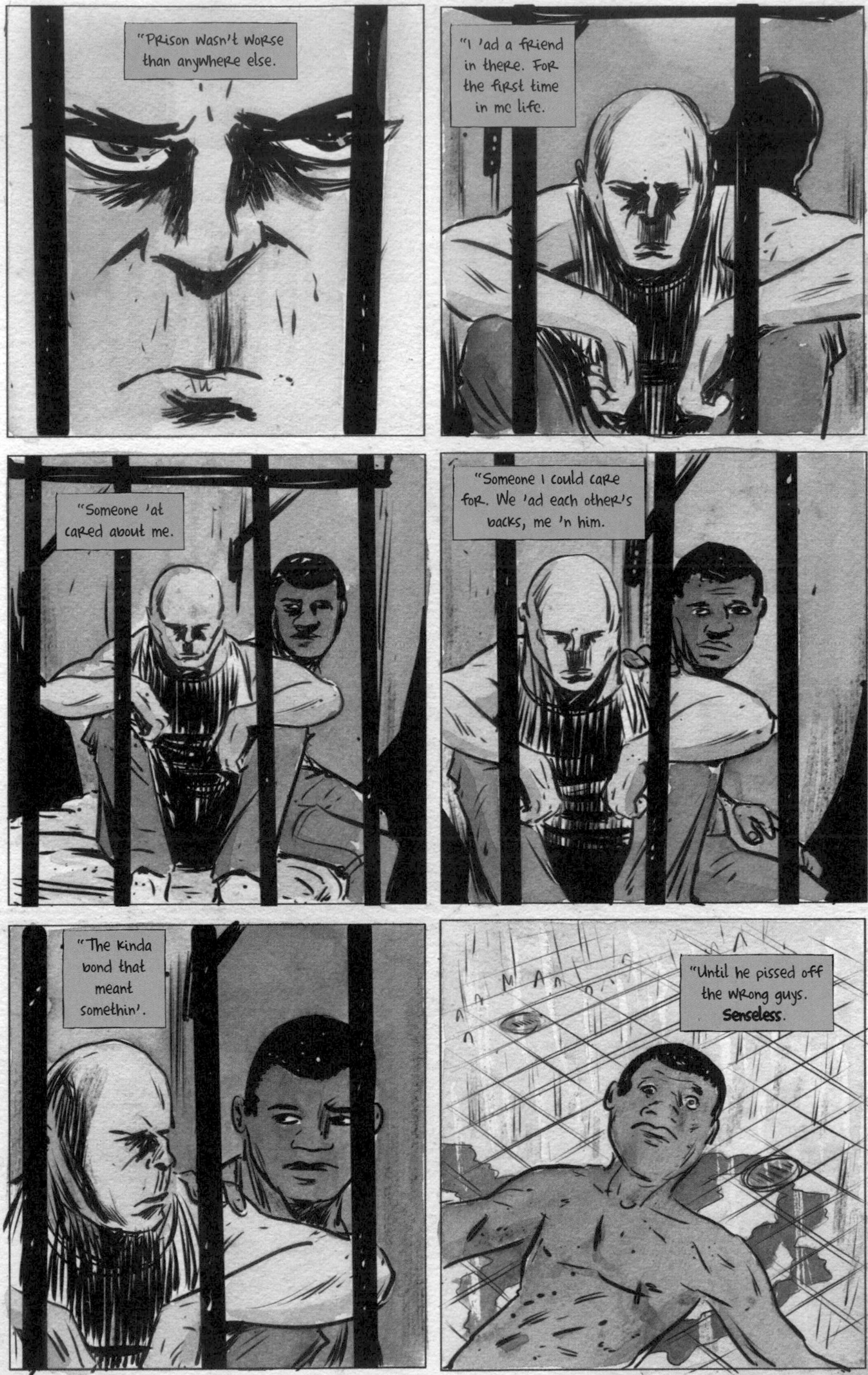
"Prison wasn't worse than anywhere else.
"I 'ad a friend in there. For the first time in me life.
"Someone 'at cared about me.
"Someone I could care for. We 'ad each other's backs, me 'n him.
"The kinda bond that meant somethin'.
"Until he pissed off the wrong guys. **Senseless**.

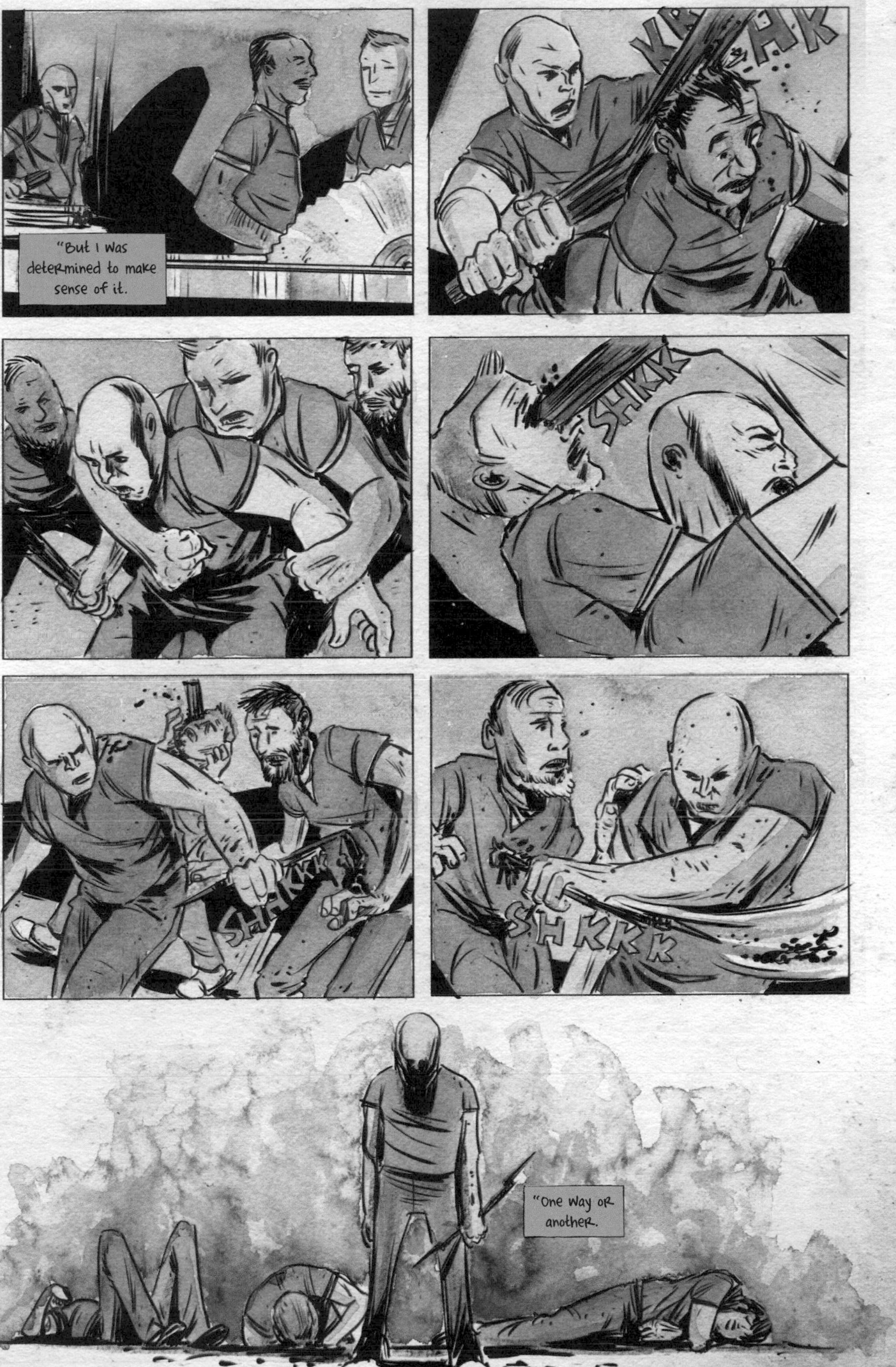
"But I was determined to make sense of it.
KRAK
SHKKK
SHKKK
SHKKK
"One way or another.

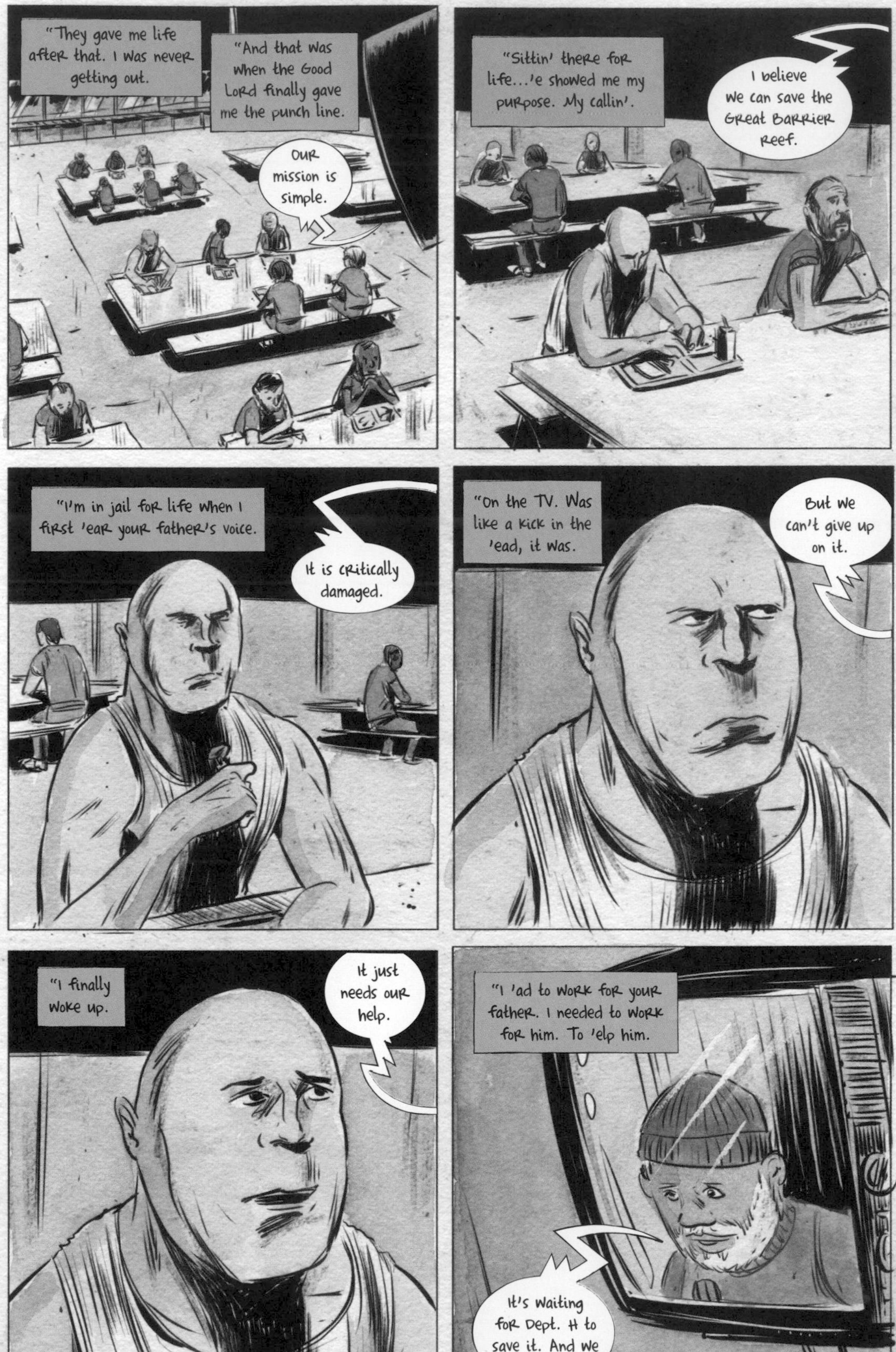
"They gave me life after that. I was never getting out.
"And that was when the Good Lord finally gave me the punch line.
Our mission is simple.
"Sittin' there for life...'e showed me my purpose. My callin'.
I believe we can save the Great Barrier Reef.
"I'm in jail for life when I first 'ear your father's voice.
It is critically damaged.
"On the TV. Was like a kick in the 'ead, it was.
But we can't give up on it.
"I finally woke up.
It just needs our help.
"I 'ad to work for your father. I needed to work for him. To 'elp him.
It's waiting for Dept. H to save it. And we will.

"an' no prison was gonna stop me from helpin' 'im.

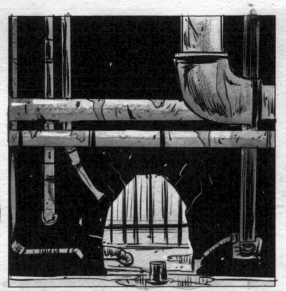

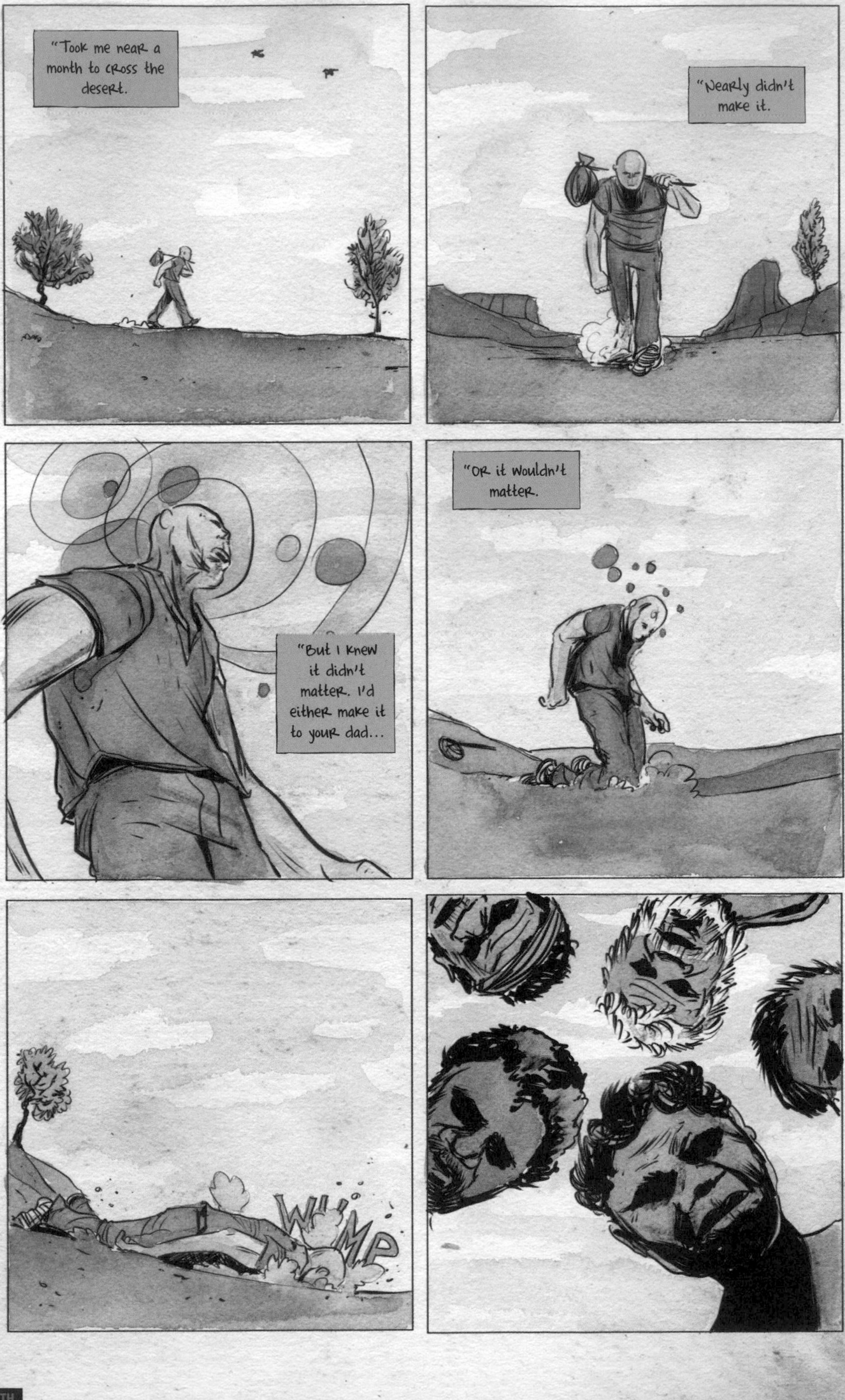
"Took me near a month to cross the desert.
"Nearly didn't make it.
"But I knew it didn't matter. I'd either make it to your dad...
"Or it wouldn't matter.
WUMP

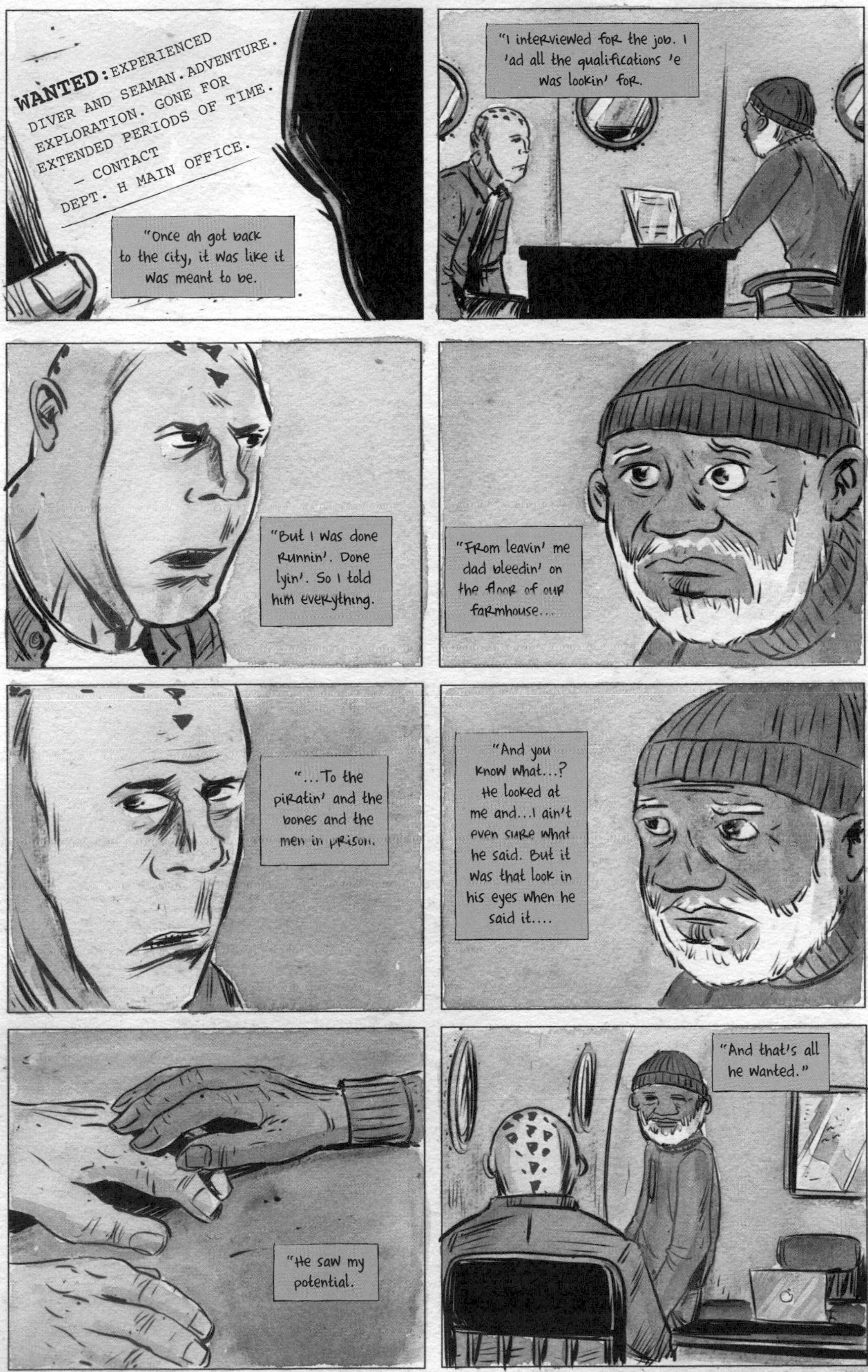
WANTED: EXPERIENCED DIVER AND SEAMAN. ADVENTURE. EXPLORATION. GONE FOR EXTENDED PERIODS OF TIME. — CONTACT DEPT. H MAIN OFFICE.
"Once ah got back to the city, it was like it was meant to be.
"I interviewed for the job. I 'ad all the qualifications 'e was lookin' for.
"But I was done runnin'. Done lyin'. So I told him everything.
"From leavin' me dad bleedin' on the floor of our farmhouse...
"...To the piratin' and the bones and the men in prison.
"And you know what...? He looked at me and...I ain't even sure what he said. But it was that look in his eyes when he said it....
"He saw my potential.
"And that's all he wanted."

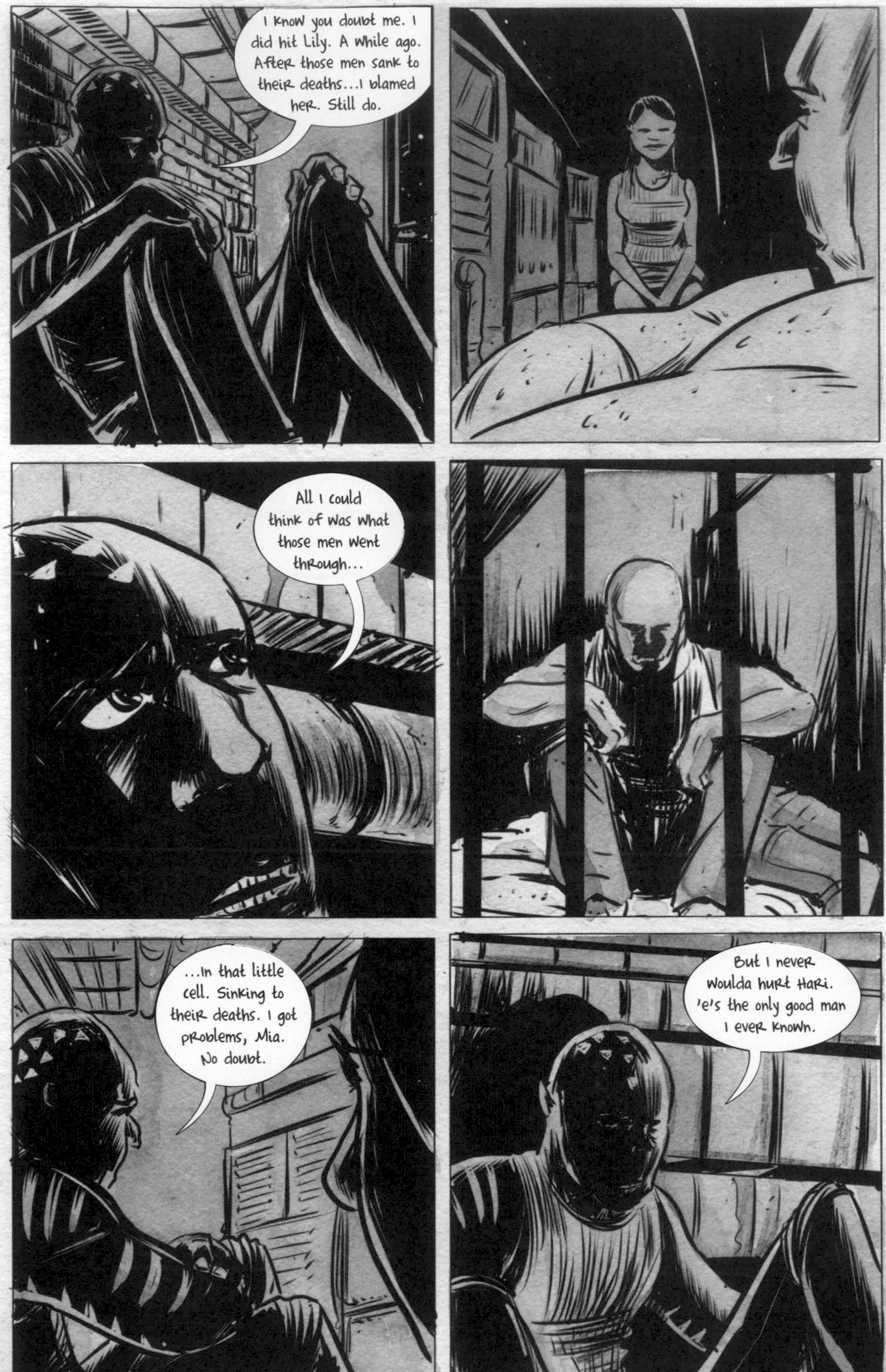
I know you doubt me. I did hit Lily. A while ago. After those men sank to their deaths...I blamed her. Still do.
All I could think of was what those men went through...
...In that little cell. Sinking to their deaths. I got problems, Mia. No doubt.
But I never woulda hurt Hari. 'e's the only good man I ever known.

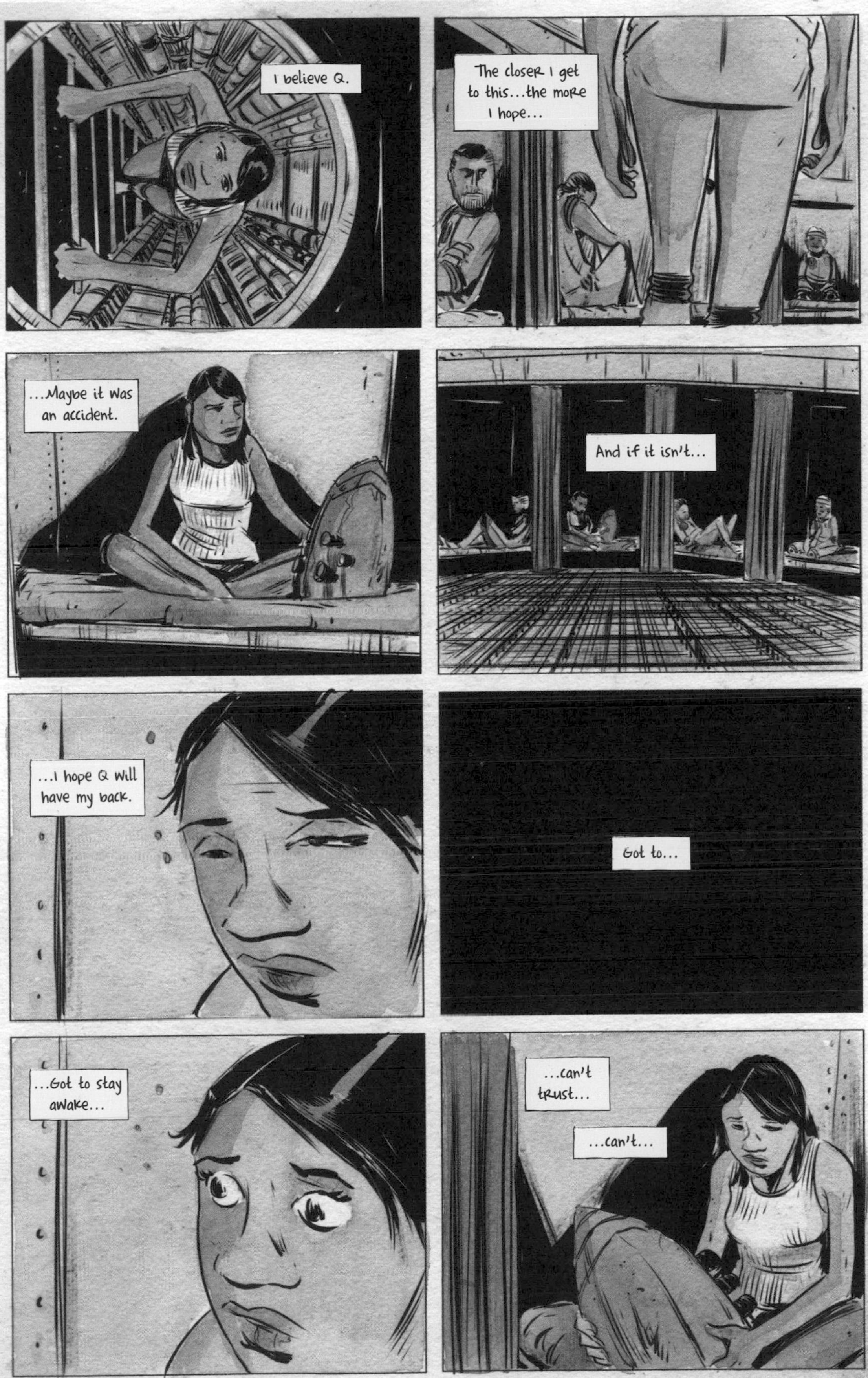
I believe Q.
The closer I get to this...the more I hope...
...Maybe it was an accident.
And if it isn't...
...I hope Q will have my back.
Got to...
...Got to stay awake...
...can't trust...
...can't...

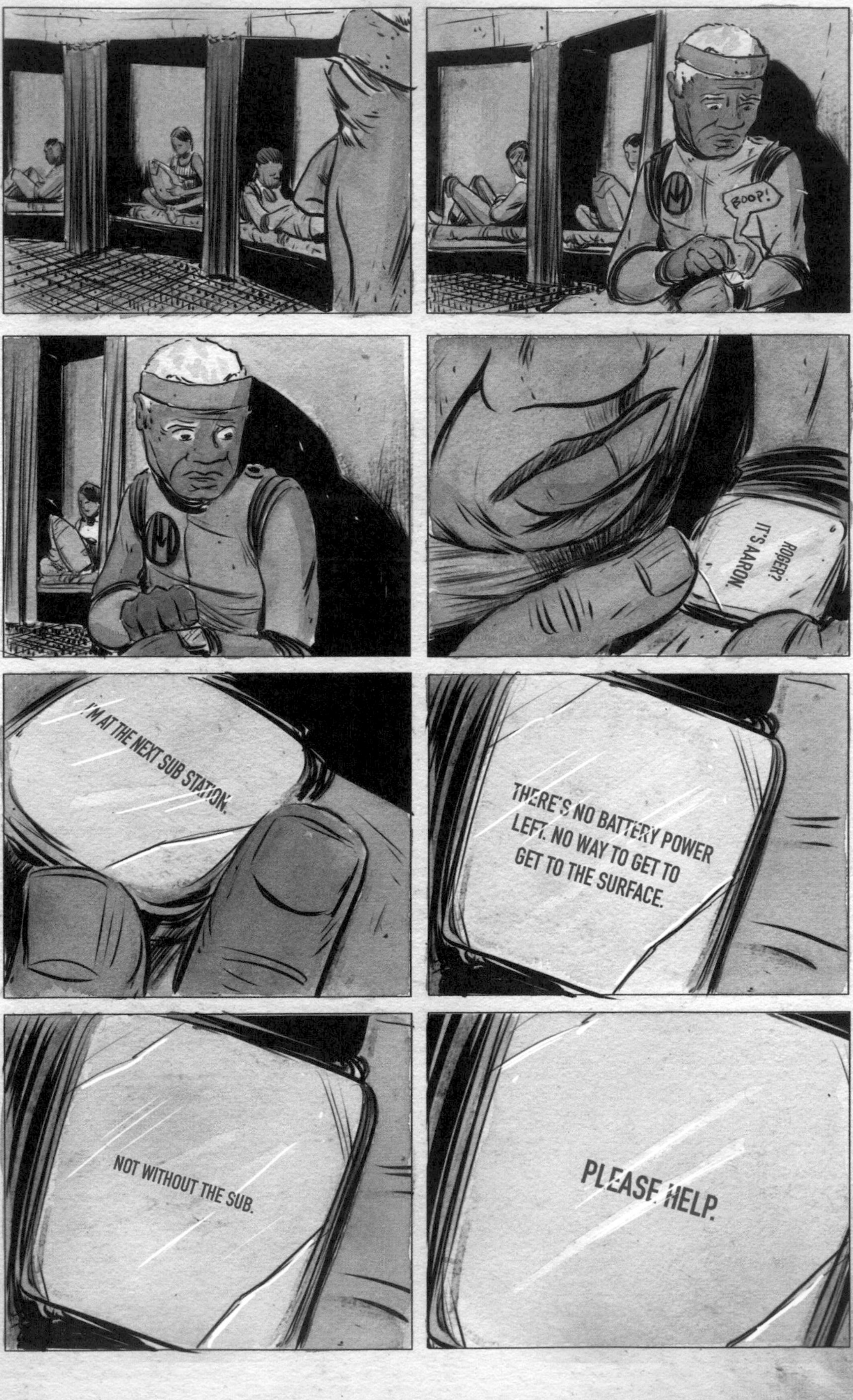
BOOP!
ROGER?
IT'S AARON.
I'M AT THE NEXT SUB STATION.
THERE'S NO BATTERY POWER LEFT. NO WAY TO GET TO GET TO THE SURFACE.
NOT WITHOUT THE SUB.
PLEASE HELP.

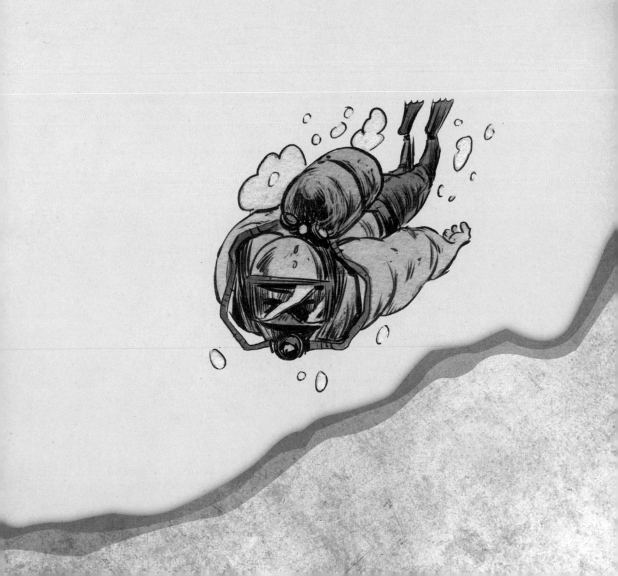

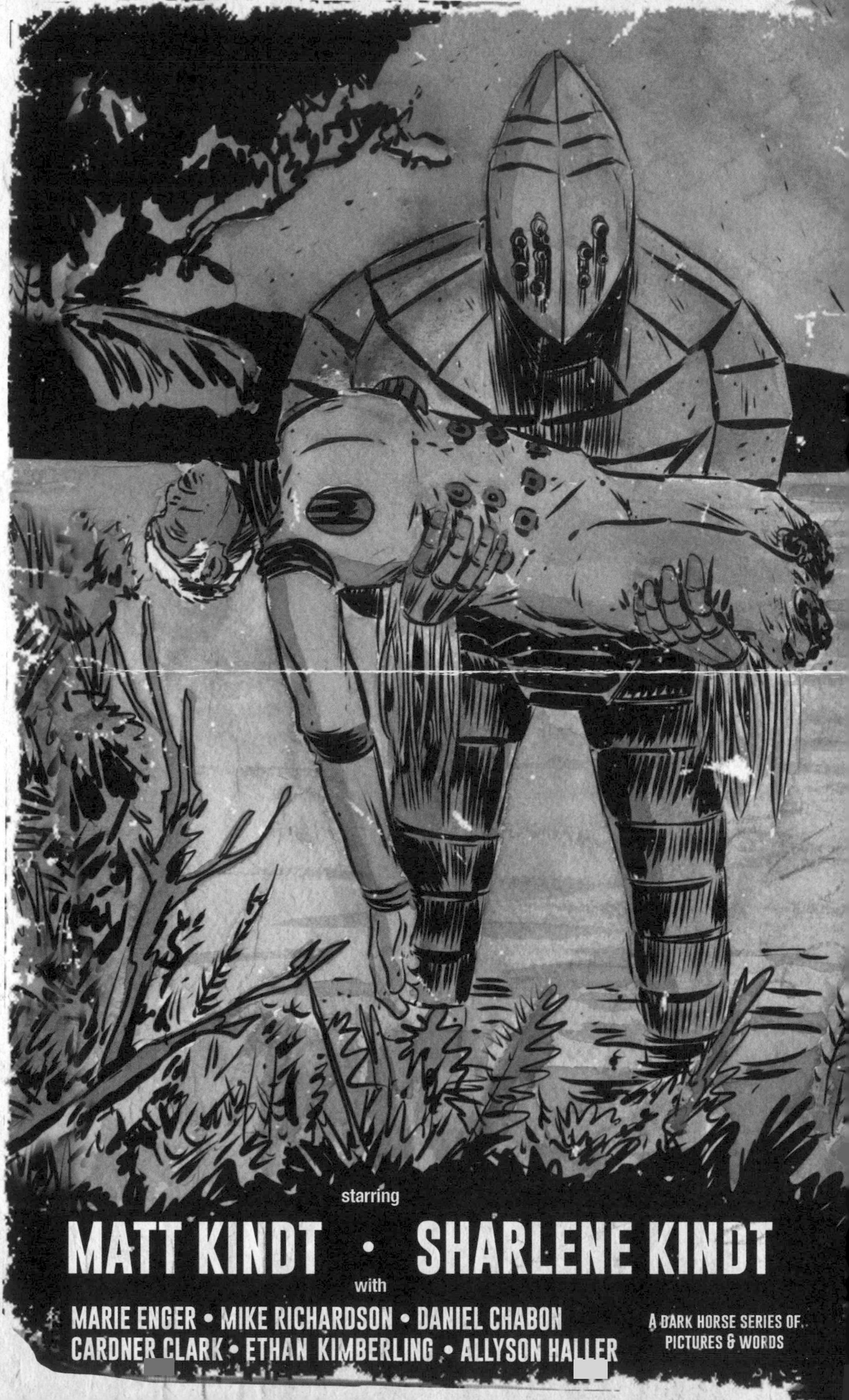
starring
MATT KINDT • SHARLENE KINDT
with
MARIE ENGER • MIKE RICHARDSON • DANIEL CHABON
CARDNER CLARK • ETHAN KIMBERLING • ALLYSON HALLER
A DARK HORSE SERIES OF PICTURES & WORDS

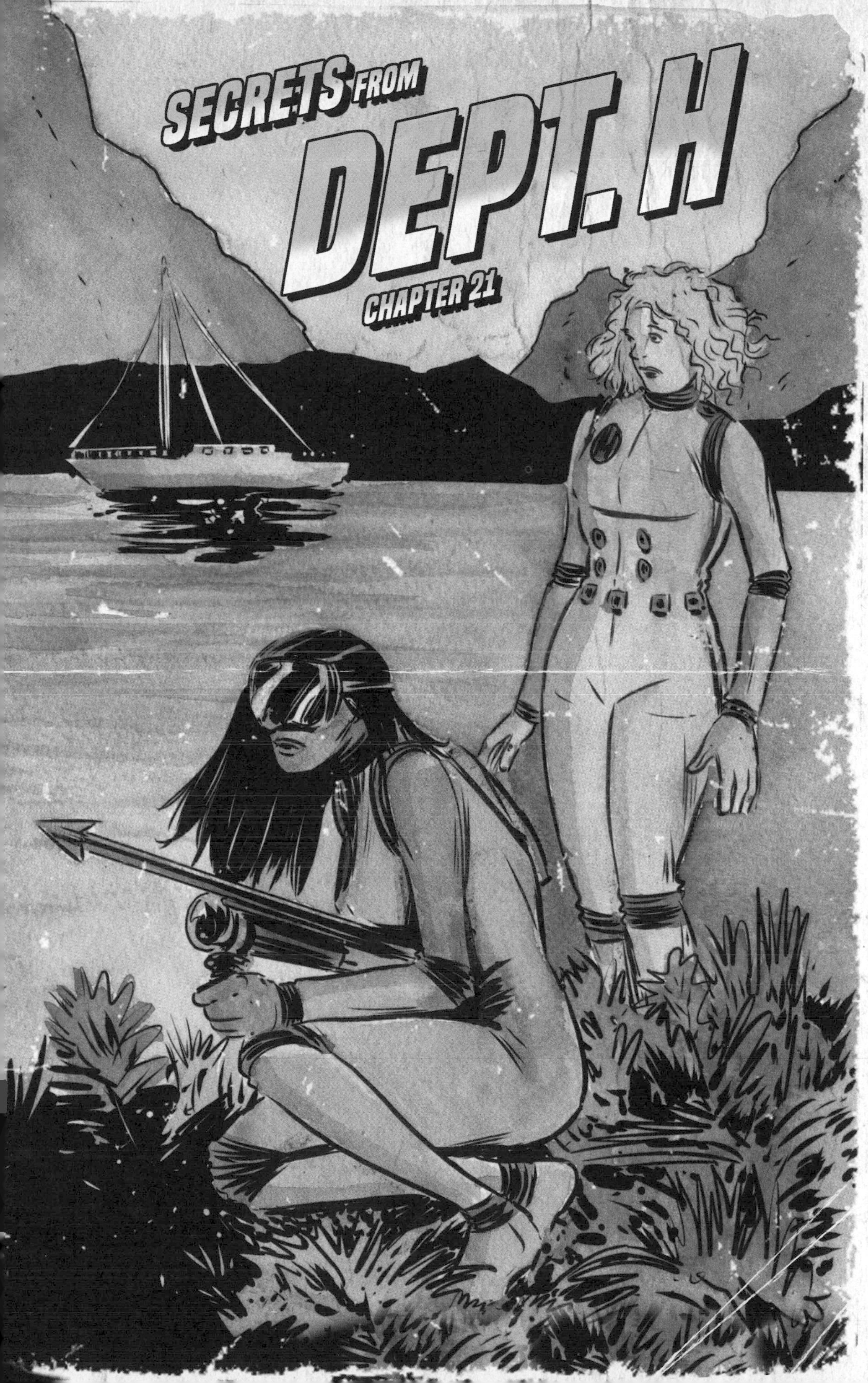
SECRETS FROM
DEPT. H
CHAPTER 21

THERE'S NO BATTERY POWER LEFT. NO WAY TO GET TO THE SURFACE.

NOT WITHOUT THE SUB.

PLEASE HELP.

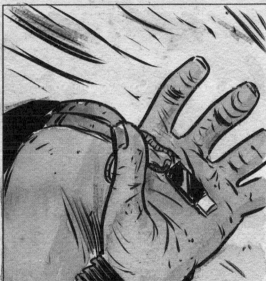

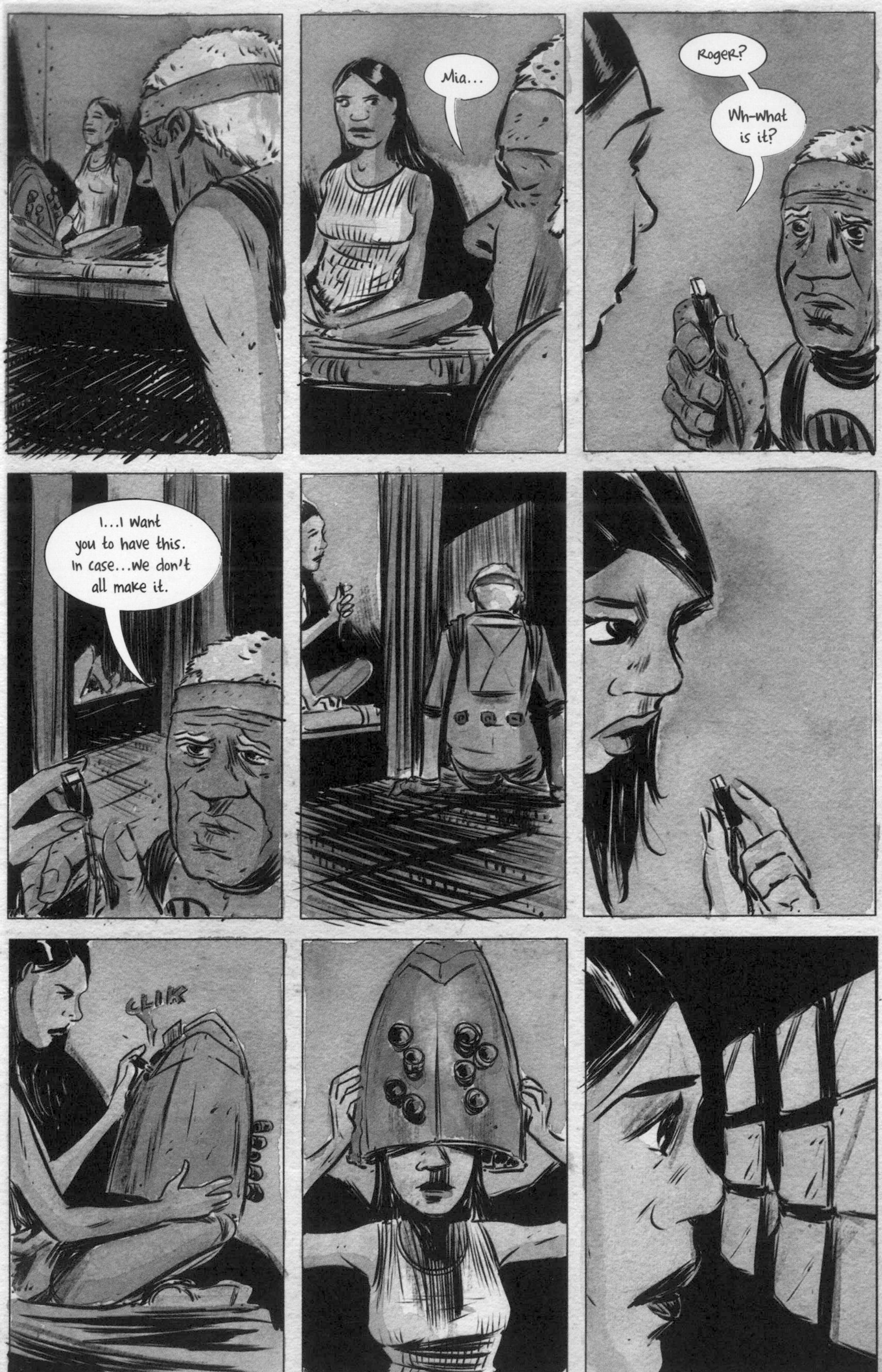
Mia...
Roger?
Wh-what is it?
I...I want you to have this. In case...we don't all make it.
CLIK

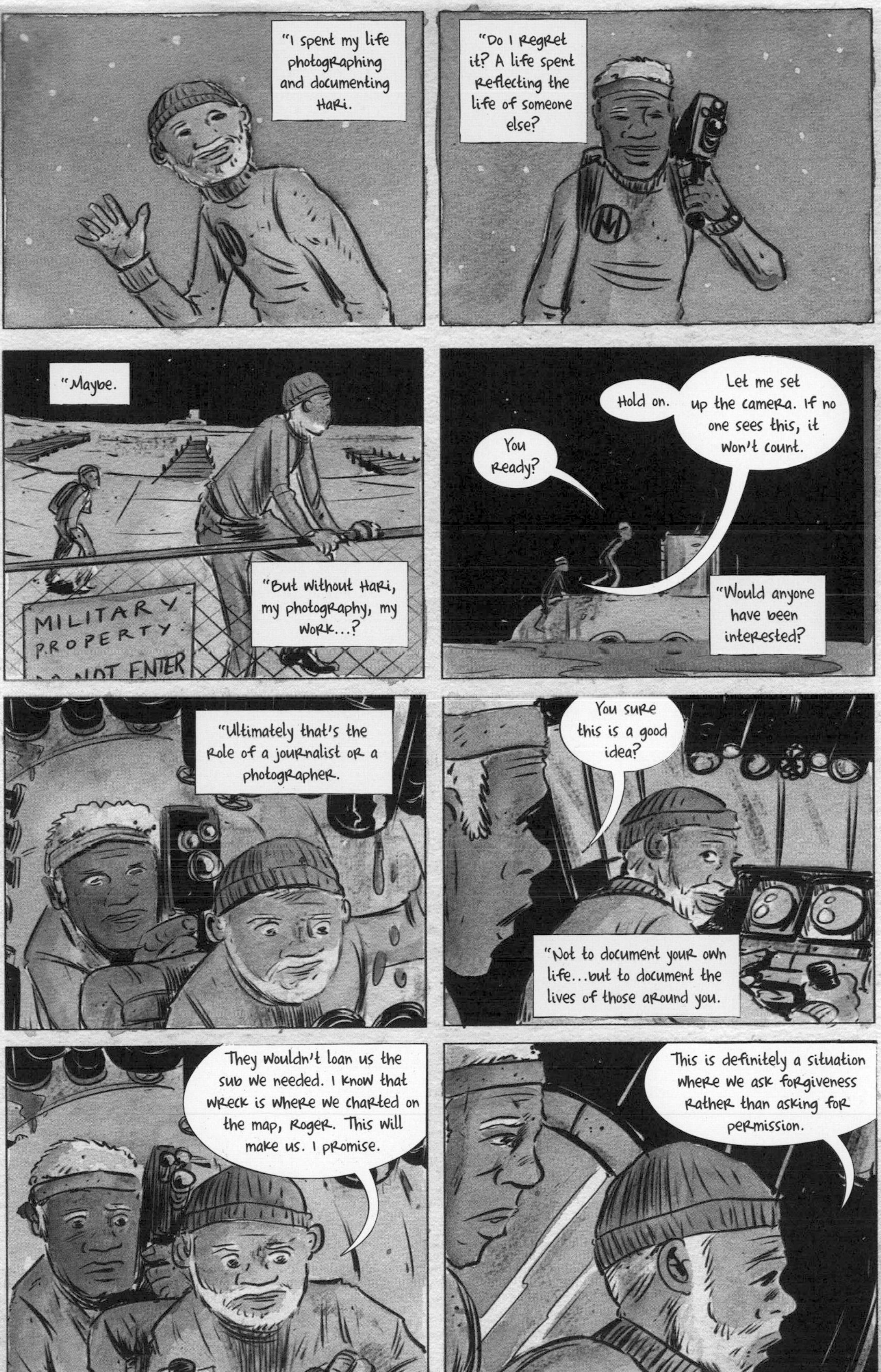
"I spent my life photographing and documenting Hari.
"Do I regret it? A life spent reflecting the life of someone else?
"Maybe.
MILITARY PROPERTY
DO NOT ENTER
"But without Hari, my photography, my work...?
Hold on.
Let me set up the camera. If no one sees this, it won't count.
You ready?
"Would anyone have been interested?
"Ultimately that's the role of a journalist or a photographer.
You sure this is a good idea?
"Not to document your own life...but to document the lives of those around you.
They wouldn't loan us the sub we needed. I know that wreck is where we charted on the map, Roger. This will make us. I promise.
This is definitely a situation where we ask forgiveness rather than asking for permission.

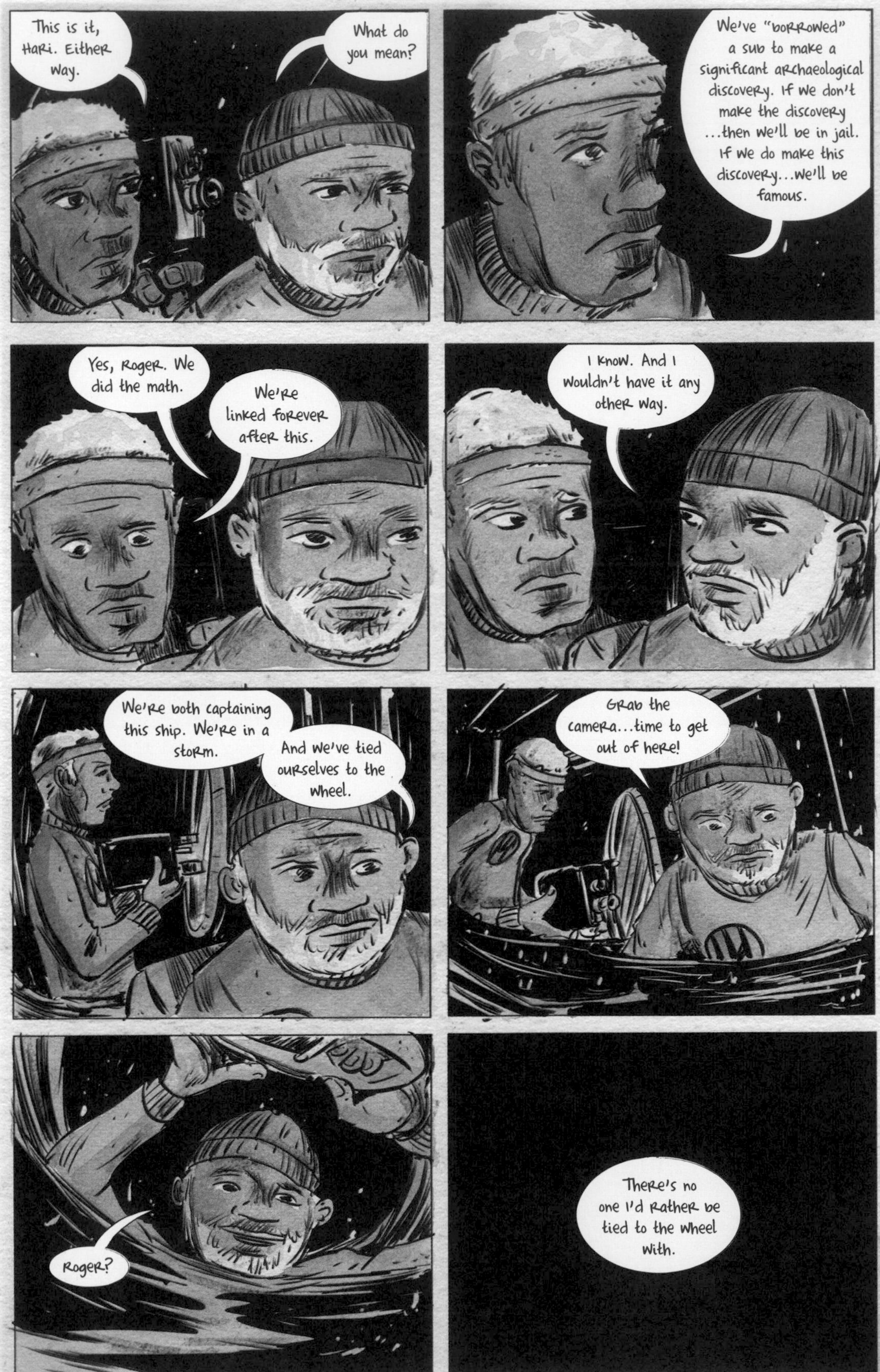
This is it, Hari. Either way.
What do you mean?
We've "borrowed" a sub to make a significant archaeological discovery. If we don't make the discovery ...then we'll be in jail. If we do make this discovery...we'll be famous.
Yes, Roger. We did the math.
We're linked forever after this.
I know. And I wouldn't have it any other way.
We're both captaining this ship. We're in a storm.
And we've tied ourselves to the wheel.
Grab the camera...time to get out of here!
Roger?
There's no one I'd rather be tied to the wheel with.

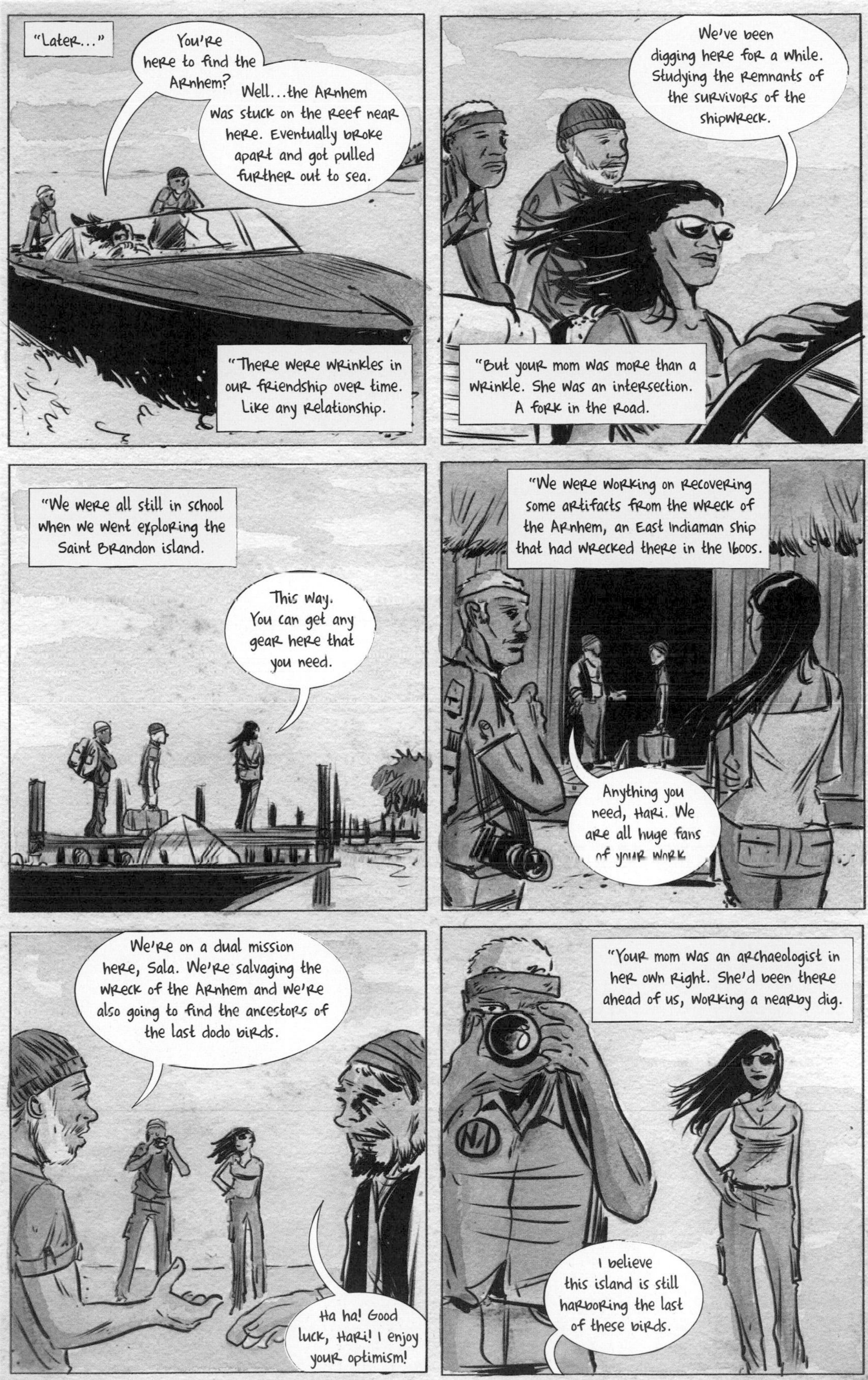
"Later..."
You're here to find the Arnhem?
Well...the Arnhem was stuck on the reef near here. Eventually broke apart and got pulled further out to sea.
"There were wrinkles in our friendship over time. Like any relationship.
We've been digging here for a while. Studying the remnants of the survivors of the shipwreck.
"But your mom was more than a wrinkle. She was an intersection. A fork in the road.
"We were all still in school when we went exploring the Saint Brandon island.
This way. You can get any gear here that you need.
"We were working on recovering some artifacts from the wreck of the Arnhem, an East Indiaman ship that had wrecked there in the 1600s.
Anything you need, Hari. We are all huge fans of your work
We're on a dual mission here, Sala. We're salvaging the wreck of the Arnhem and we're also going to find the ancestors of the last dodo birds.
Ha ha! Good luck, Hari! I enjoy your optimism!
"Your mom was an archaeologist in her own right. She'd been there ahead of us, working a nearby dig.
I believe this island is still harboring the last of these birds.

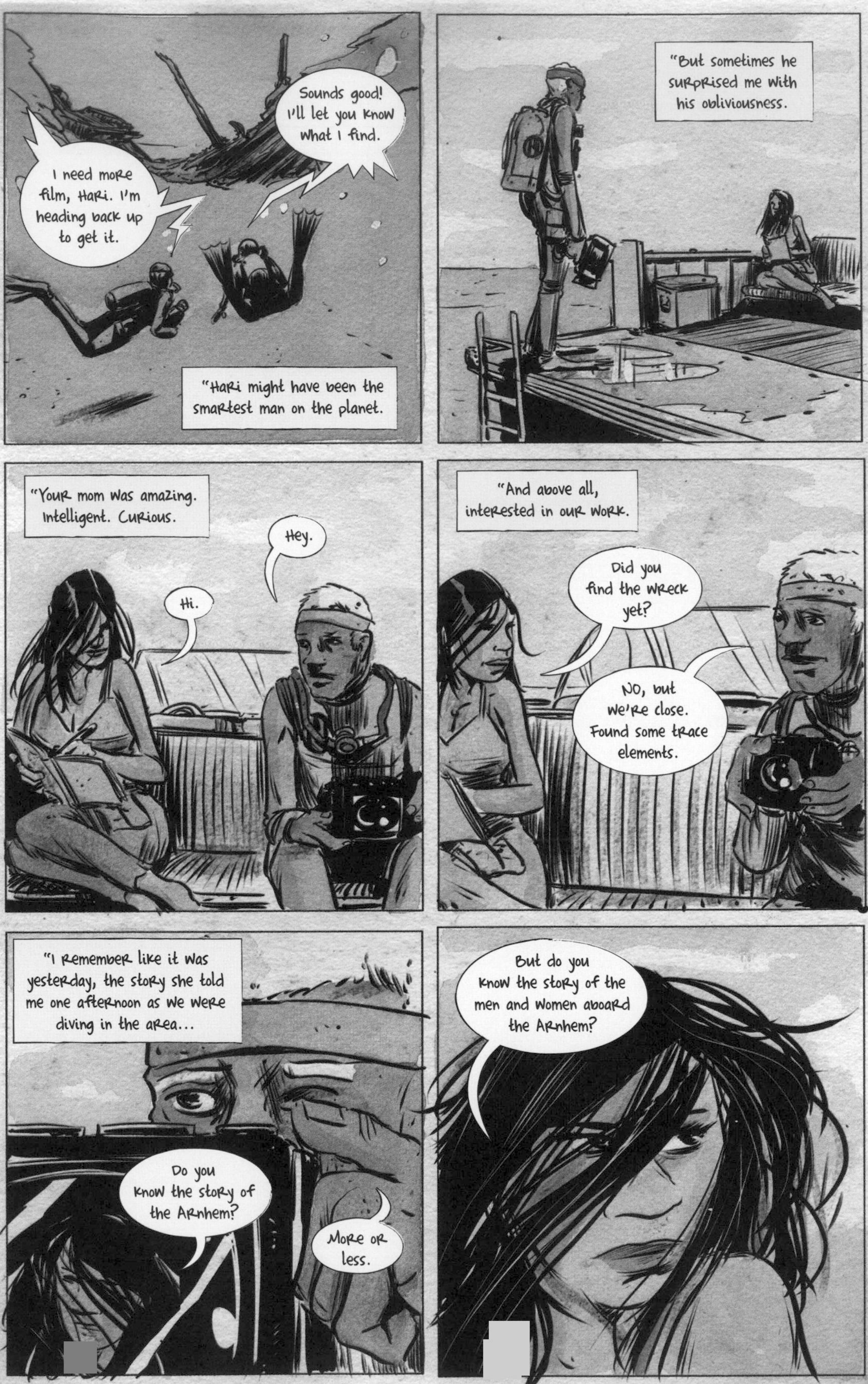
I need more film, Hari. I'm heading back up to get it.
Sounds good! I'll let you know what I find.
"Hari might have been the smartest man on the planet.
"But sometimes he surprised me with his obliviousness.
"Your mom was amazing. Intelligent. Curious.
Hi.
Hey.
"And above all, interested in our work.
Did you find the wreck yet?
No, but we're close. Found some trace elements.
"I remember like it was yesterday, the story she told me one afternoon as we were diving in the area...
Do you know the story of the Arnhem?
More or less.
But do you know the story of the men and women aboard the Arnhem?

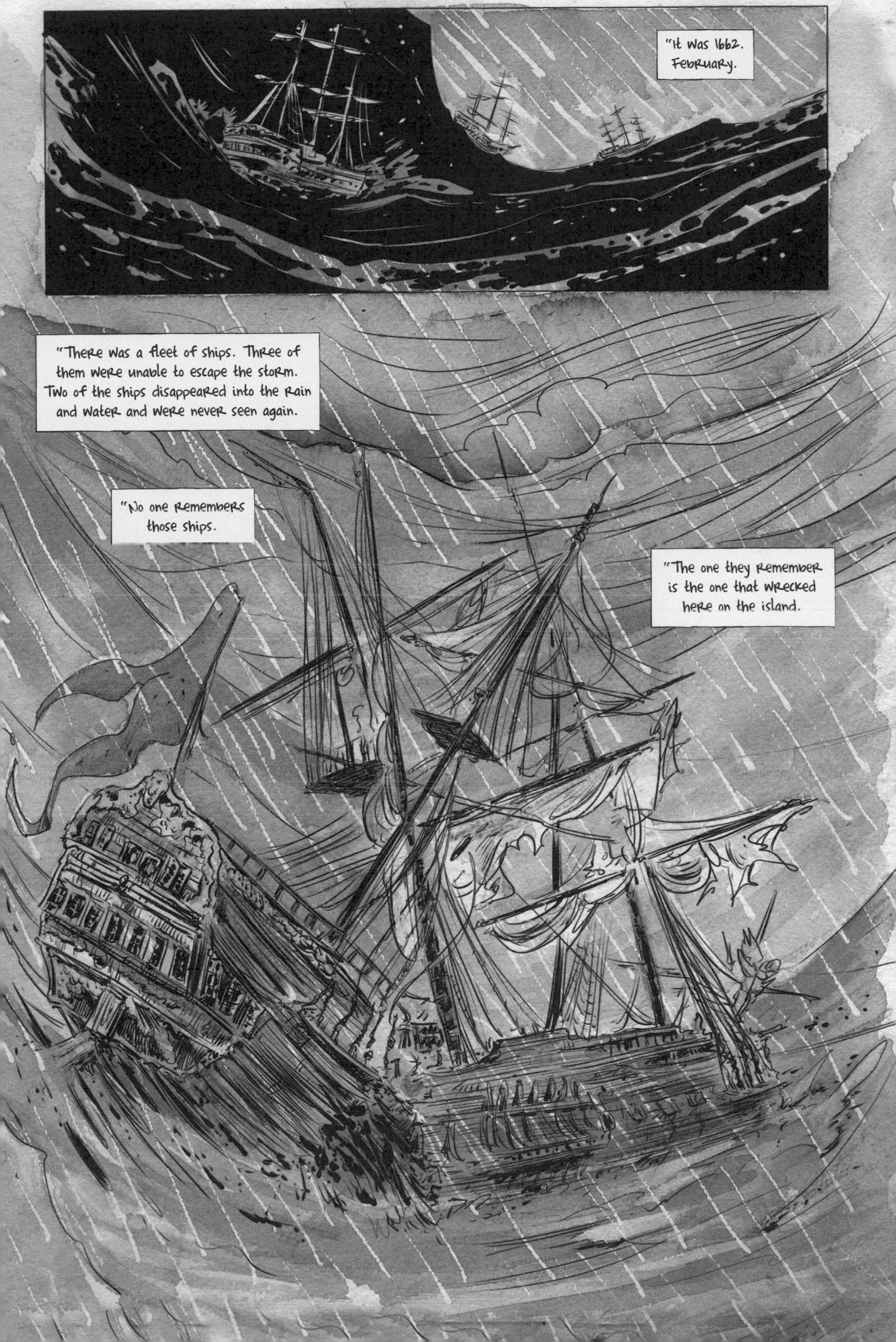
"It was 1662. February.
"There was a fleet of ships. Three of them were unable to escape the storm. Two of the ships disappeared into the rain and water and were never seen again.
"No one remembers those ships.
"The one they remember is the one that wrecked here on the island.

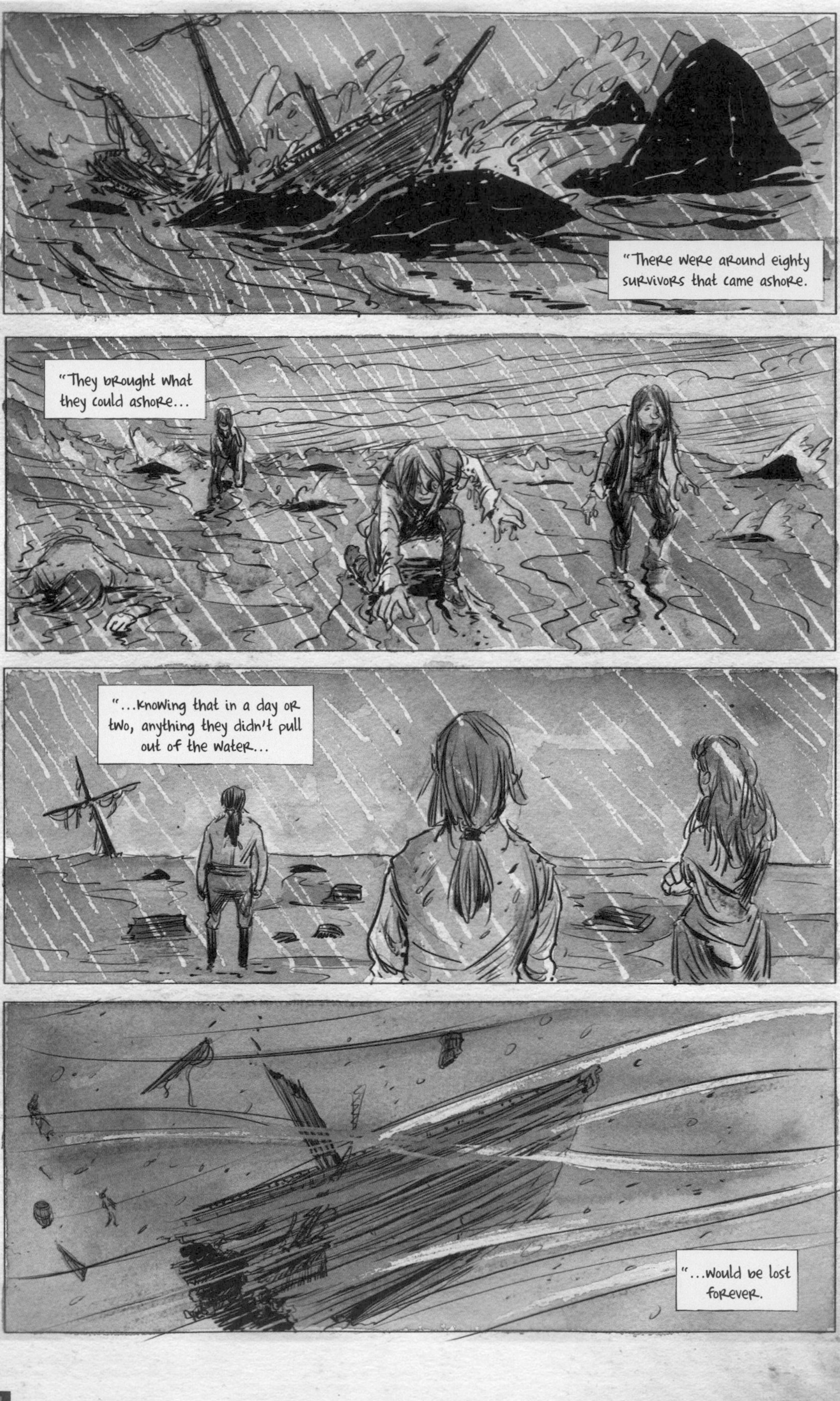
"There were around eighty survivors that came ashore.
"They brought what they could ashore...
"...knowing that in a day or two, anything they didn't pull out of the water...
"...would be lost forever.

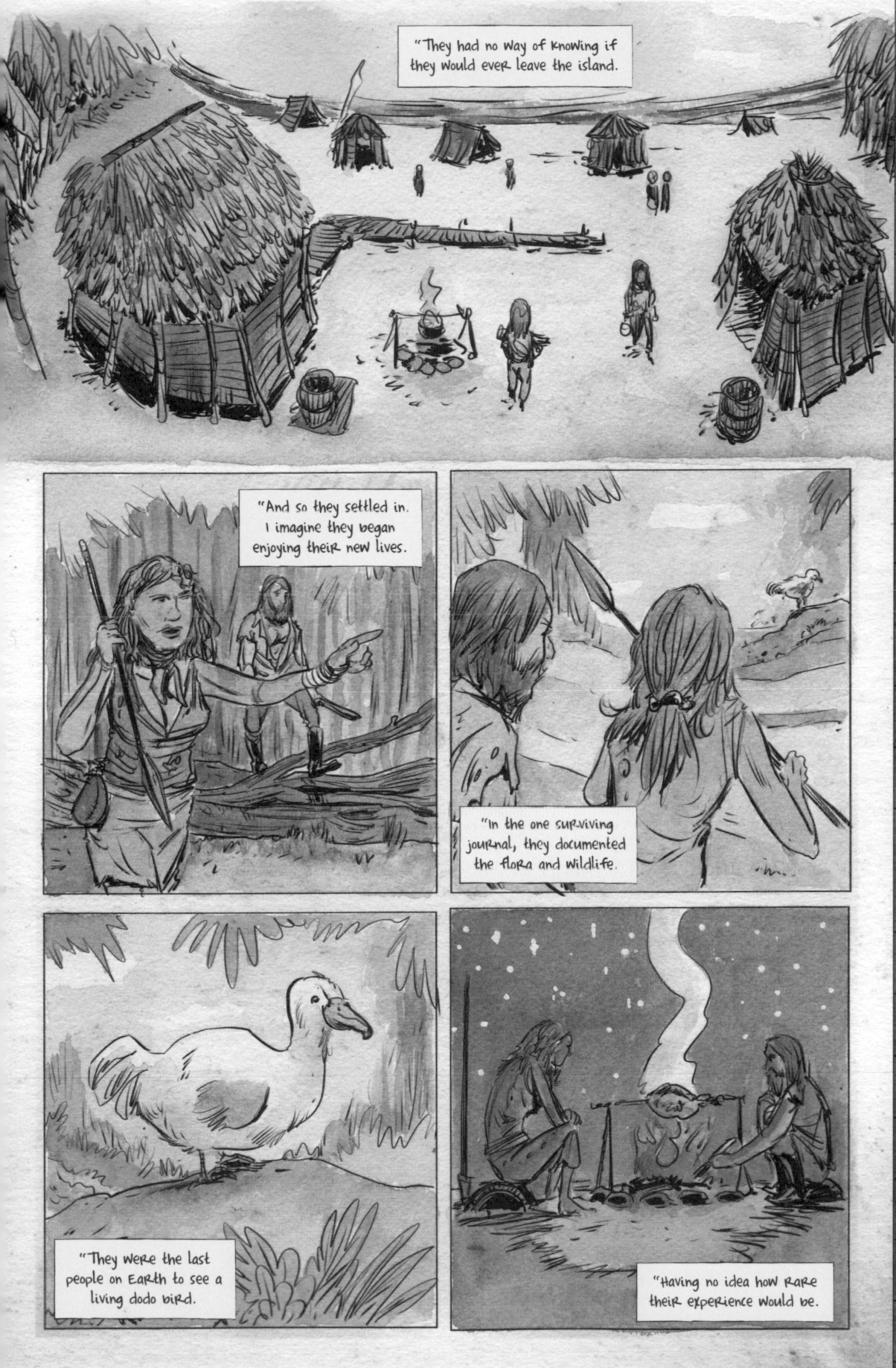
"They had no way of knowing if they would ever leave the island.
"And so they settled in. I imagine they began enjoying their new lives.
"In the one surviving journal, they documented the flora and wildlife.
"They were the last people on Earth to see a living dodo bird.
"Having no idea how rare their experience would be.

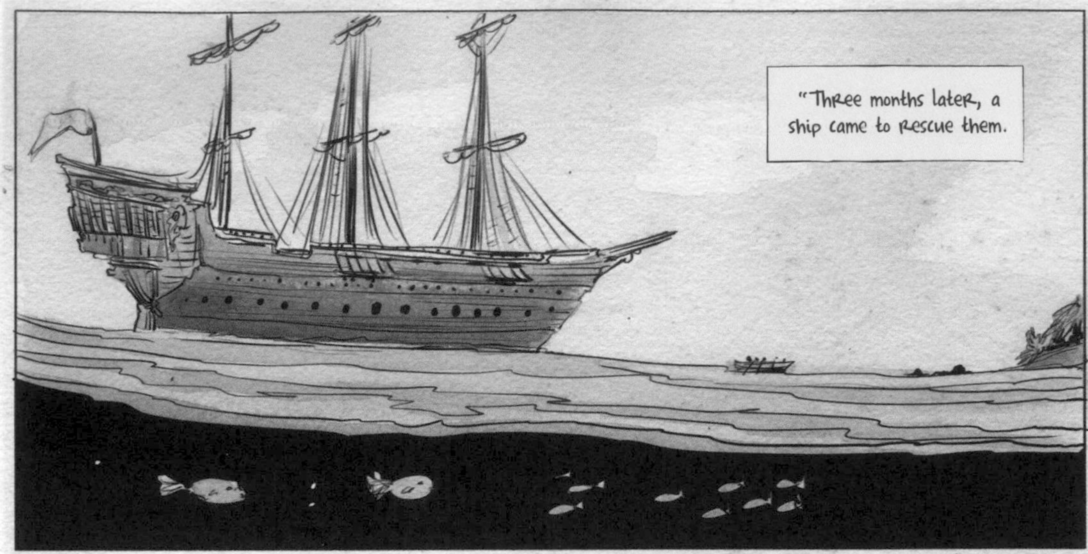
"Three months later, a ship came to rescue them.

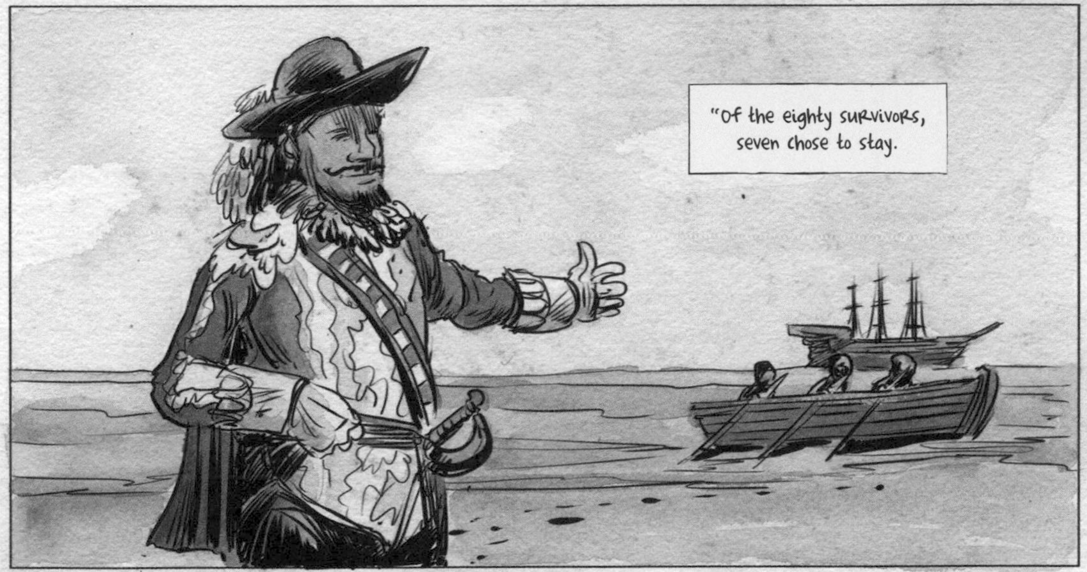
"Of the eighty survivors, seven chose to stay.

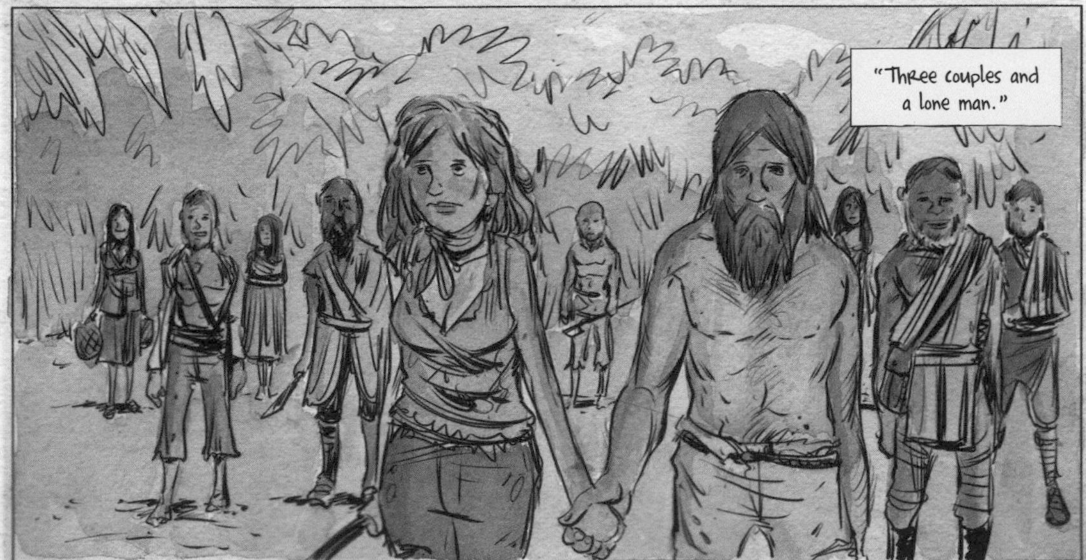
"Three couples and a lone man."

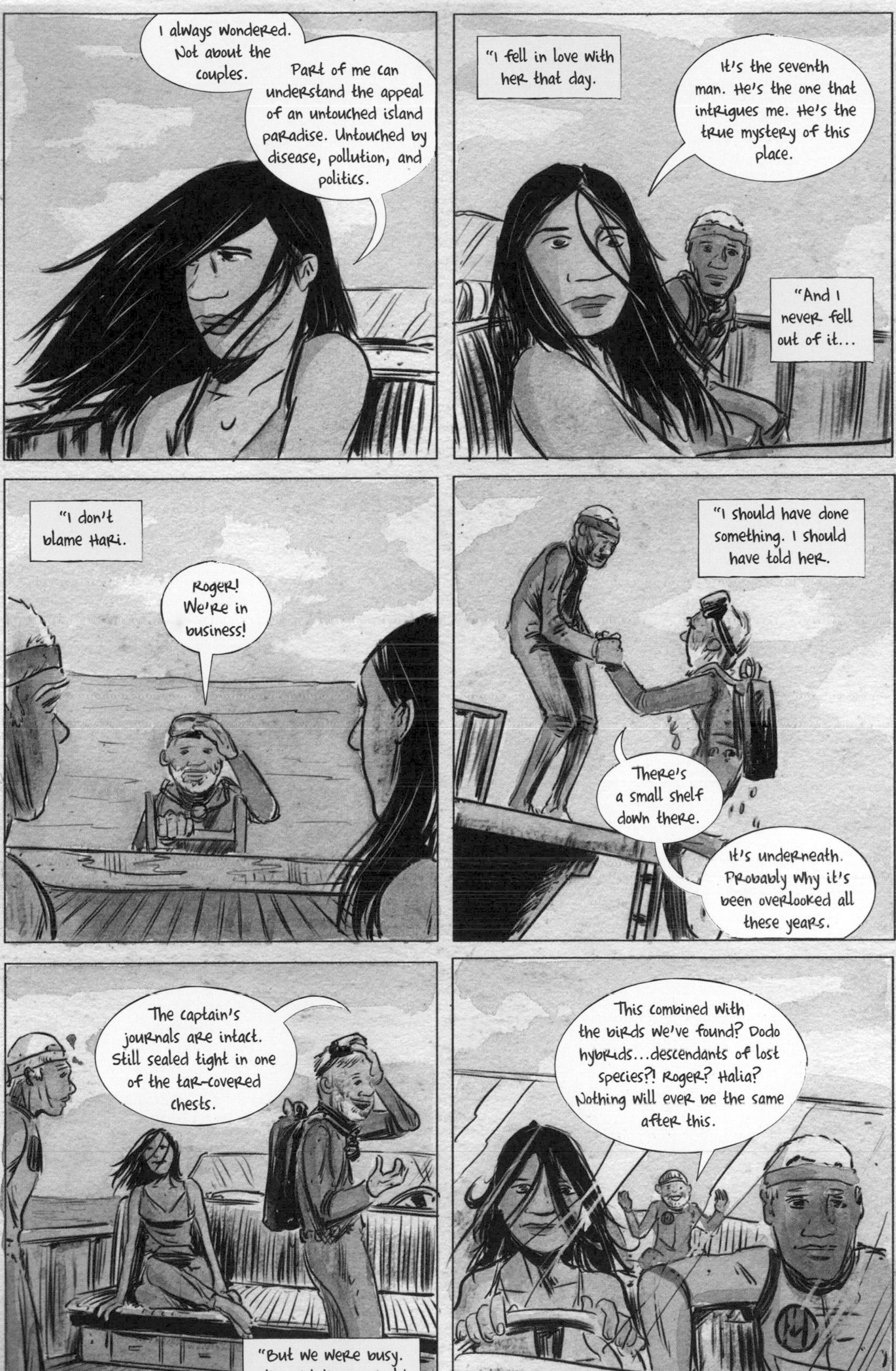
I always wondered. Not about the couples.
Part of me can understand the appeal of an untouched island paradise. Untouched by disease, pollution, and politics.
"I fell in love with her that day.
It's the seventh man. He's the one that intrigues me. He's the true mystery of this place.
"And I never fell out of it...
"I don't blame Hari.
Roger! We're in business!
"I should have done something. I should have told her.
There's a small shelf down there.
It's underneath. Probably why it's been overlooked all these years.
The captain's journals are intact. Still sealed tight in one of the tar-covered chests.
"But we were busy. I thought there would be time.
This combined with the birds we've found? Dodo hybrids...descendants of lost species?! Roger? Halia? Nothing will ever be the same after this.

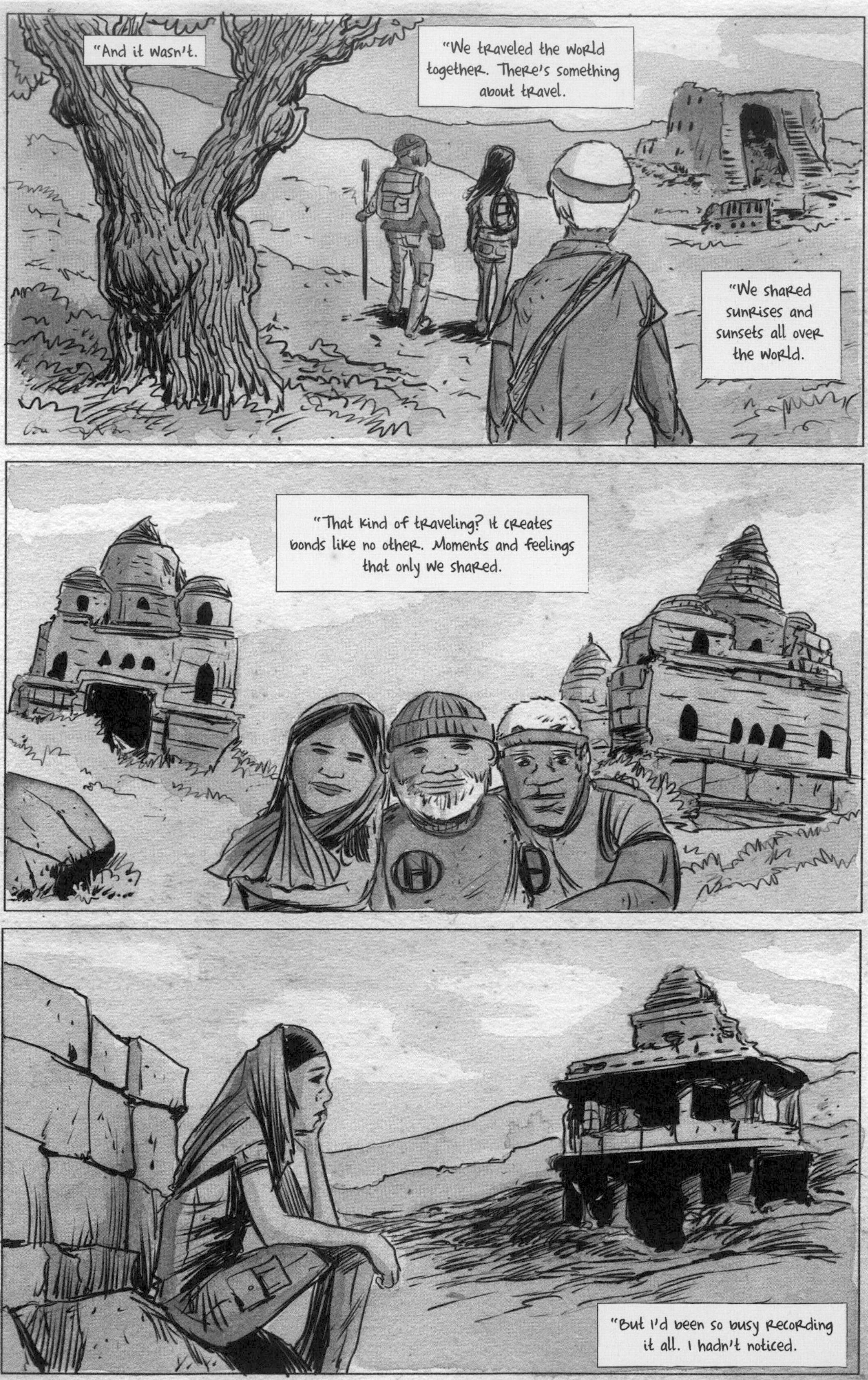
"And it wasn't.
"We traveled the world together. There's something about travel.
"We shared sunrises and sunsets all over the world.
"That kind of traveling? It creates bonds like no other. Moments and feelings that only we shared.
"But I'd been so busy recording it all. I hadn't noticed.

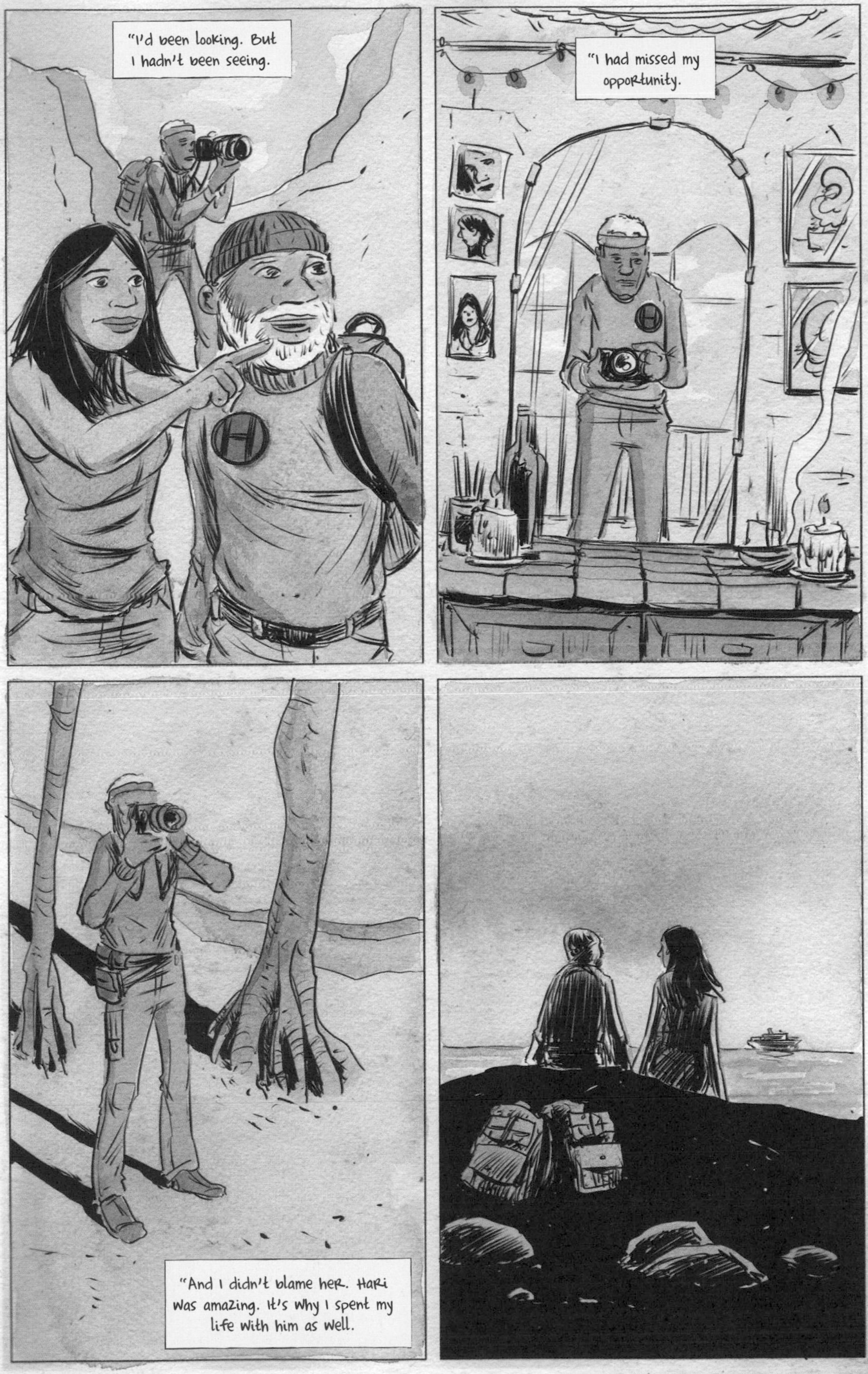
"I'd been looking. But I hadn't been seeing.
"I had missed my opportunity.
"And I didn't blame her. Hari was amazing. It's why I spent my life with him as well.

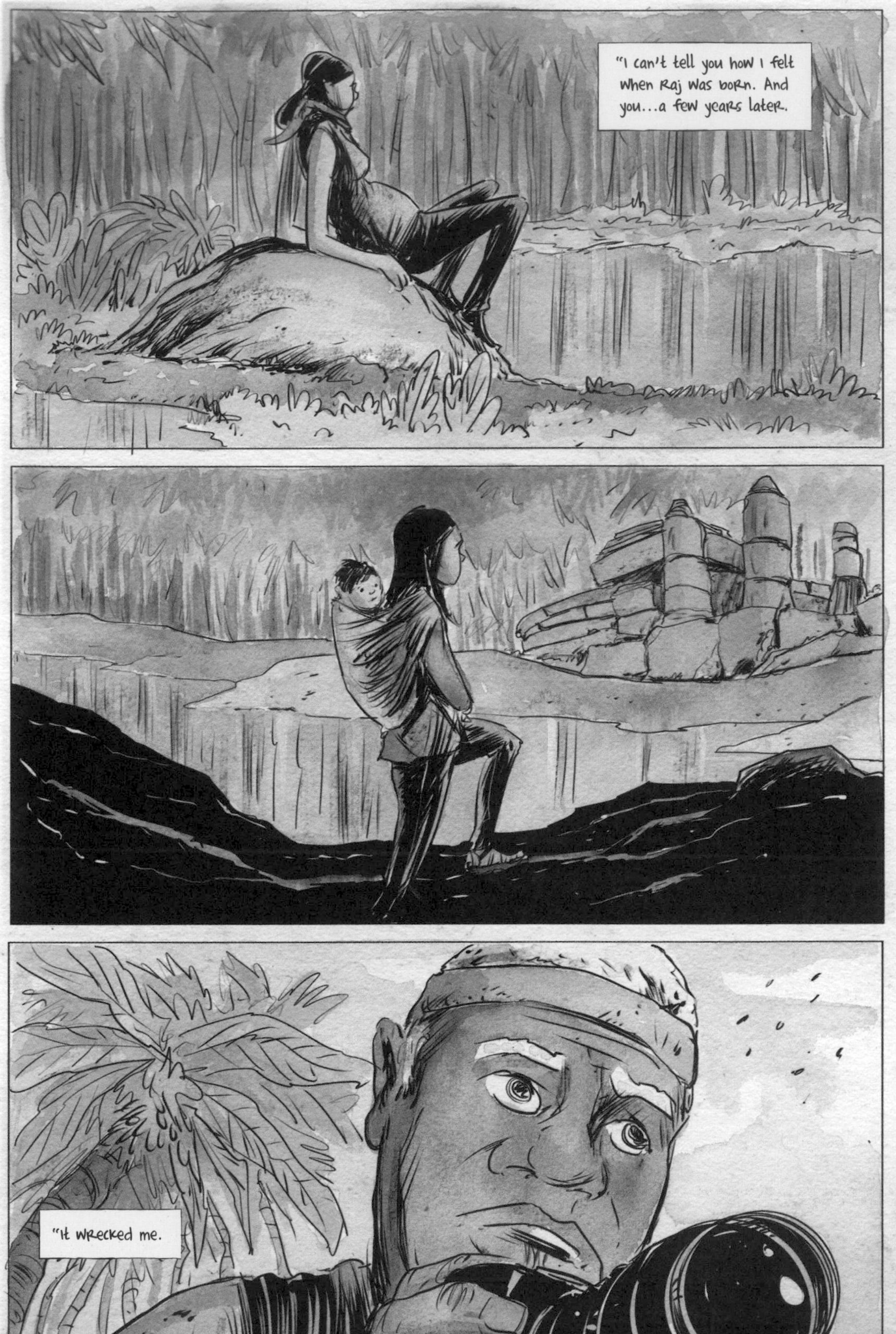
"I can't tell you how I felt when Raj was born. And you...a few years later.
"It wrecked me.

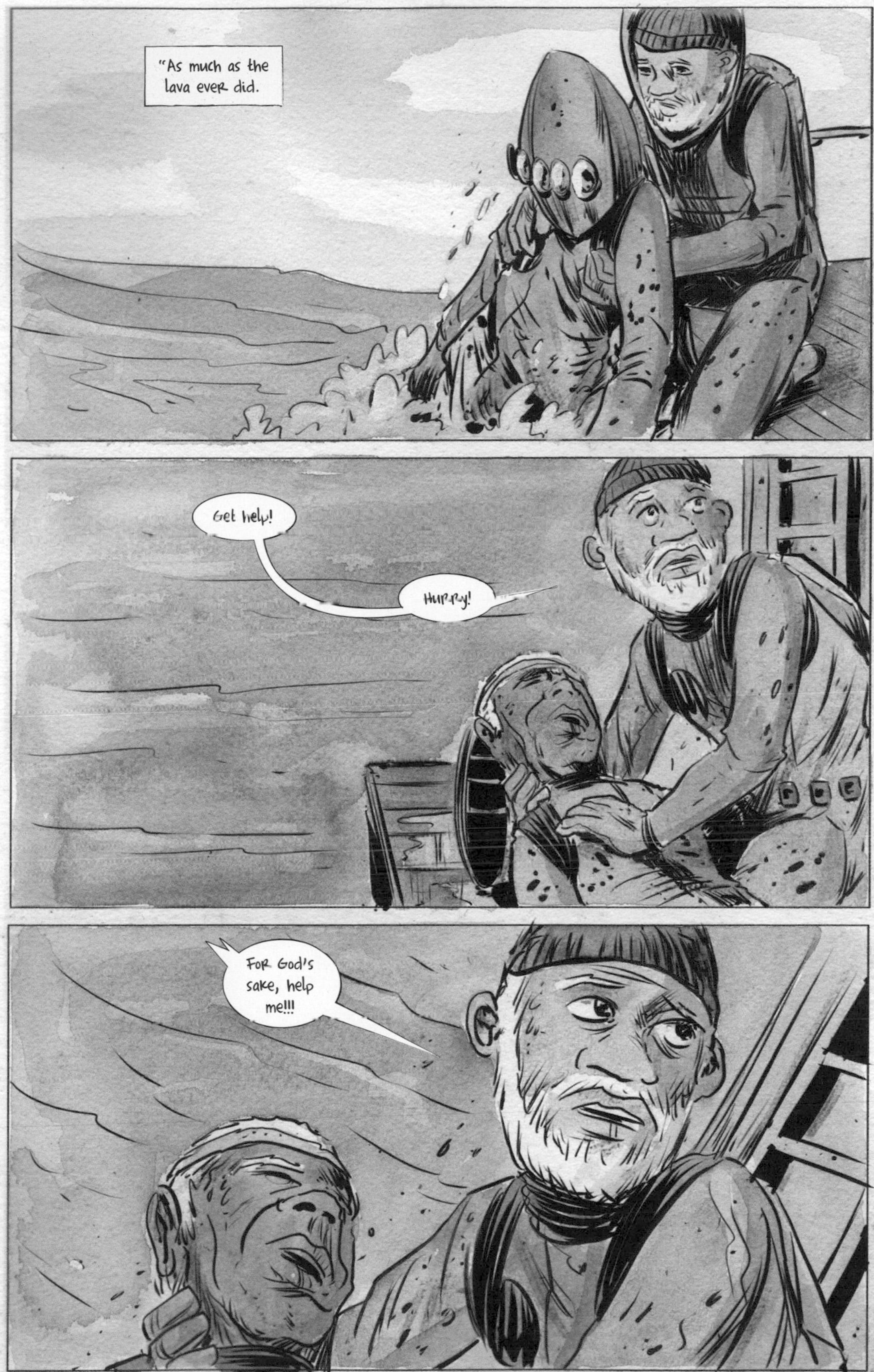
"As much as the lava ever did.
Get help!
Hurry!
For God's sake, help me!!!

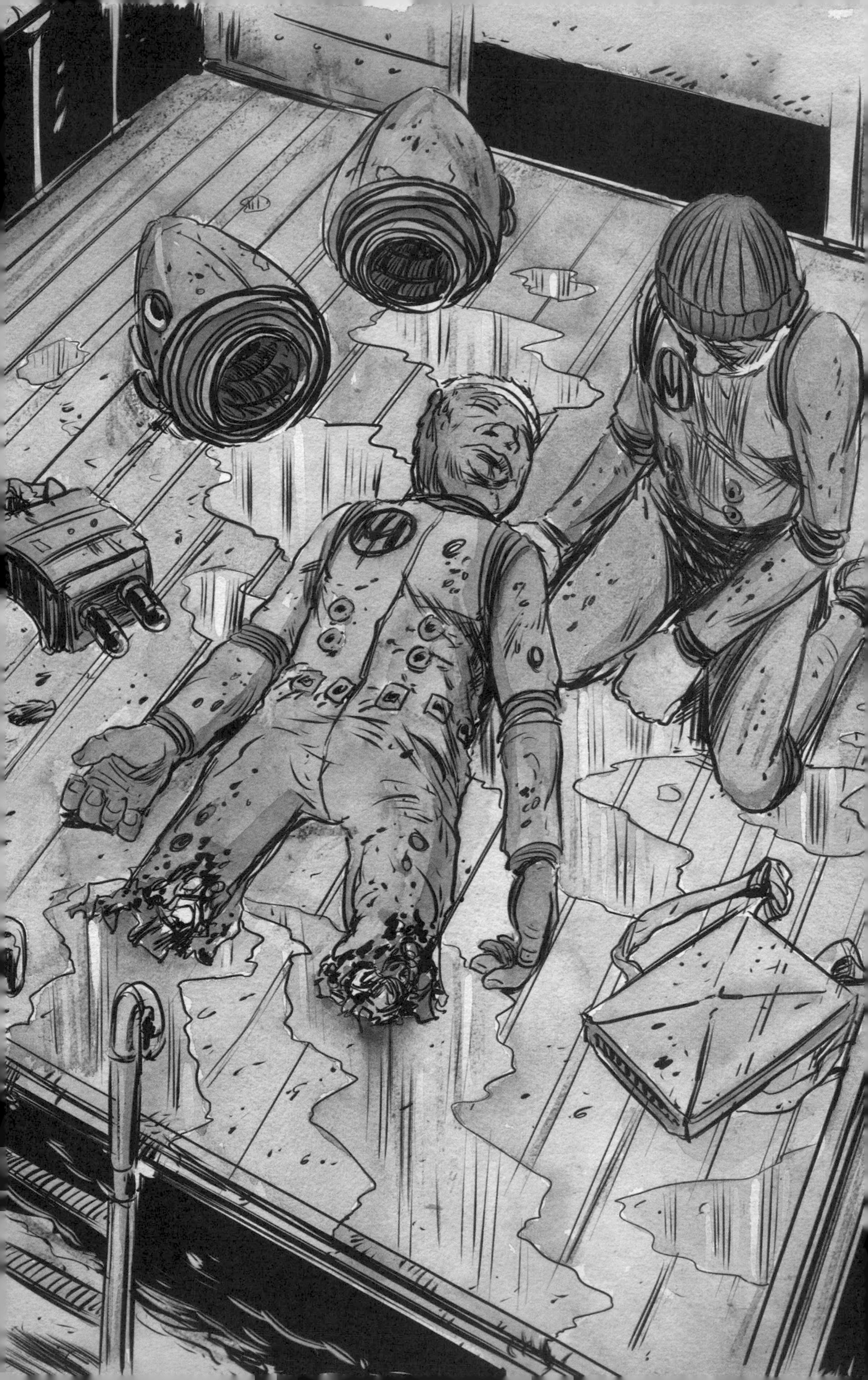

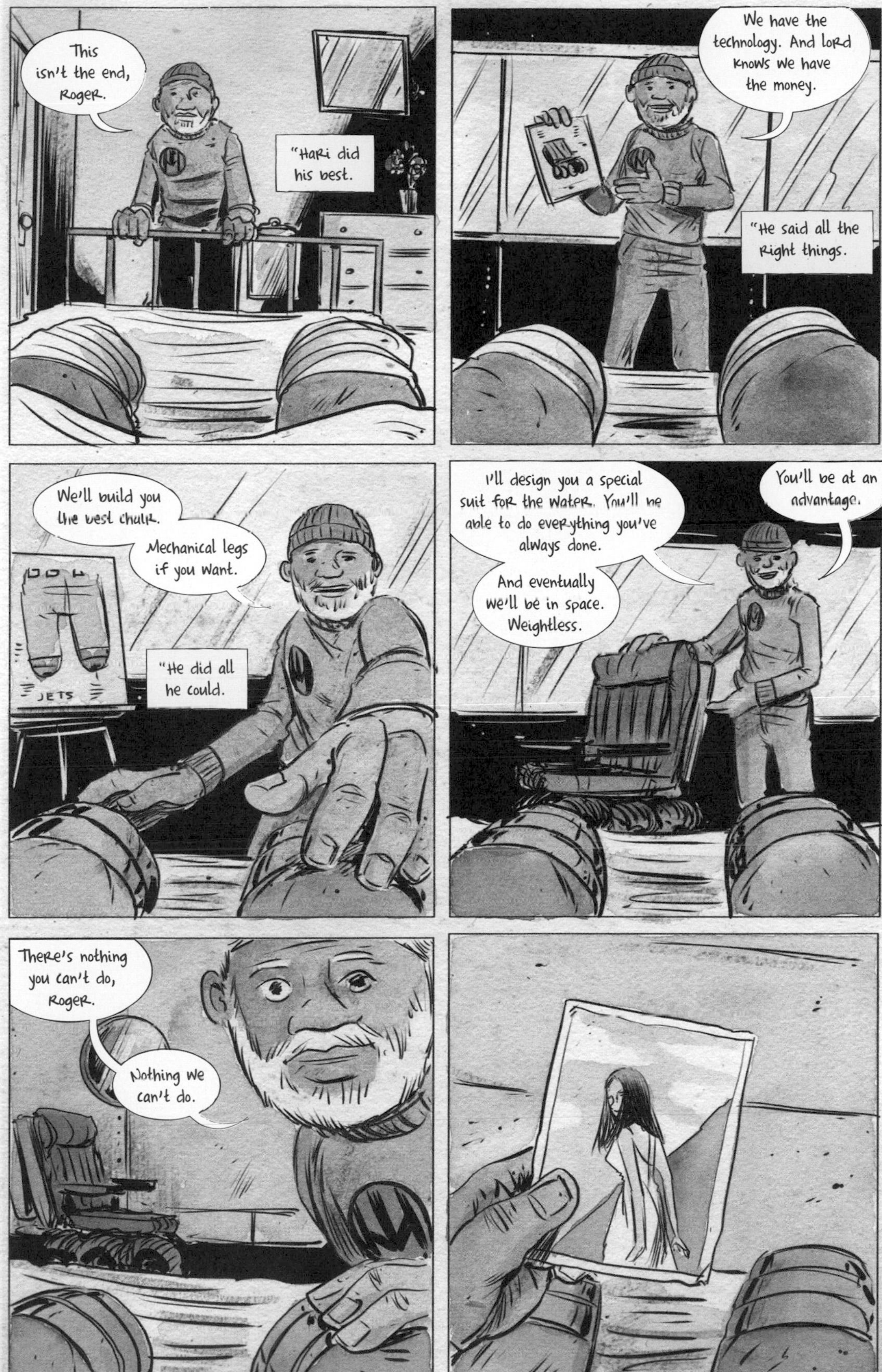
This isn't the end, Roger.
"Hari did his best.
We have the technology. And lord knows we have the money.
"He said all the right things.
We'll build you the best chair.
Mechanical legs if you want.
JETS
"He did all he could.
I'll design you a special suit for the water. You'll be able to do everything you've always done.
And eventually we'll be in space. Weightless.
You'll be at an advantage.
There's nothing you can't do, Roger.
Nothing we can't do.

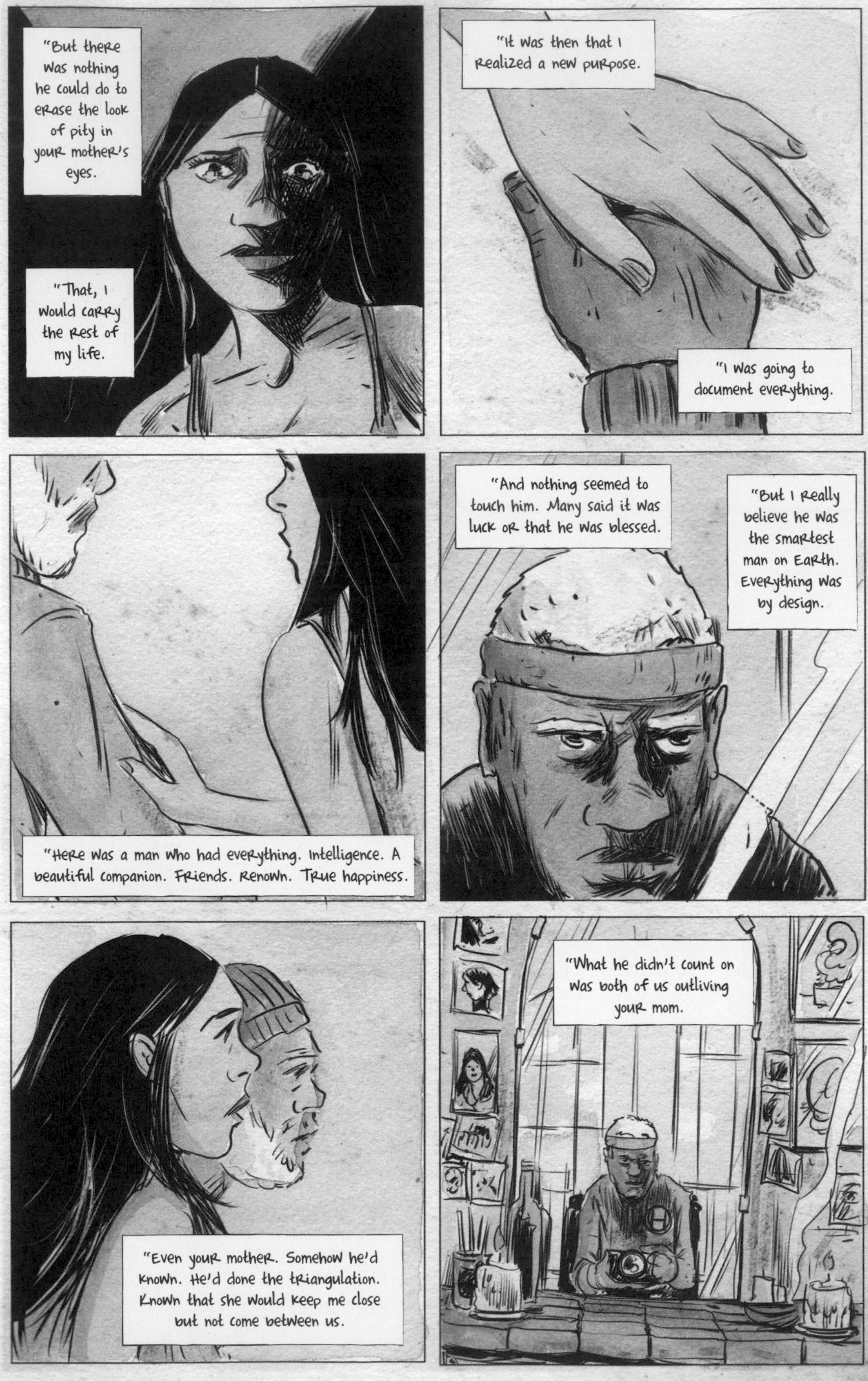
"But there was nothing he could do to erase the look of pity in your mother's eyes.
"That, I would carry the rest of my life.
"It was then that I realized a new purpose.
"I was going to document everything.
"Here was a man who had everything. Intelligence. A beautiful companion. Friends. Renown. True happiness.
"And nothing seemed to touch him. Many said it was luck or that he was blessed.
"But I really believe he was the smartest man on Earth. Everything was by design.
"Even your mother. Somehow he'd known. He'd done the triangulation. Known that she would keep me close but not come between us.
"What he didn't count on was both of us outliving your mom.

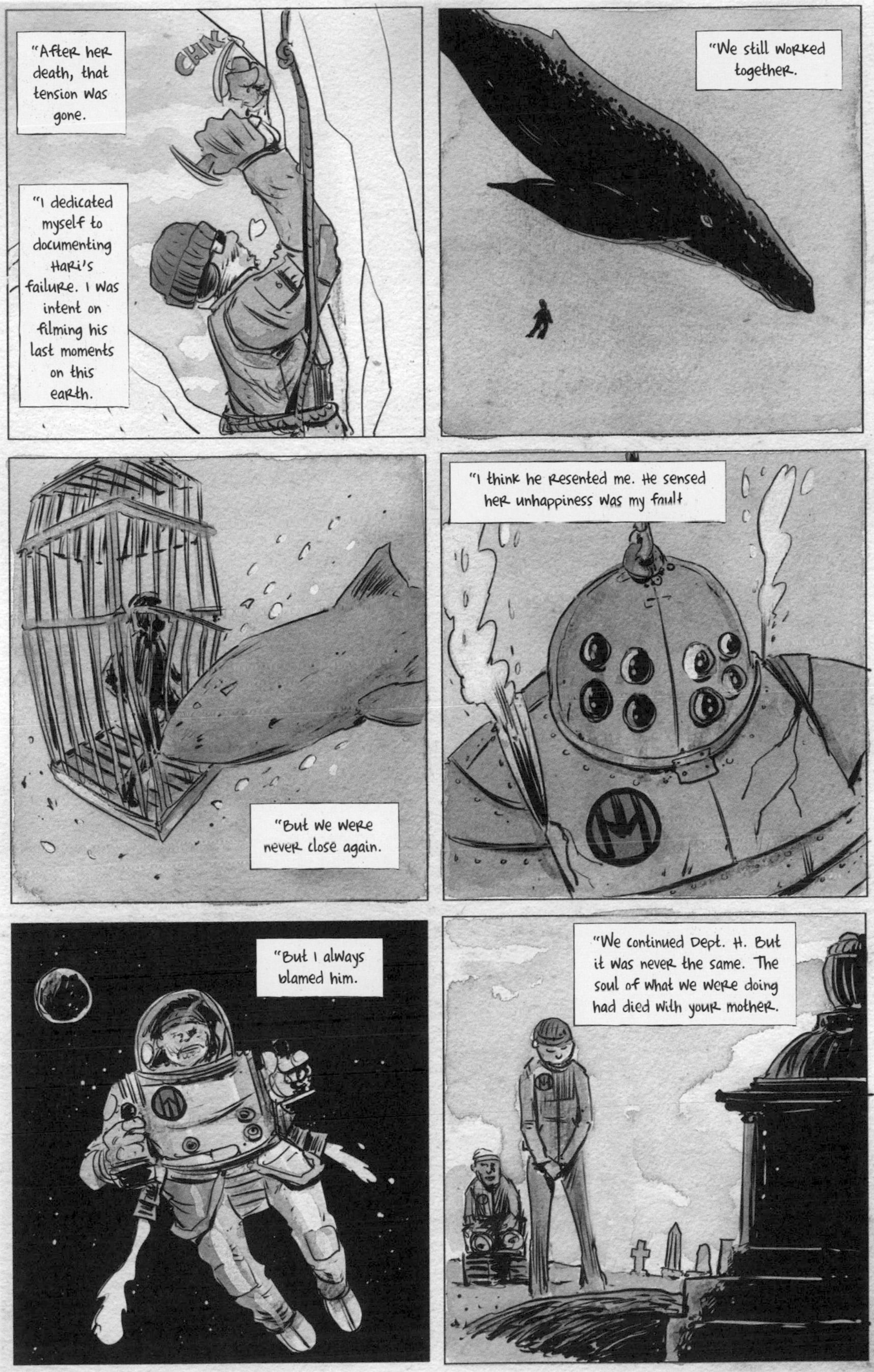
"After her death, that tension was gone.
"I dedicated myself to documenting Hari's failure. I was intent on filming his last moments on this earth.
CHK
"We still worked together.
"But we were never close again.
"I think he resented me. He sensed her unhappiness was my fault
"But I always blamed him.
"We continued Dept. H. But it was never the same. The soul of what we were doing had died with your mother.

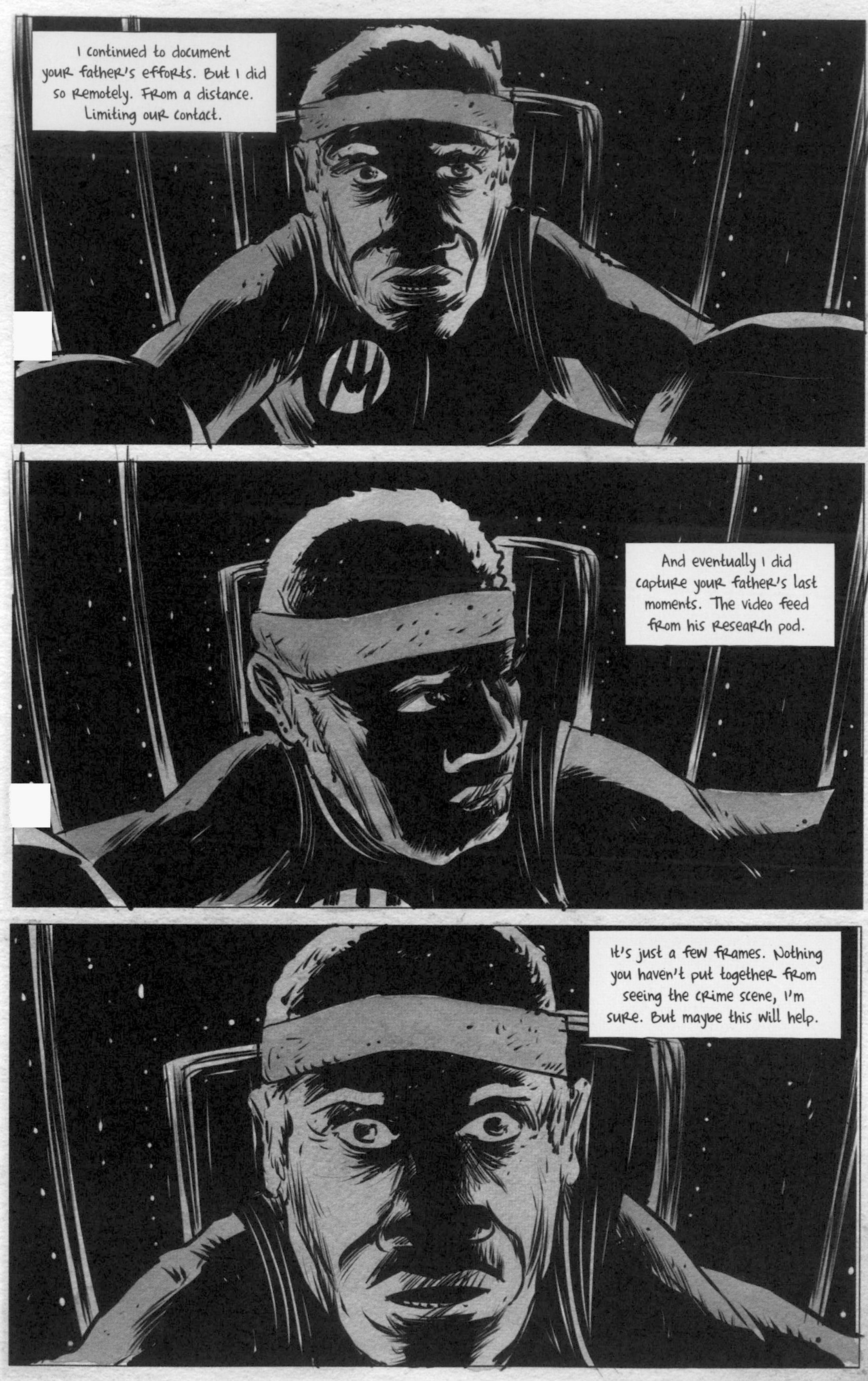
I continued to document your father's efforts. But I did so remotely. From a distance. Limiting our contact.
And eventually I did capture your father's last moments. The video feed from his research pod.
It's just a few frames. Nothing you haven't put together from seeing the crime scene, I'm sure. But maybe this will help.

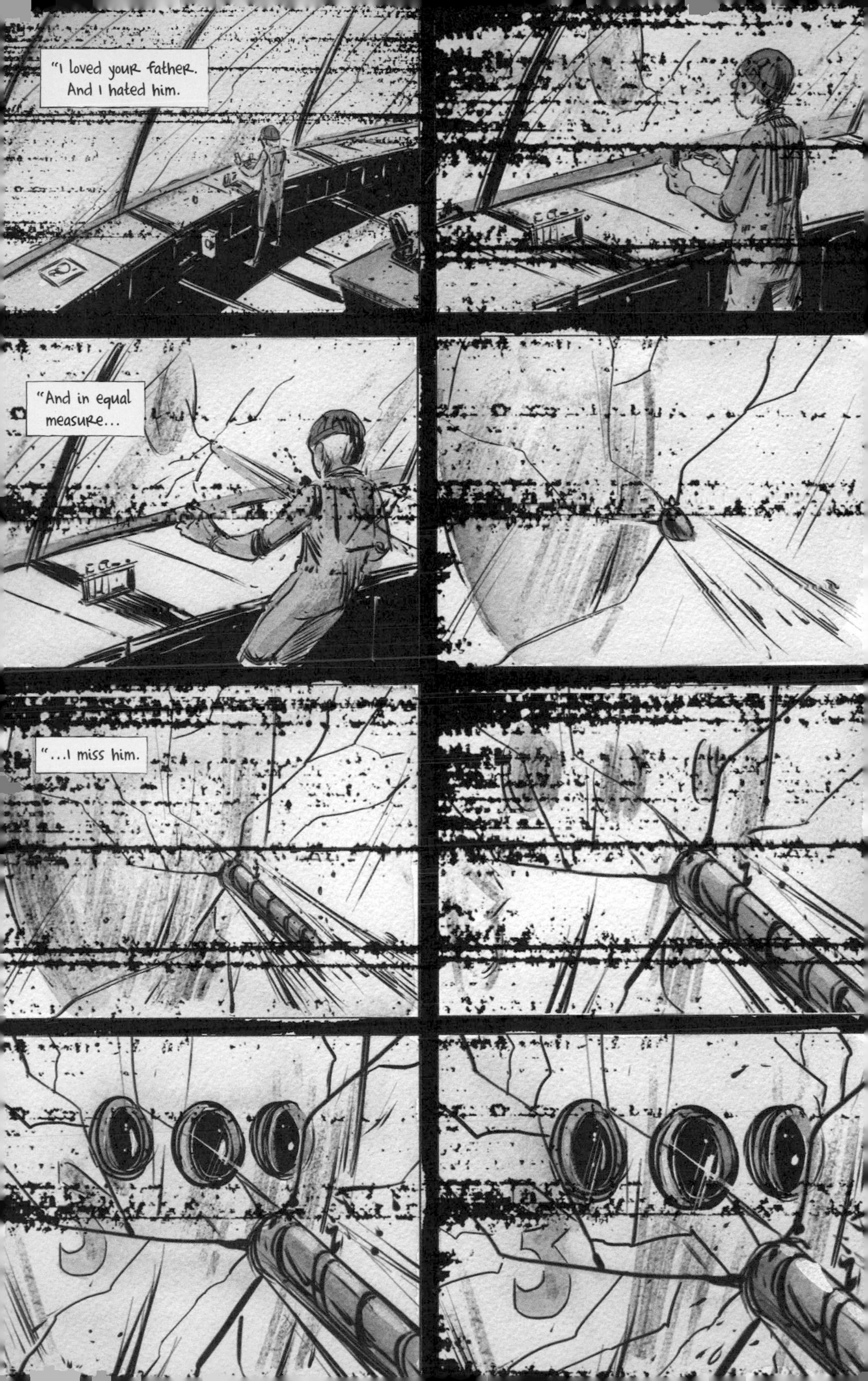
"I loved your father. And I hated him.
"And in equal measure...
"...I miss him.

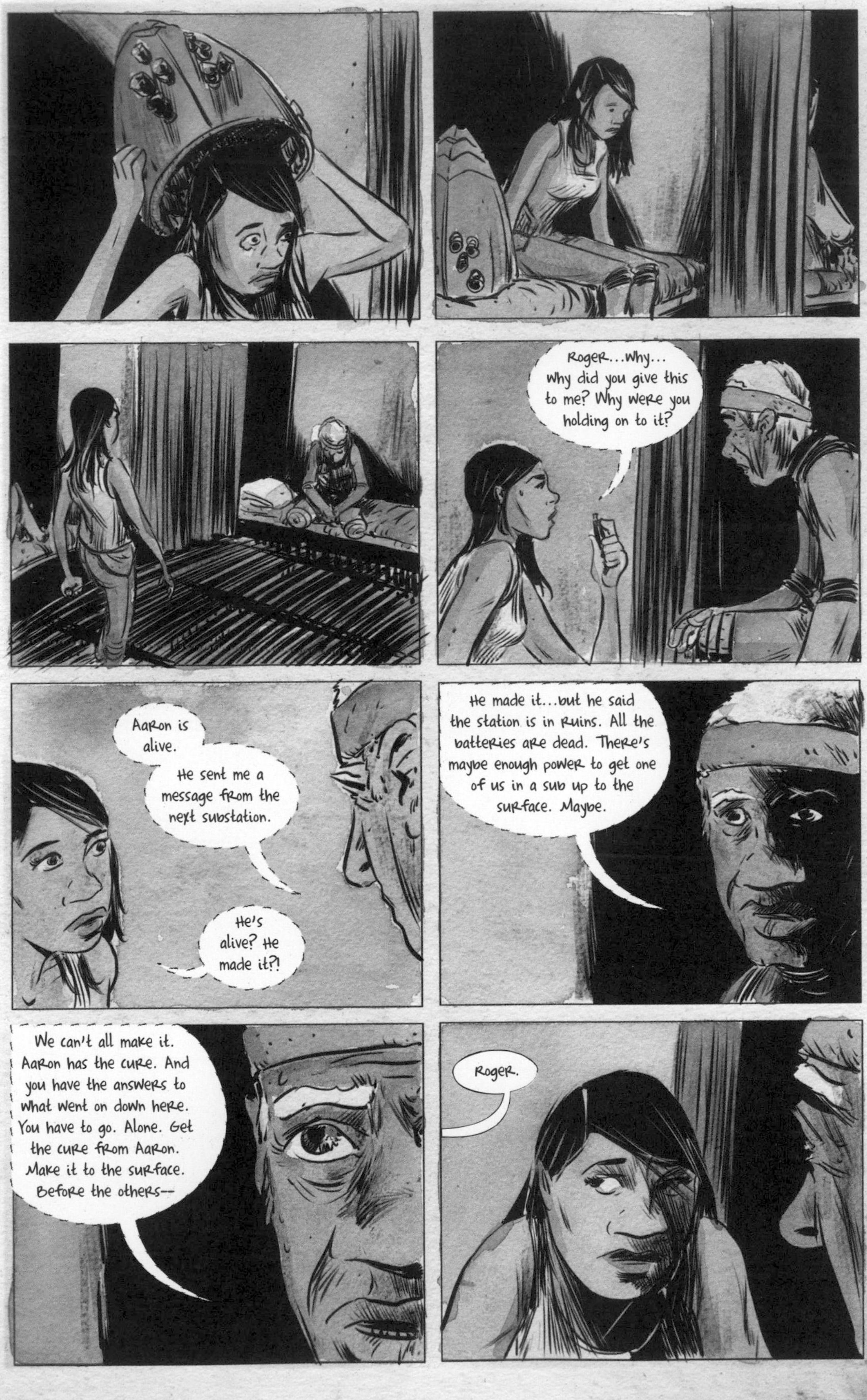
Roger...Why...
Why did you give this to me? Why were you holding on to it?
Aaron is alive.
He sent me a message from the next substation.
He's alive? He made it?!
He made it...but he said the station is in ruins. All the batteries are dead. There's maybe enough power to get one of us in a sub up to the surface. Maybe.
We can't all make it. Aaron has the cure. And you have the answers to what went on down here. You have to go. Alone. Get the cure from Aaron. Make it to the surface. Before the others--
Roger.

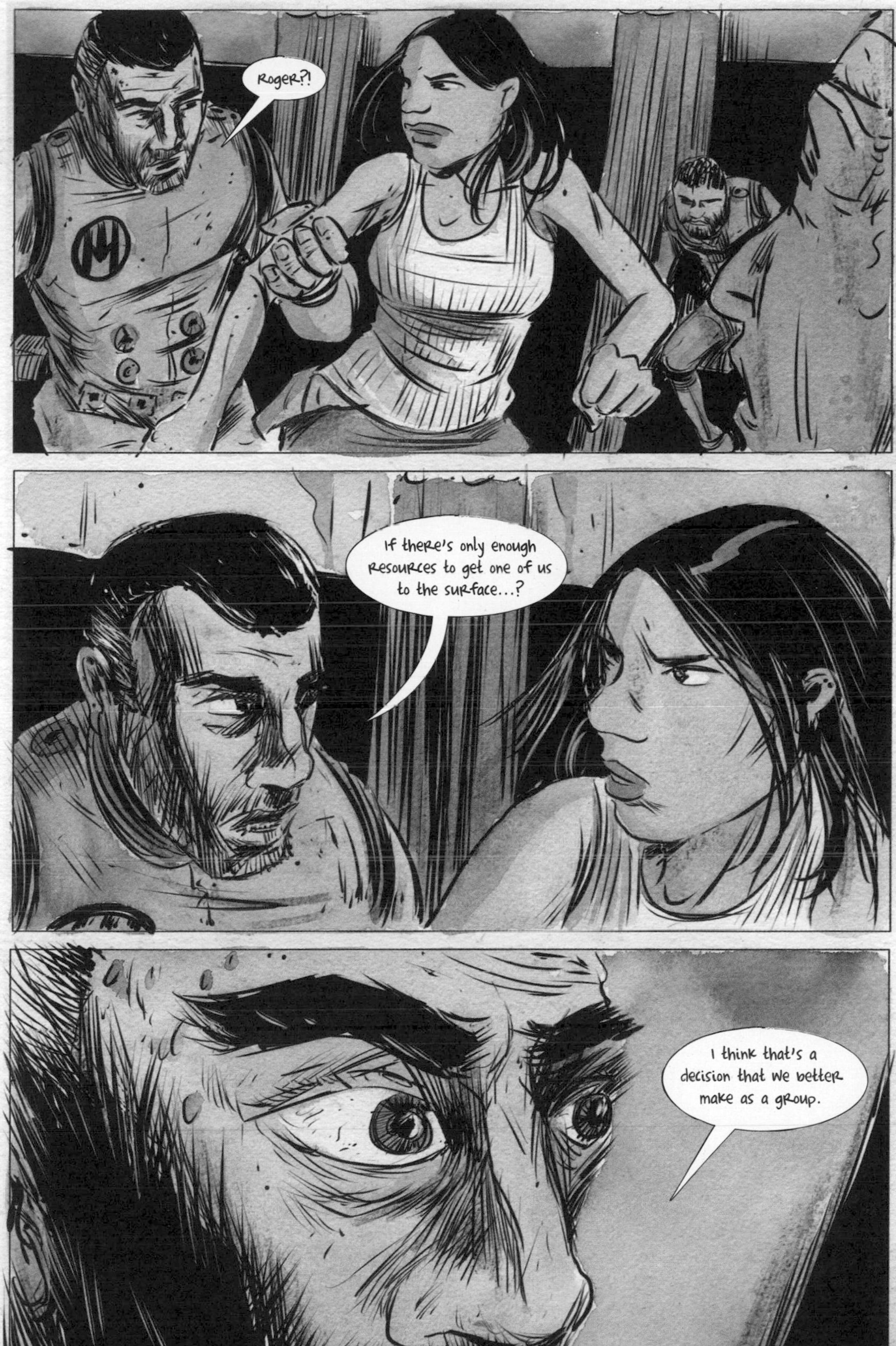
Roger?!
If there's only enough resources to get one of us to the surface...?
I think that's a decision that we better make as a group.

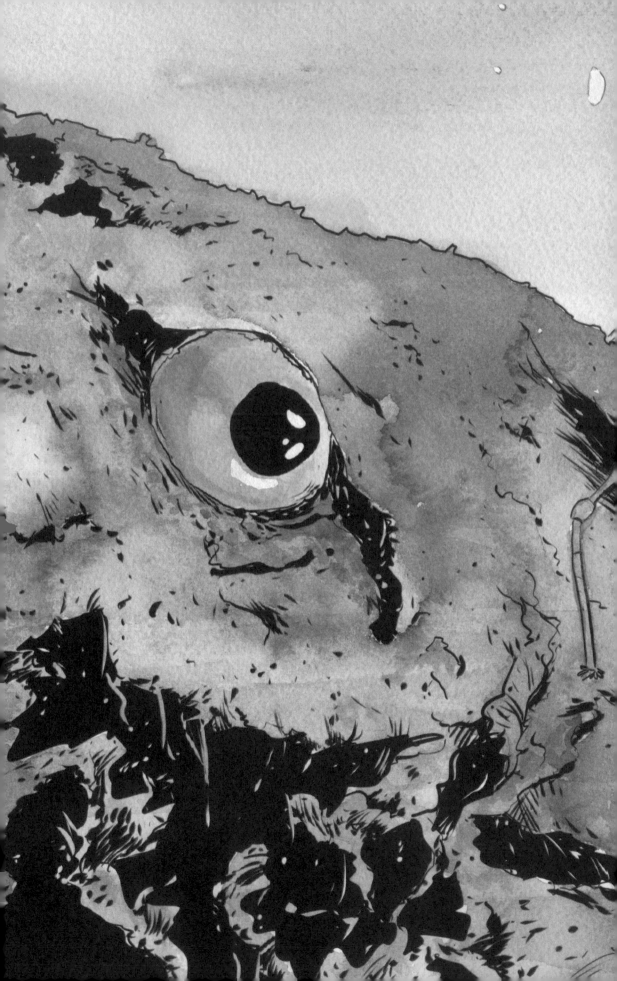

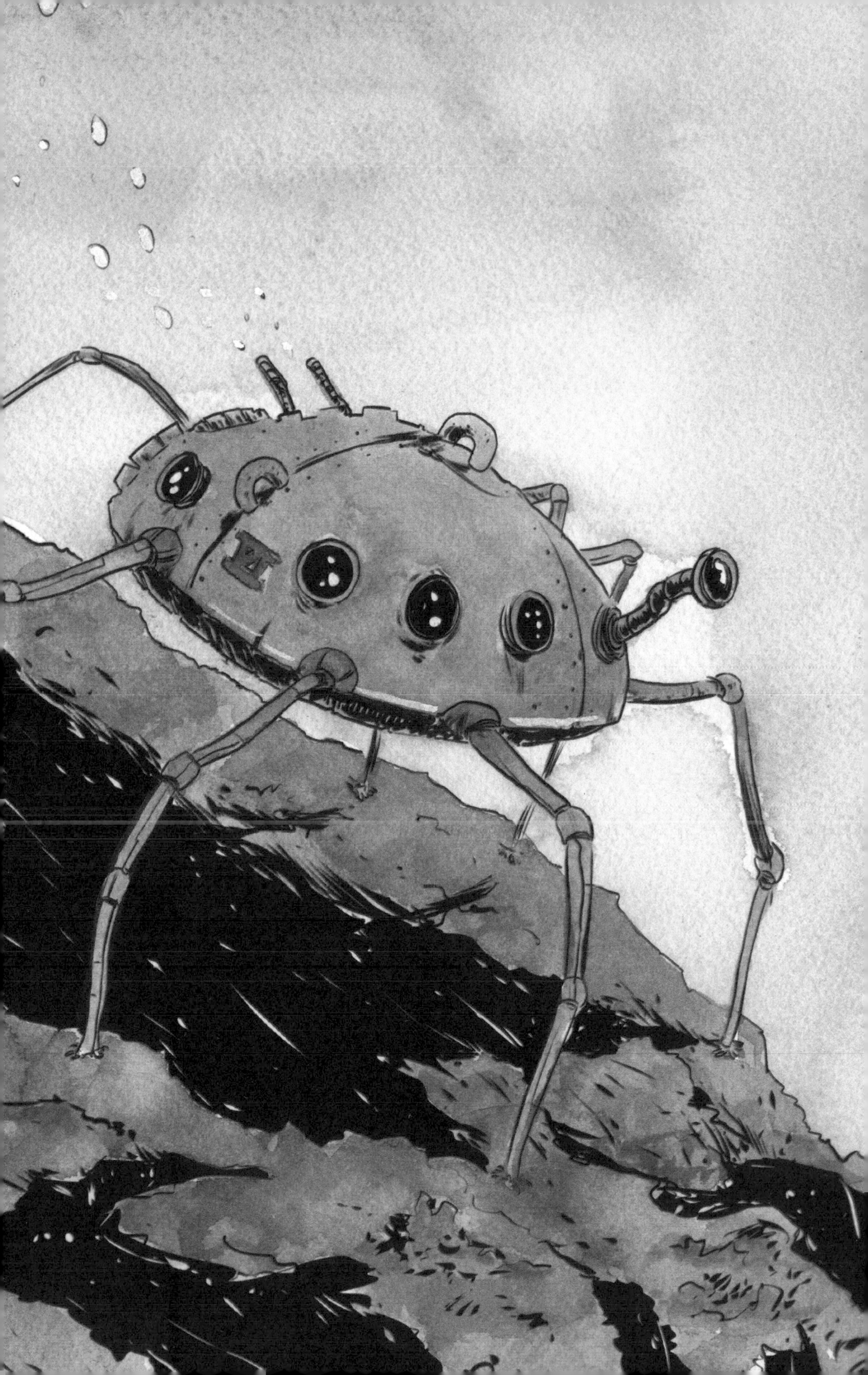

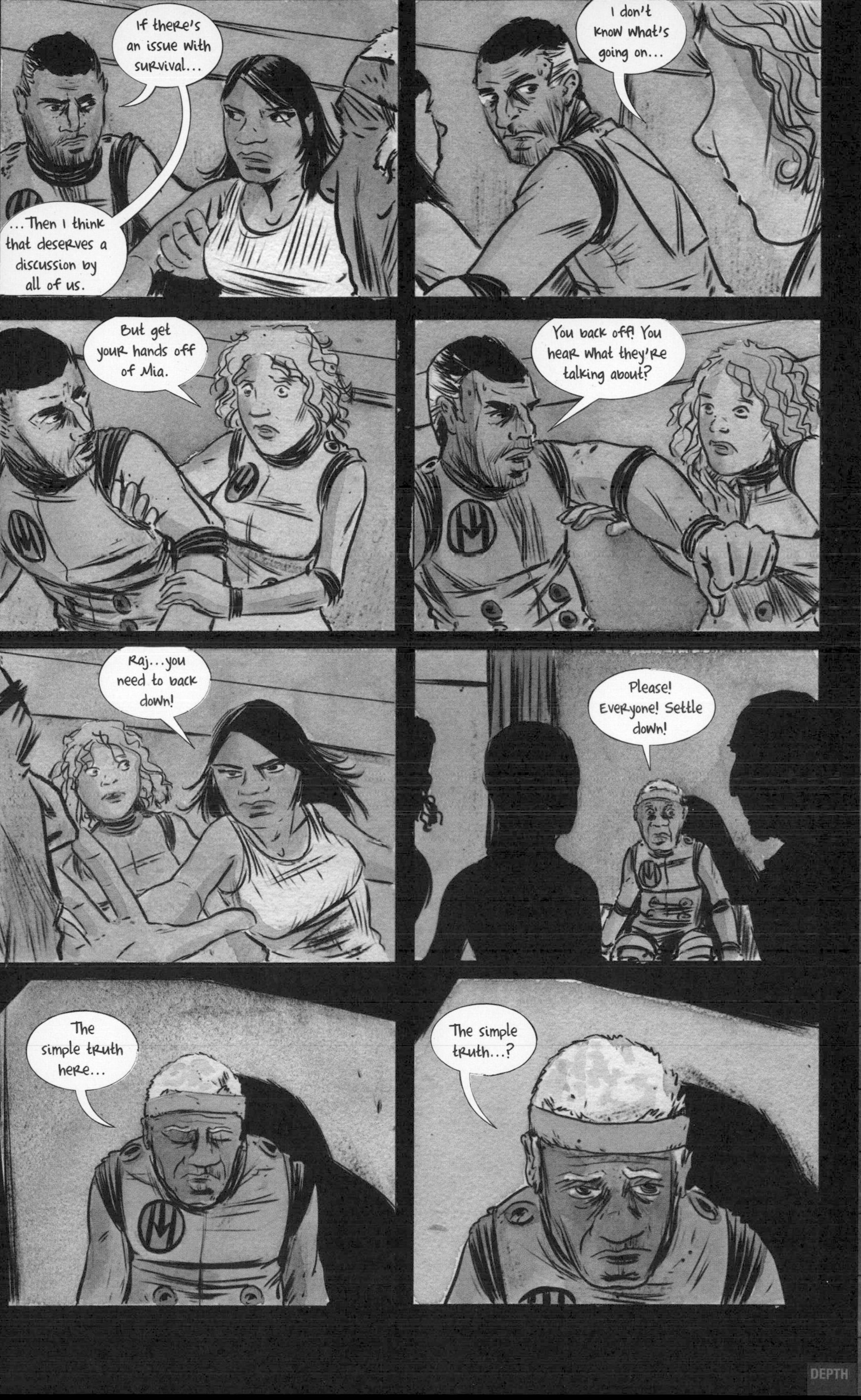
If there's an issue with survival...
...Then I think that deserves a discussion by all of us.
I don't know what's going on...
But get your hands off of Mia.
You back off! You hear what they're talking about?
Raj...you need to back down!
Please! Everyone! Settle down!
The simple truth here...
The simple truth...?

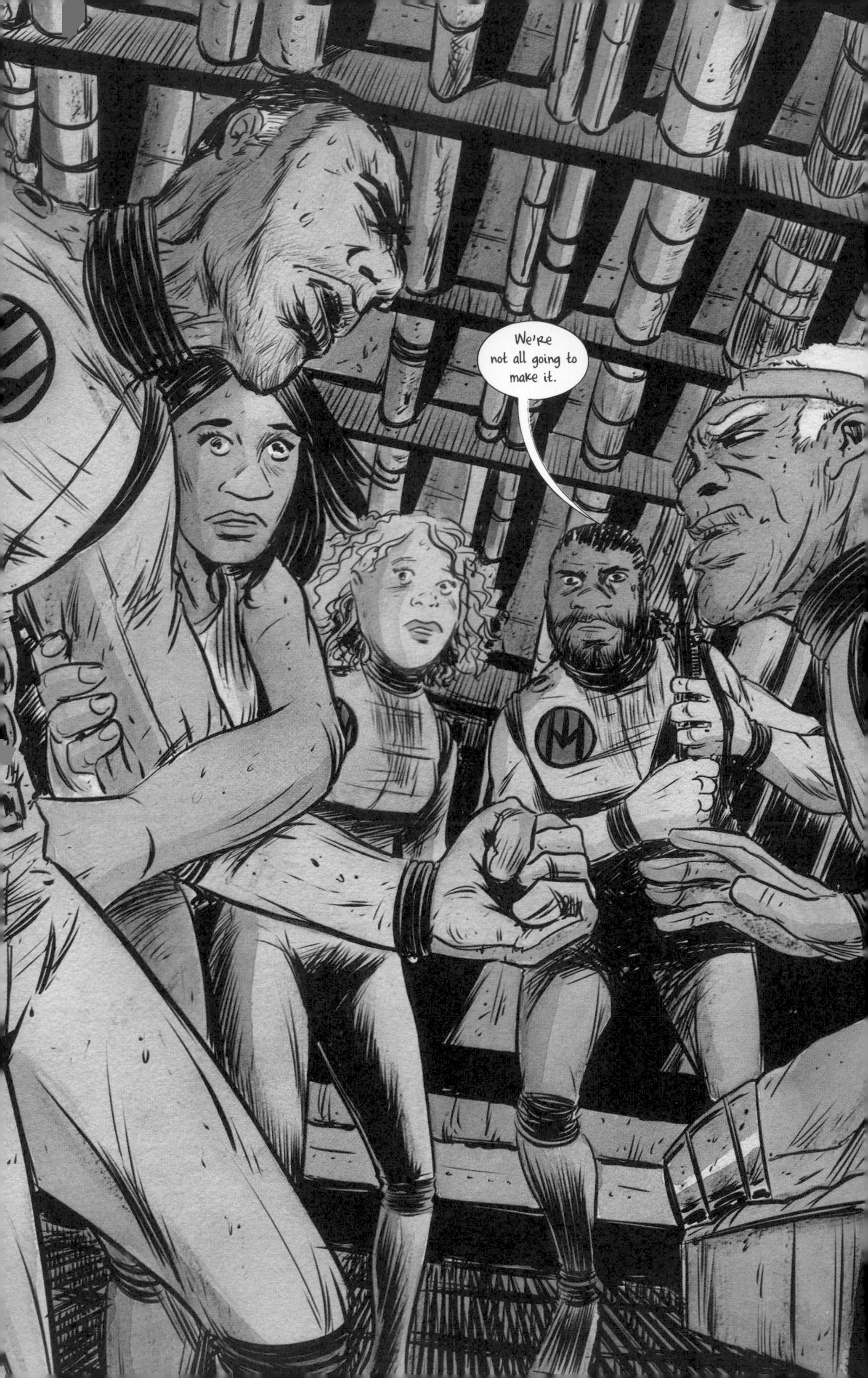
We're not all going to make it.

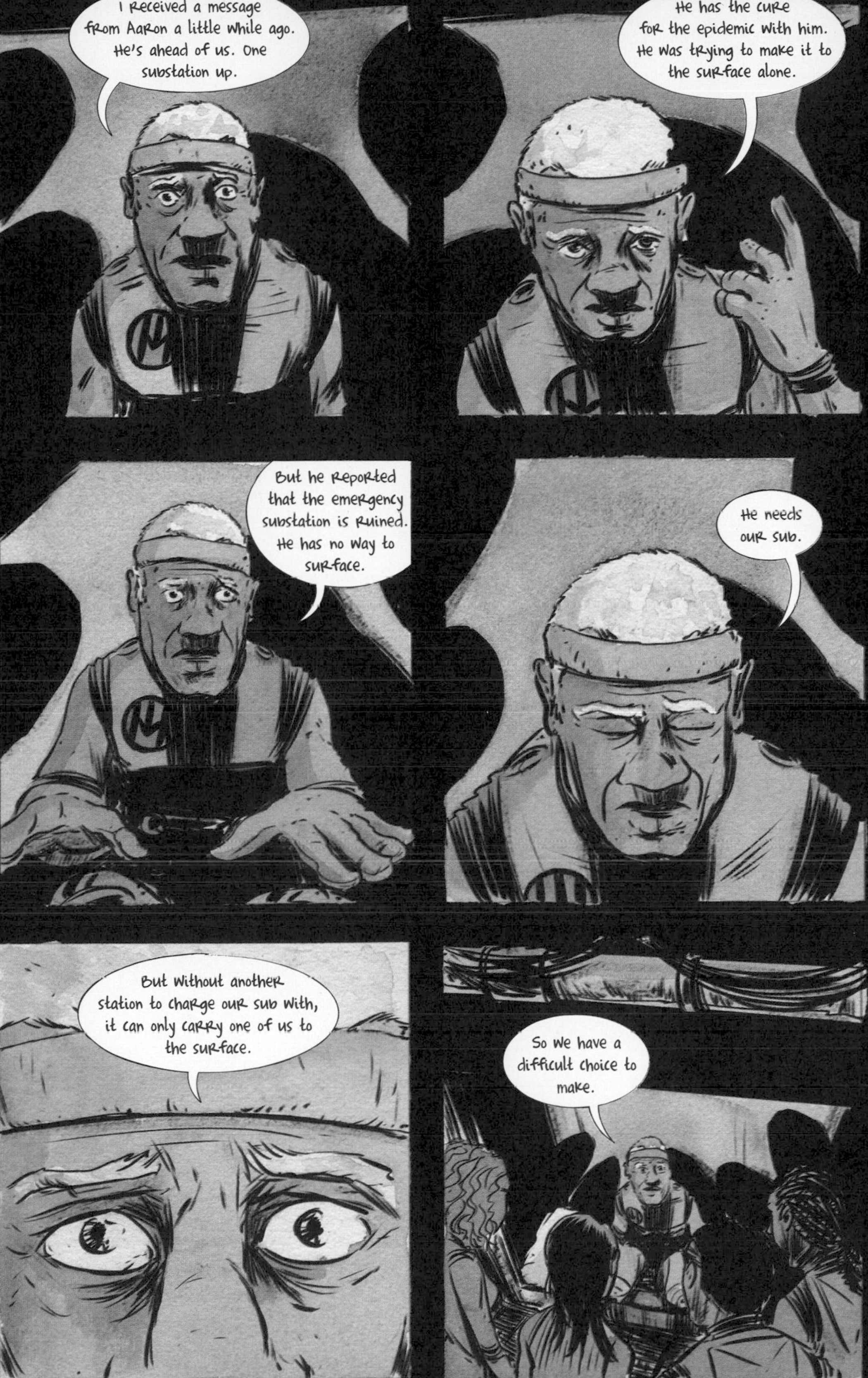
I received a message from Aaron a little while ago. He's ahead of us. One substation up.
He has the cure for the epidemic with him. He was trying to make it to the surface alone.
But he reported that the emergency substation is ruined. He has no way to surface.
He needs our sub.
But without another station to charge our sub with, it can only carry one of us to the surface.
So we have a difficult choice to make.

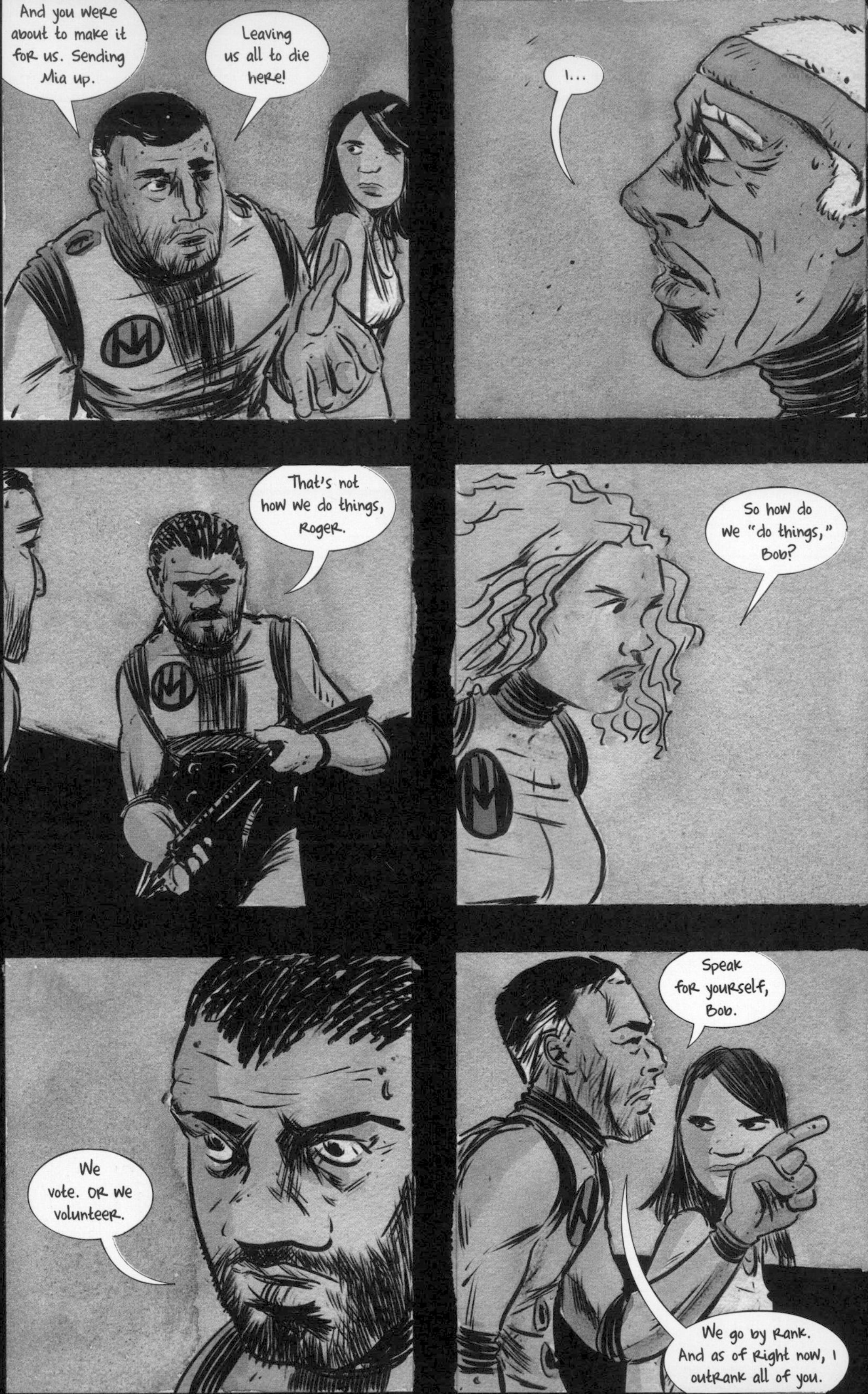
And you were about to make it for us. Sending Mia up.
Leaving us all to die here!
I...
That's not how we do things, Roger.
So how do we "do things," Bob?
We vote. Or we volunteer.
Speak for yourself, Bob.
We go by rank. And as of right now, I outrank all of you.

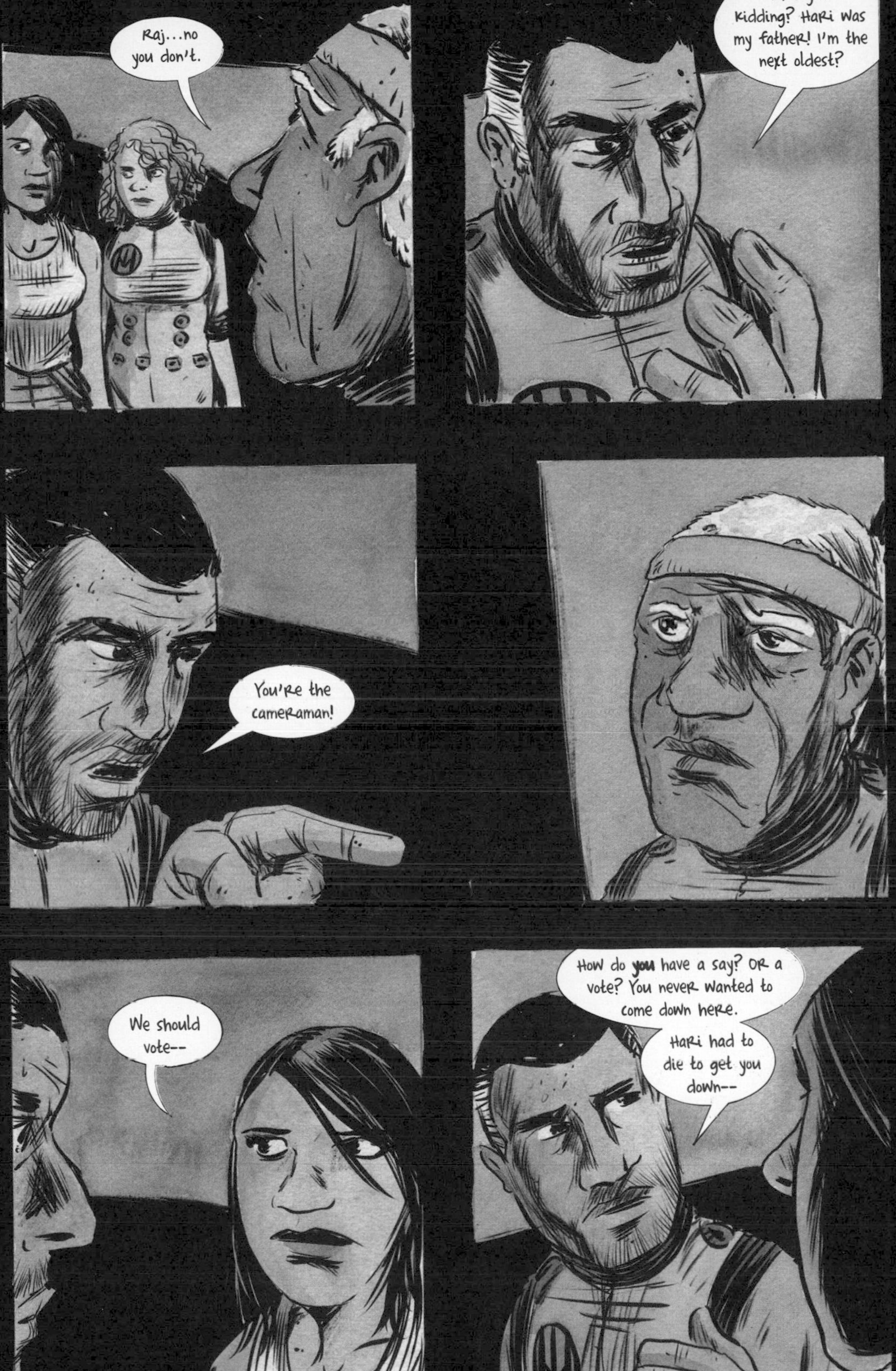
Raj...no you don't.
Are you kidding? Hari was my father! I'm the next oldest?
You're the cameraman!
We should vote--
How do you have a say? Or a vote? You never wanted to come down here.
Hari had to die to get you down--

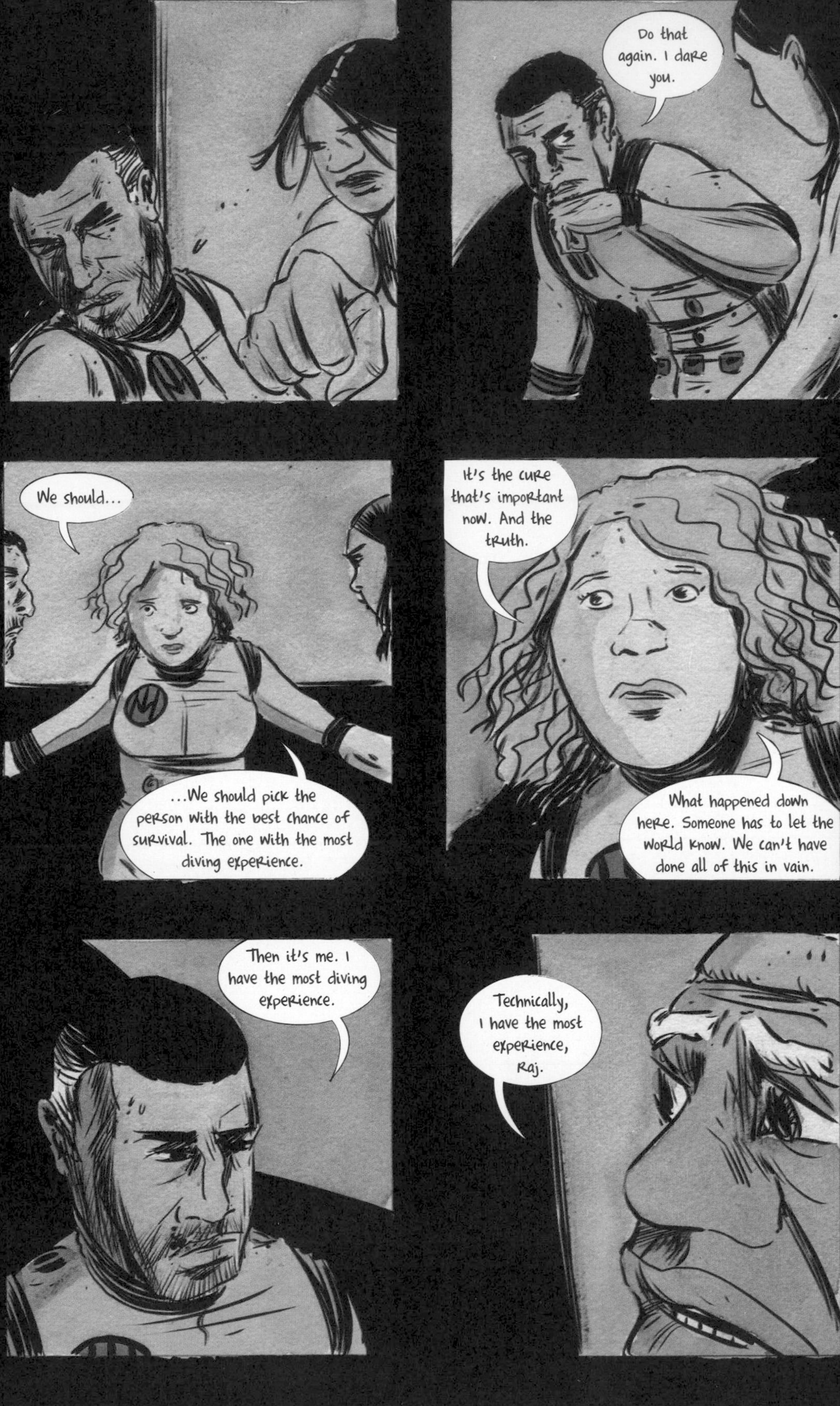
Do that again. I dare you.
We should...
...We should pick the person with the best chance of survival. The one with the most diving experience.
It's the cure that's important now. And the truth.
What happened down here. Someone has to let the world know. We can't have done all of this in vain.
Then it's me. I have the most diving experience.
Technically, I have the most experience, Raj.

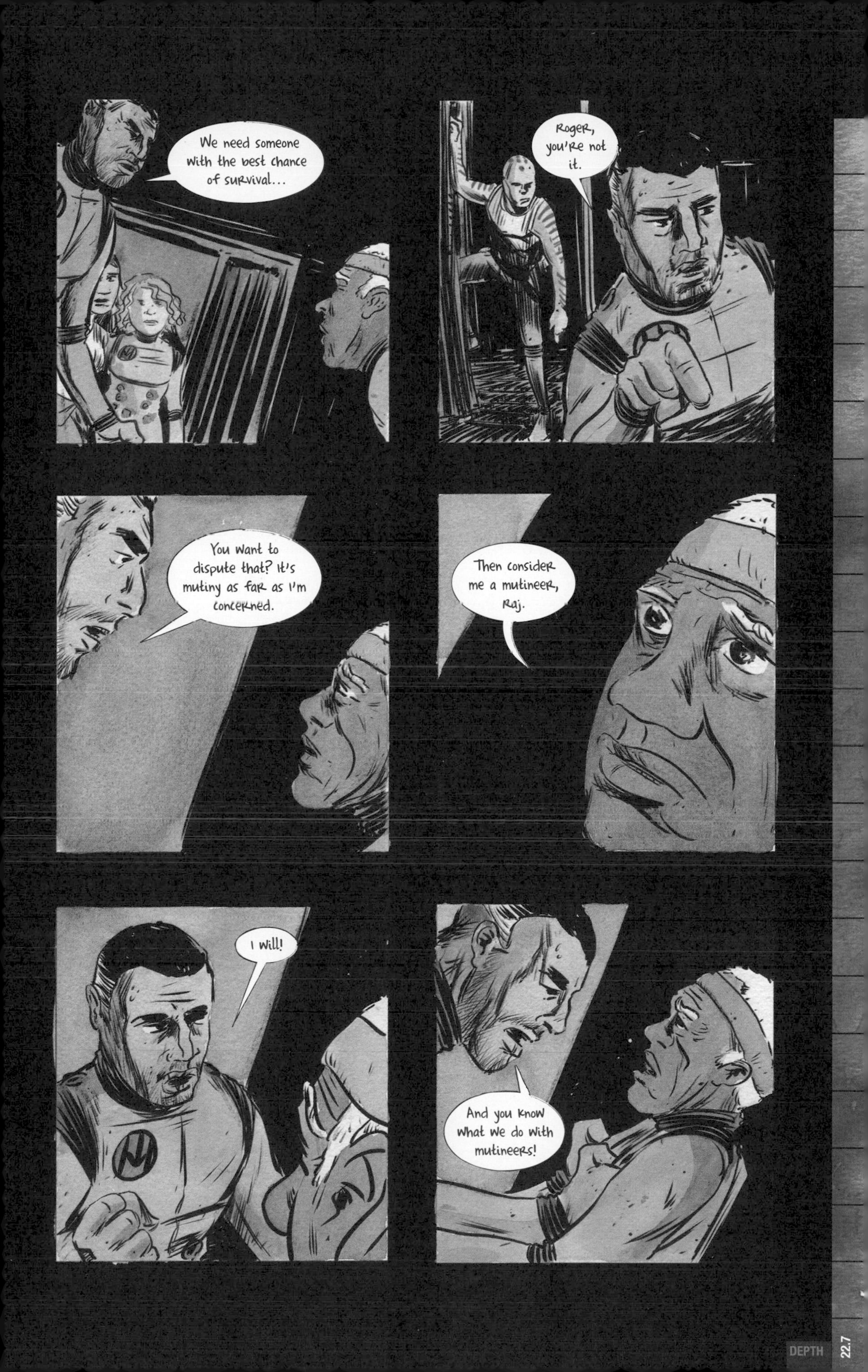
We need someone with the best chance of survival...
Roger, you're not it.
You want to dispute that? It's mutiny as far as I'm concerned.
Then consider me a mutineer, Raj.
I will!
And you know what we do with mutineers!

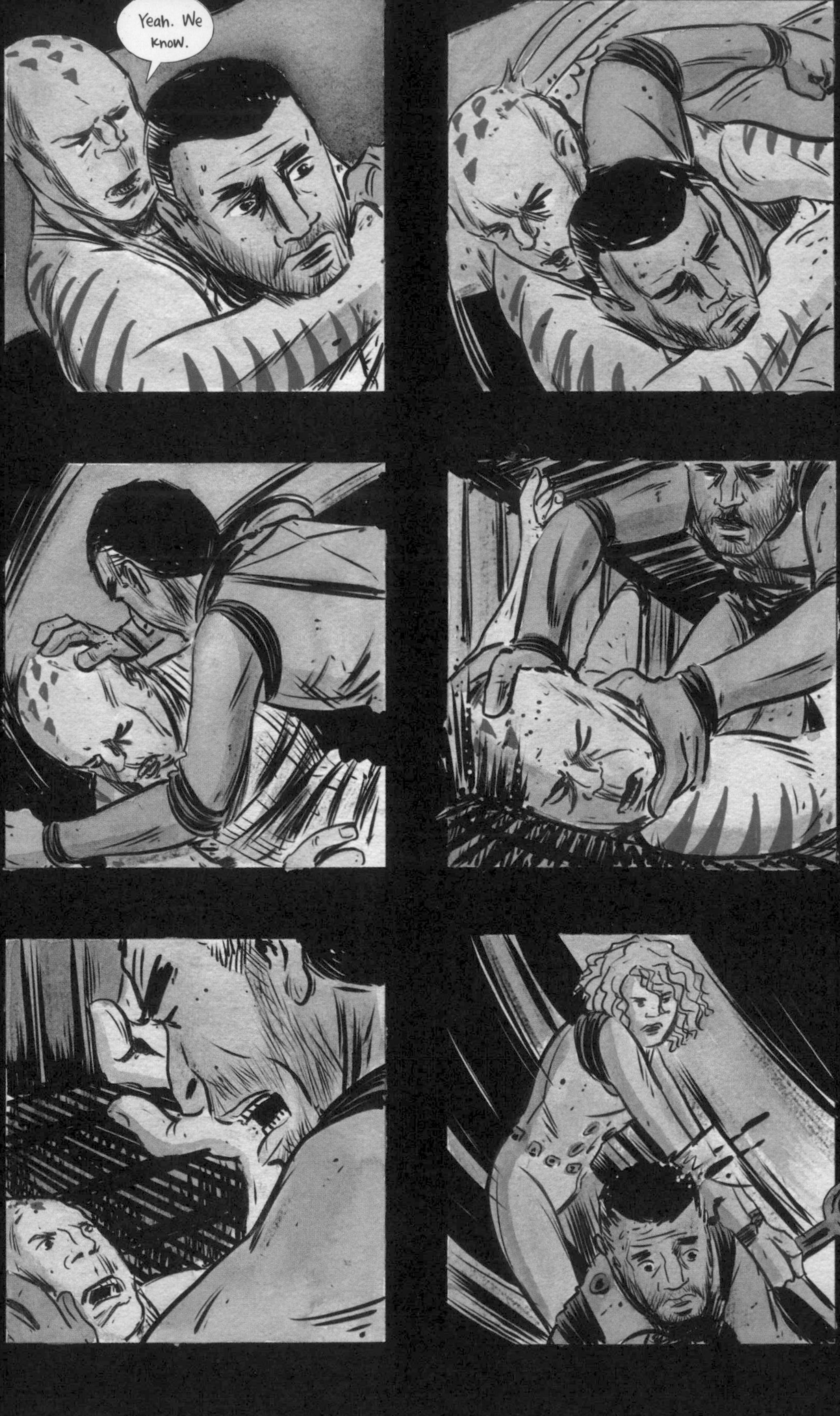
Yeah. We know.

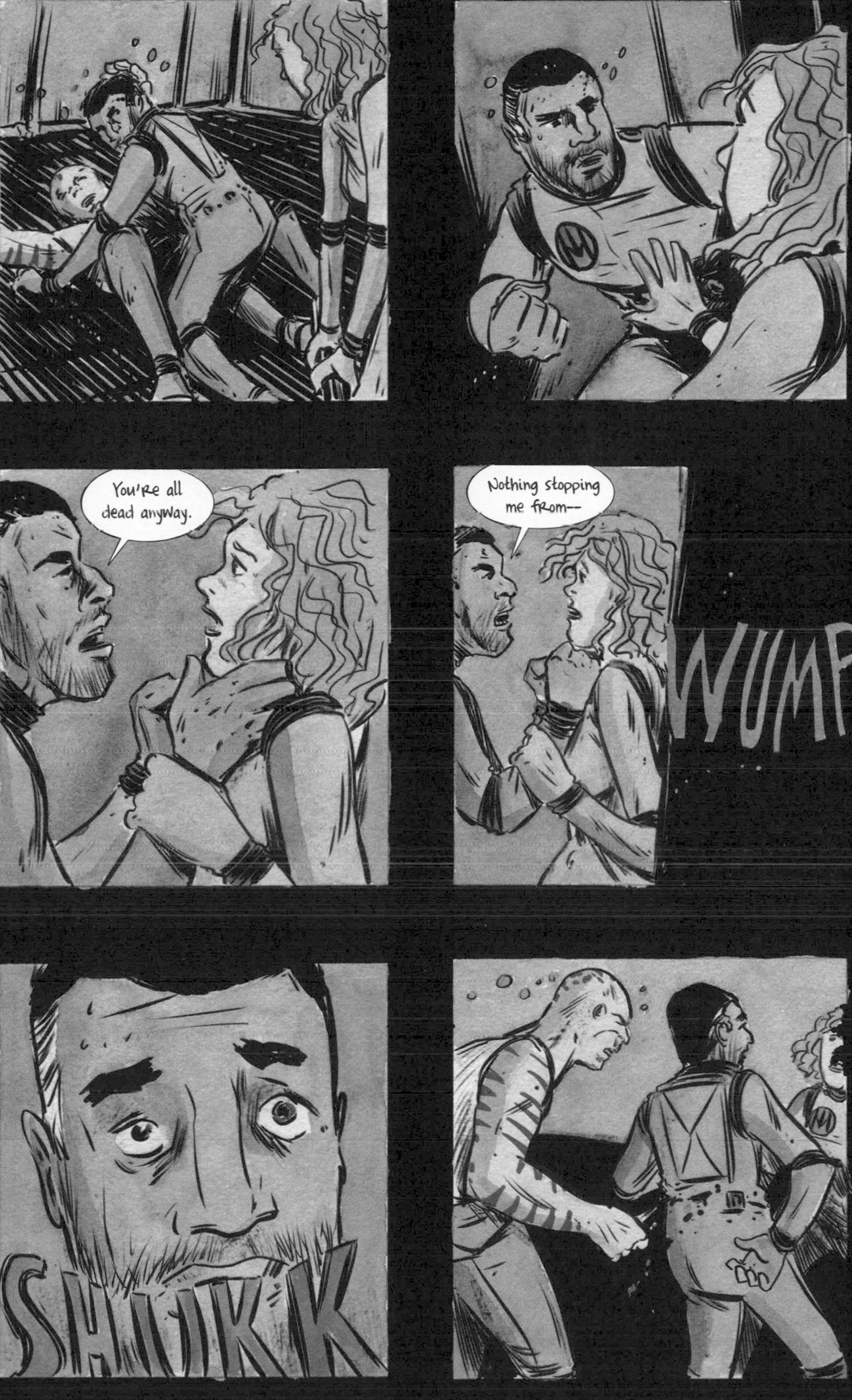
You're all dead anyway.
Nothing stopping me from--
WUMP
SHUKK

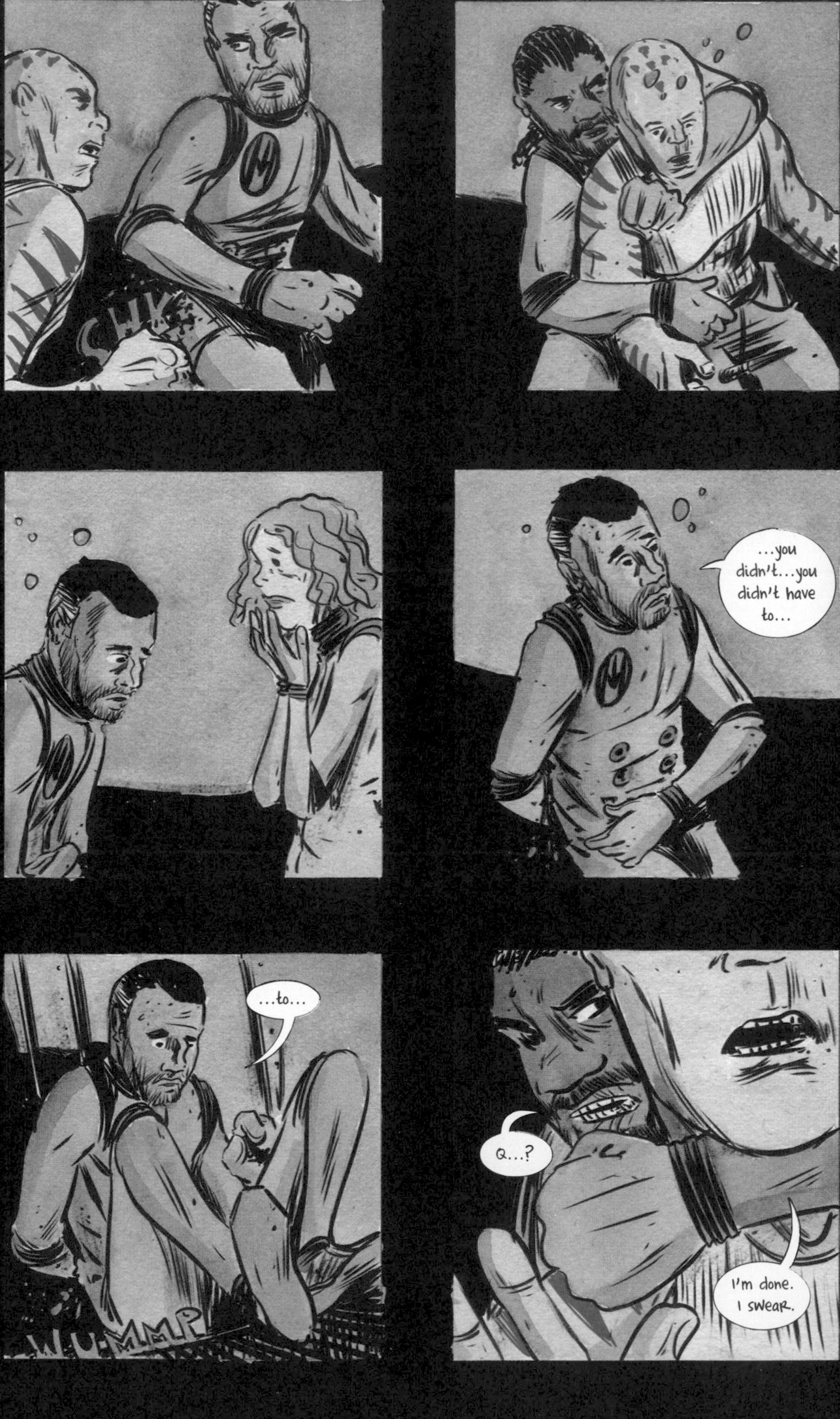

...you didn't...you didn't have to...
...to...
WUMMP
Q...?
I'm done. I swear.

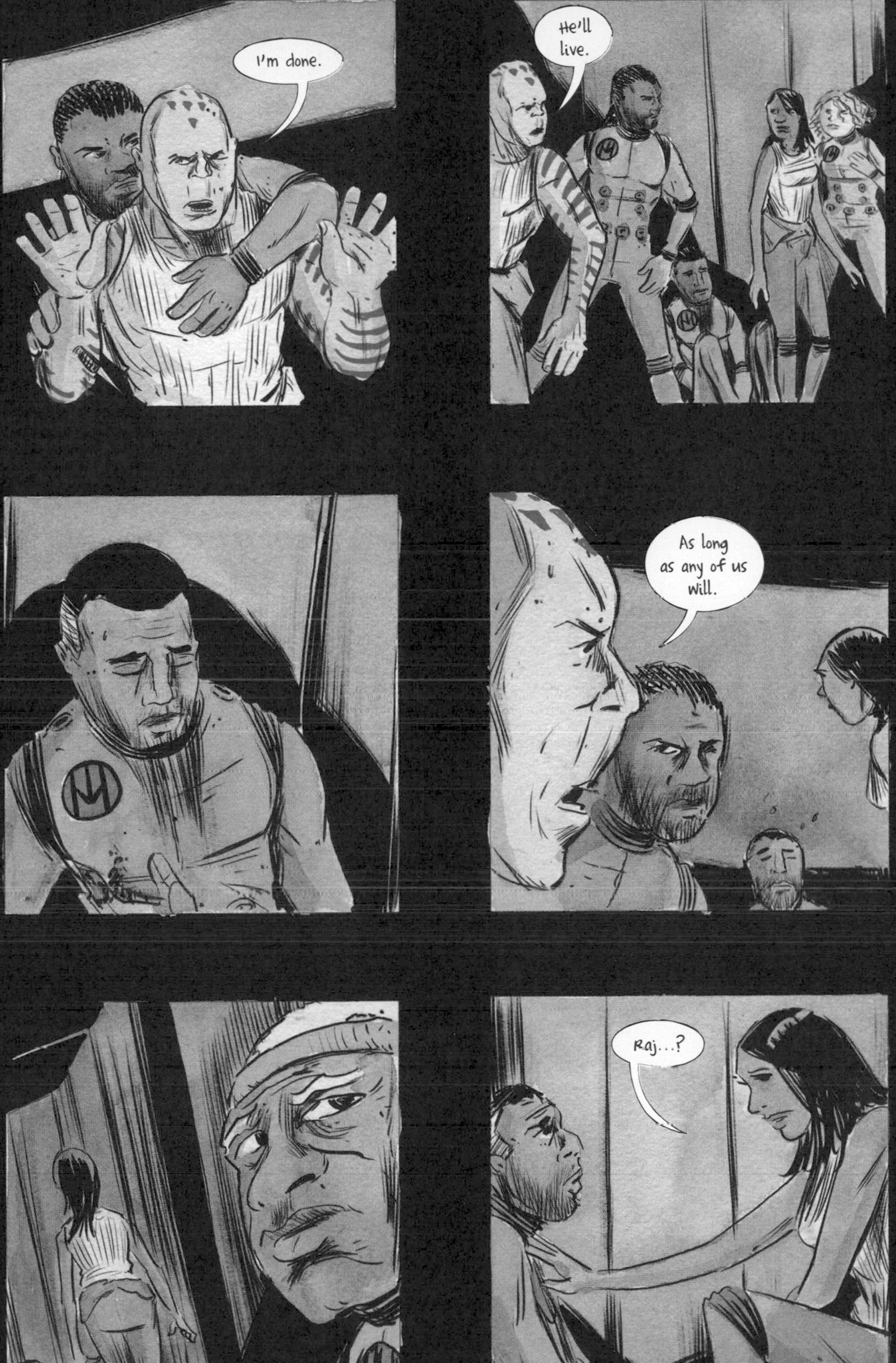

I'm done.
He'll live.
As long as any of us will.
Raj...?

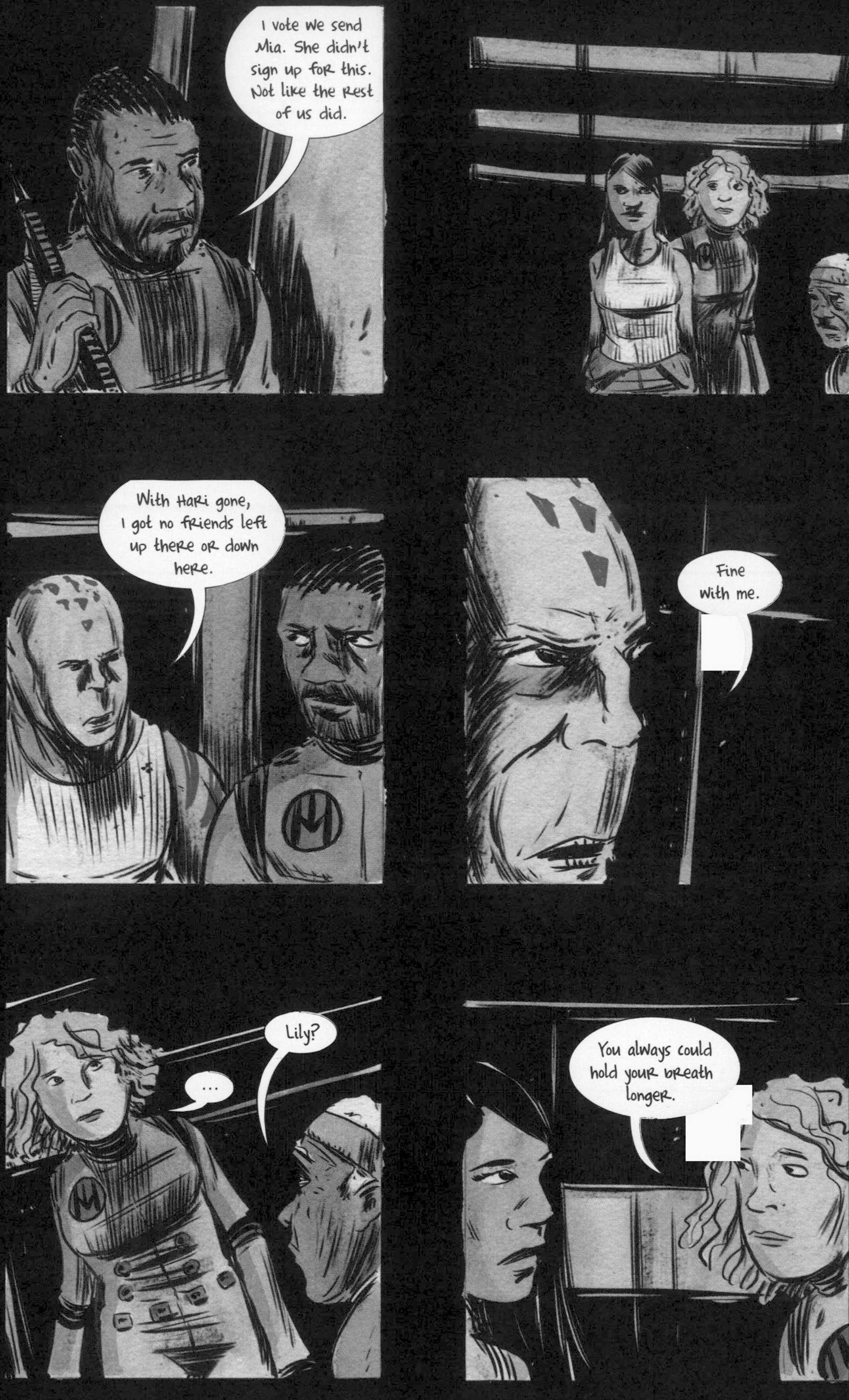
I vote we send Mia. She didn't sign up for this. Not like the rest of us did.
With Hari gone, I got no friends left up there or down here.
Fine with me.
...
Lily?
You always could hold your breath longer.

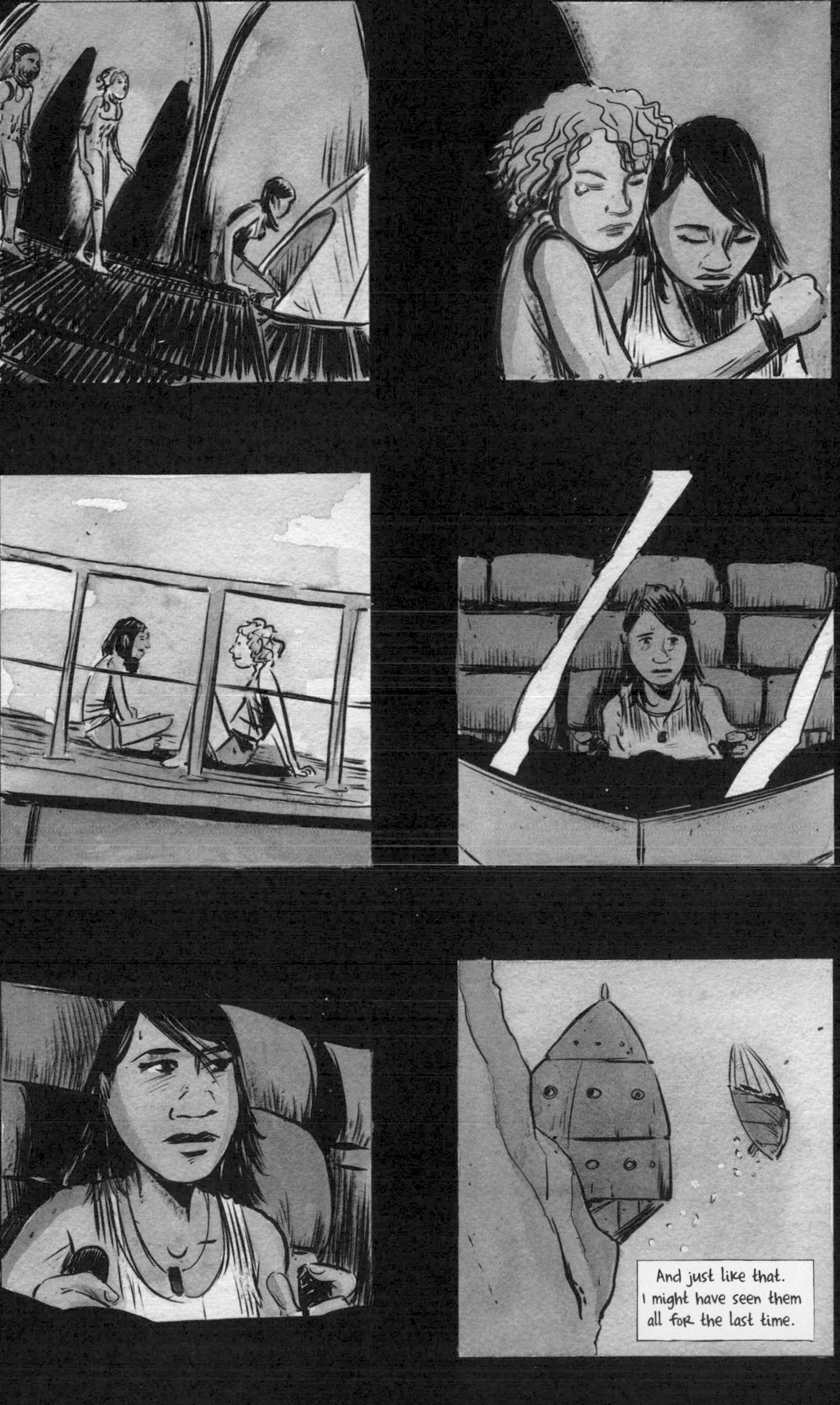
And just like that.
I might have seen them
all for the last time.

And I've got at least two hours of ascent to think about it.

Any faster and I'll get the bends.

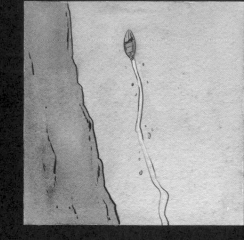

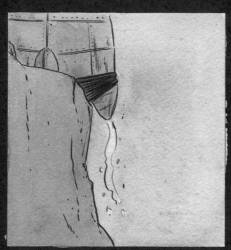

Aaron?

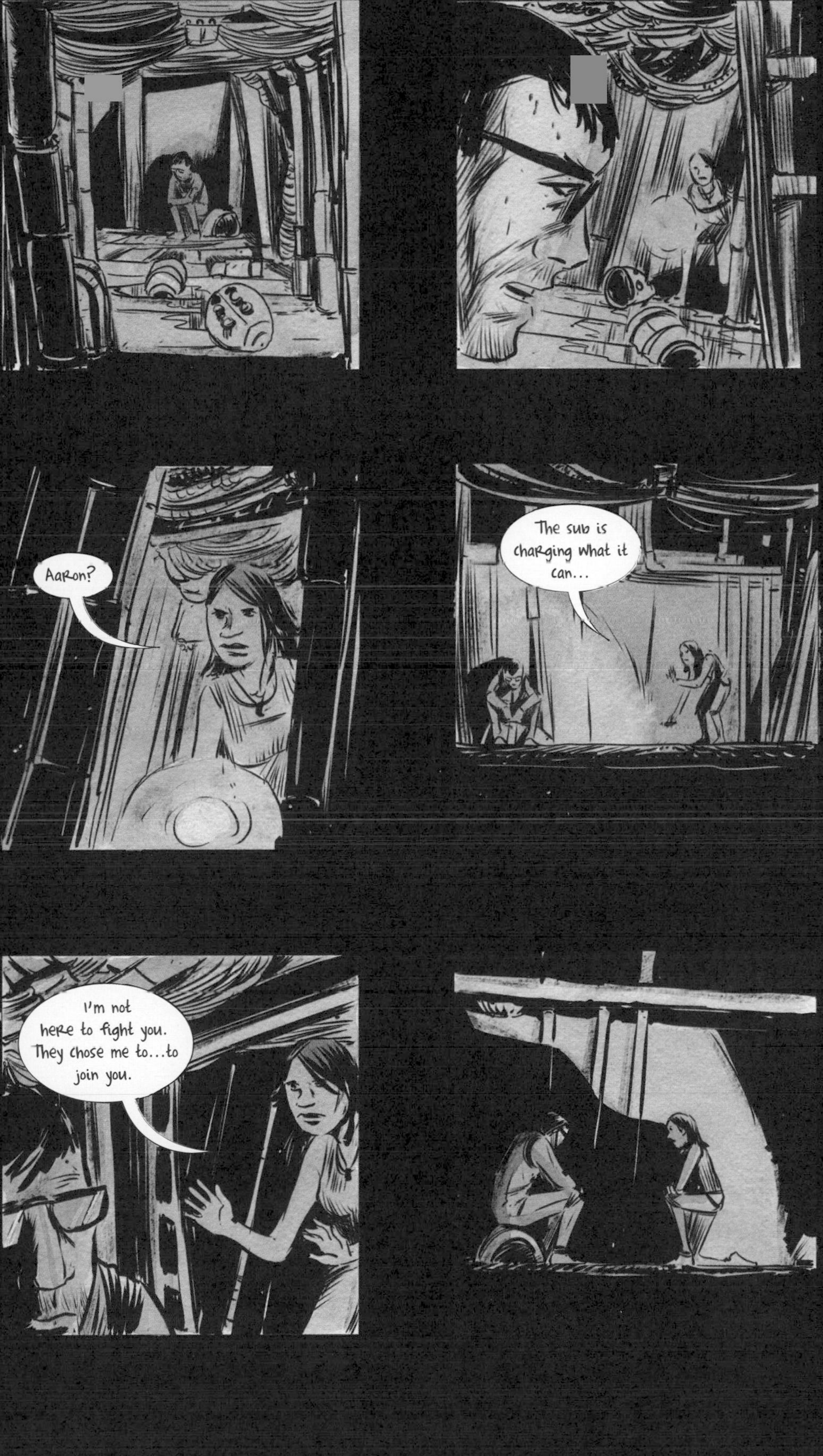
Aaron?
The sub is charging what it can...
I'm not here to fight you. They chose me to...to join you.

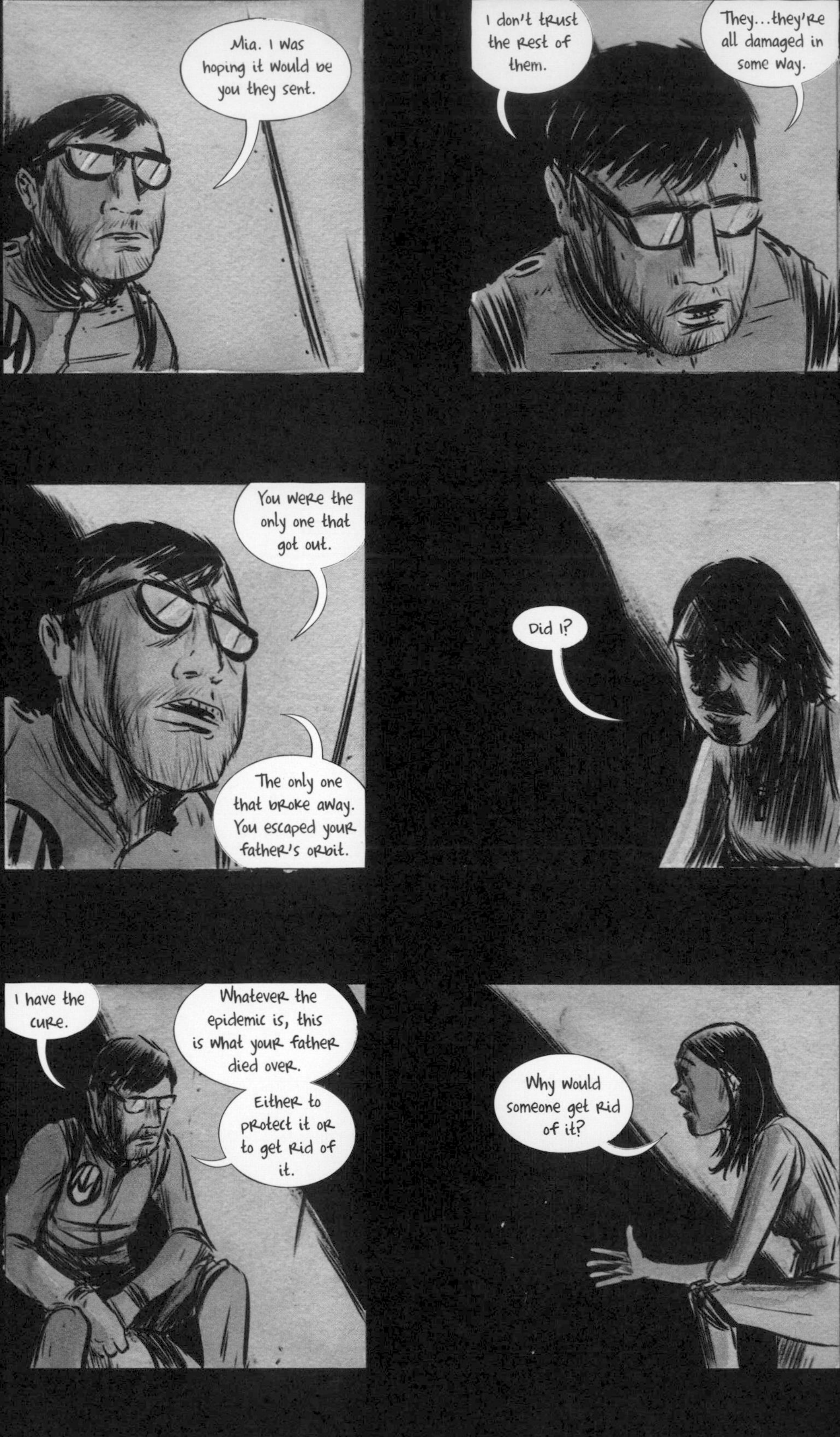
Mia. I was hoping it would be you they sent.
I don't trust the rest of them.
They...they're all damaged in some way.
You were the only one that got out.
The only one that broke away. You escaped your father's orbit.
Did I?
I have the cure.
Whatever the epidemic is, this is what your father died over.
Either to protect it or to get rid of it.
Why would someone get rid of it?

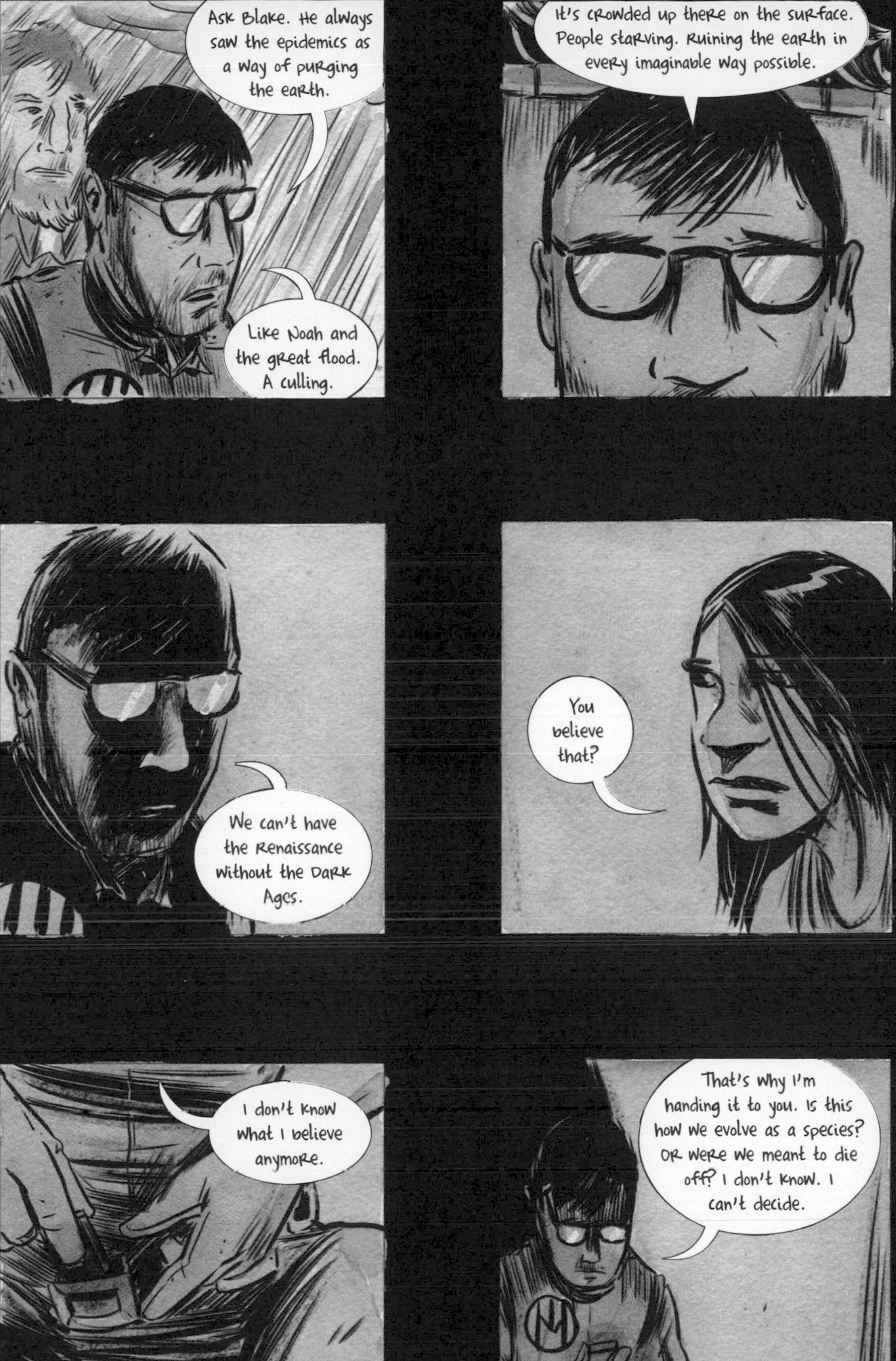
Ask Blake. He always saw the epidemics as a way of purging the earth.
Like Noah and the great flood. A culling.
It's crowded up there on the surface. People starving. Ruining the earth in every imaginable way possible.
We can't have the Renaissance without the Dark Ages.
You believe that?
I don't know what I believe anymore.
That's why I'm handing it to you. Is this how we evolve as a species? Or were we meant to die off? I don't know. I can't decide.

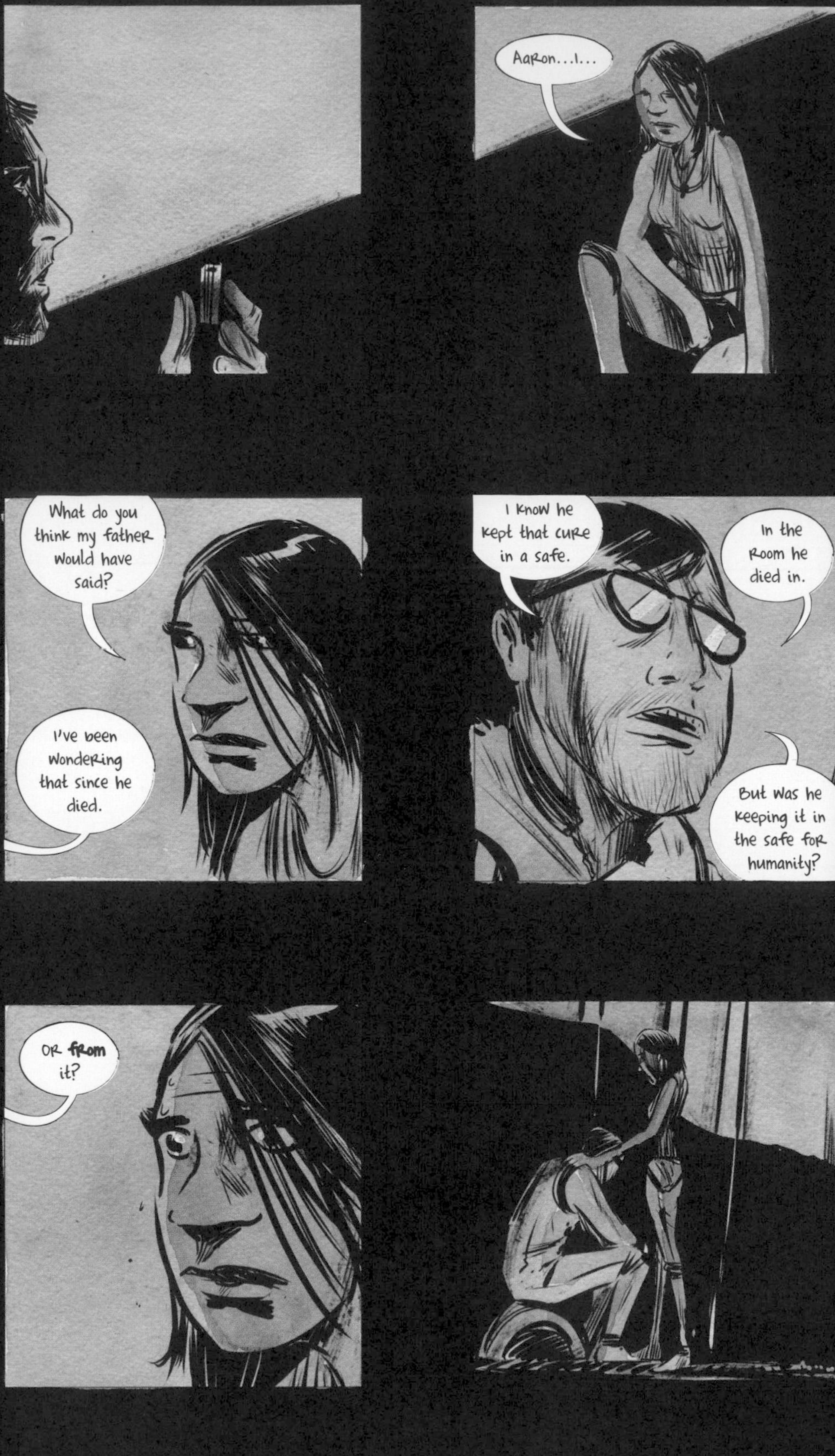

Aaron...I...
What do you think my father would have said?
I've been wondering that since he died.
I know he kept that cure in a safe.
In the room he died in.
But was he keeping it in the safe for humanity?
Or from it?

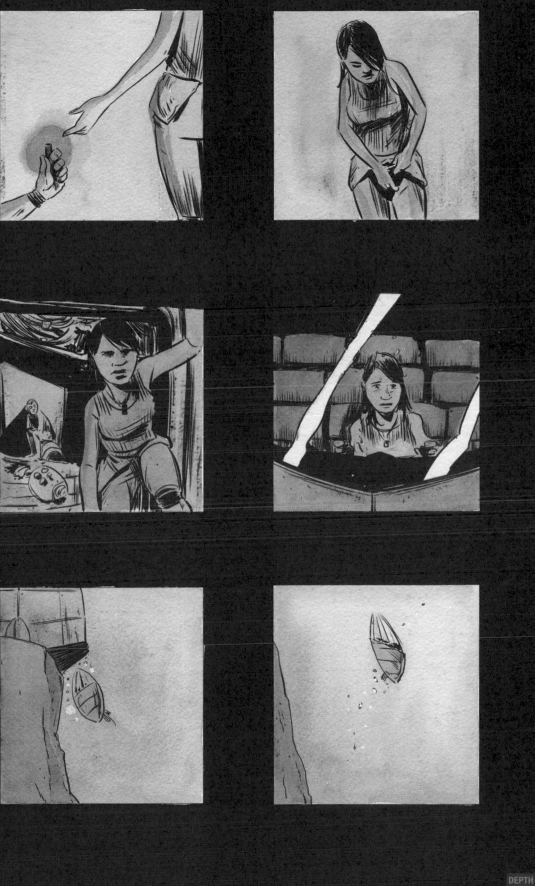

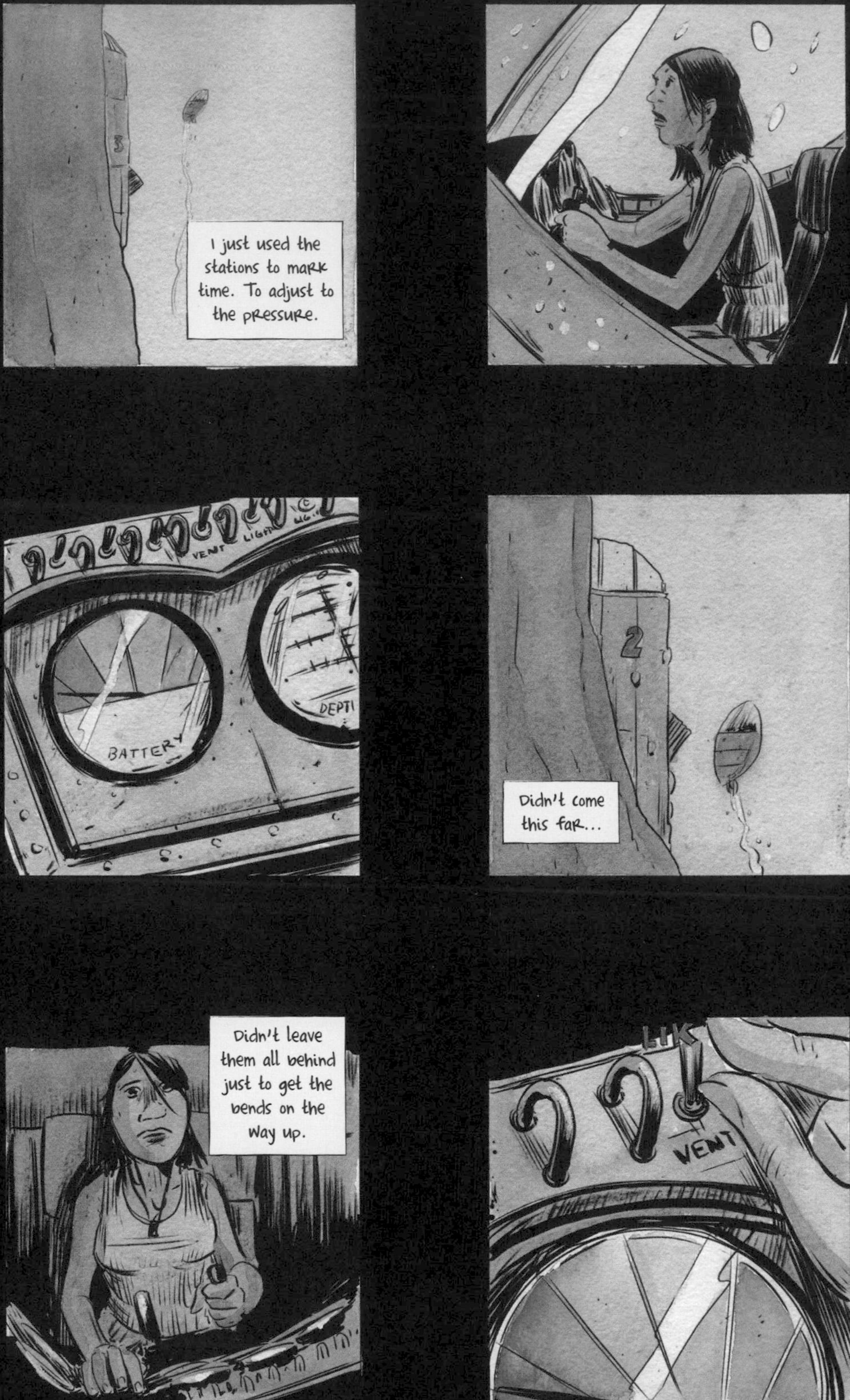
I just used the stations to mark time. To adjust to the pressure.
VENT
BATTERY
Didn't come this far...
Didn't leave them all behind just to get the bends on the way up.
LIK
VENT

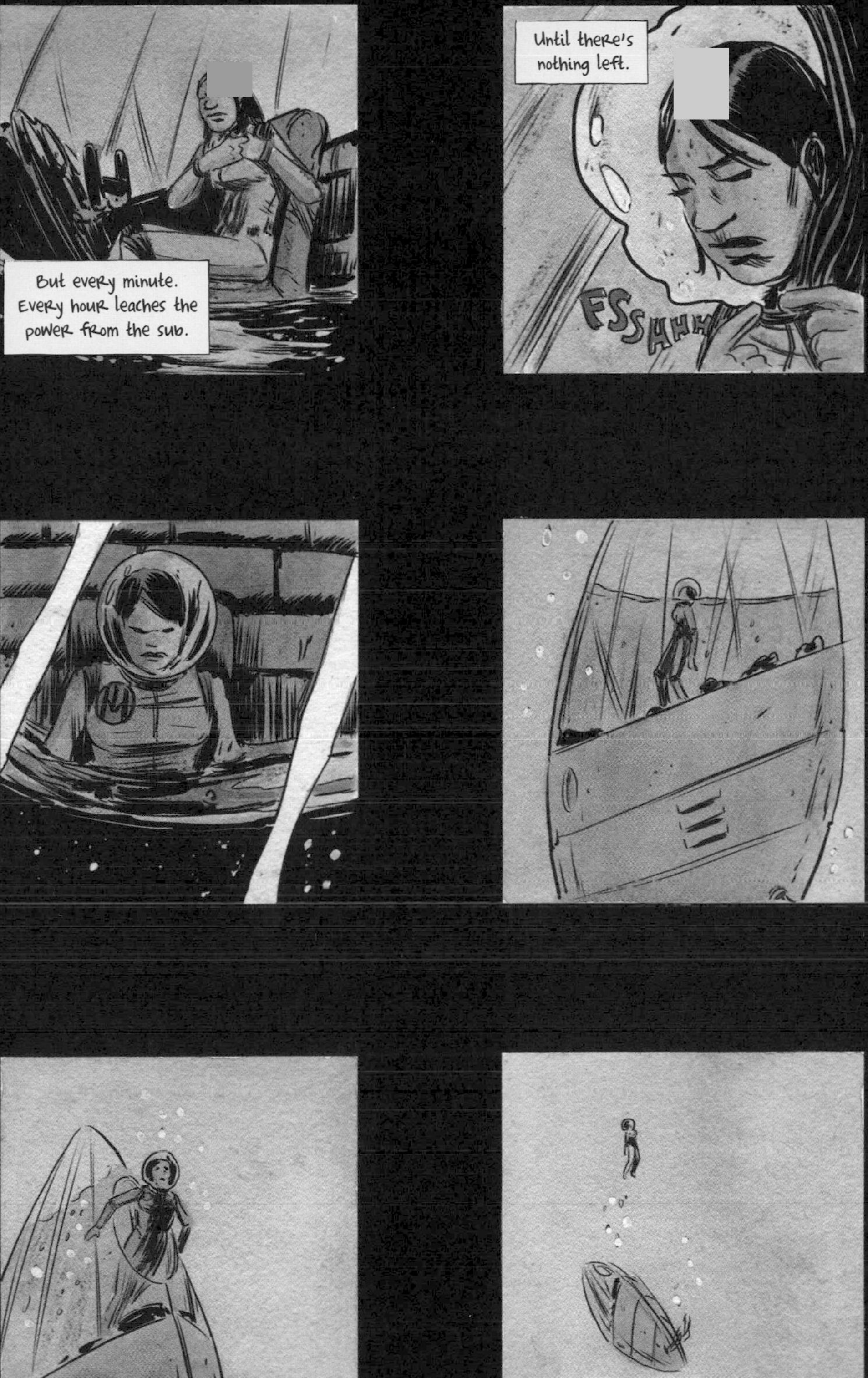
But every minute. Every hour leaches the power from the sub.
Until there's nothing left.
FSSHHH

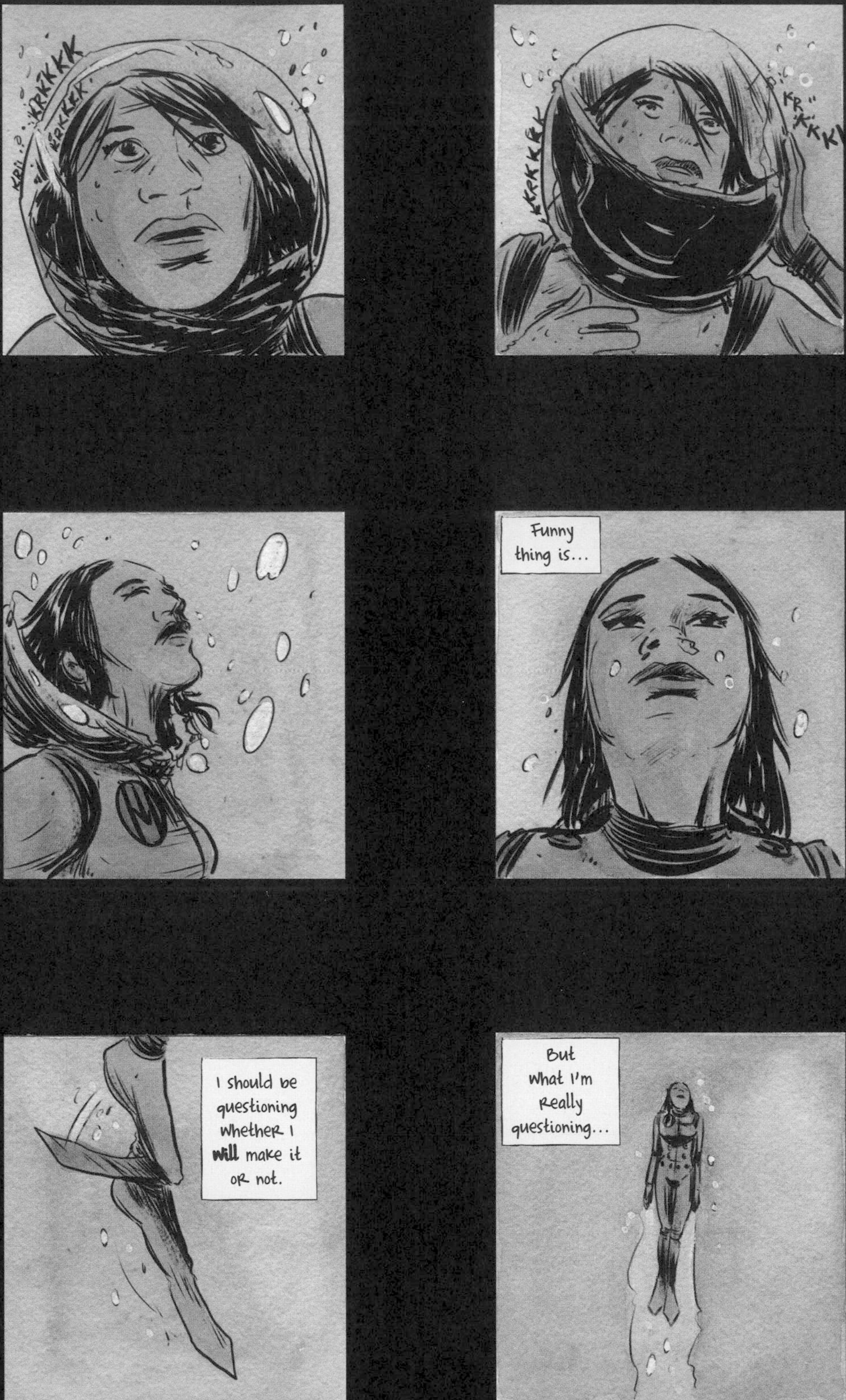
Funny thing is...
I should be questioning whether I will make it or not.
But what I'm really questioning...

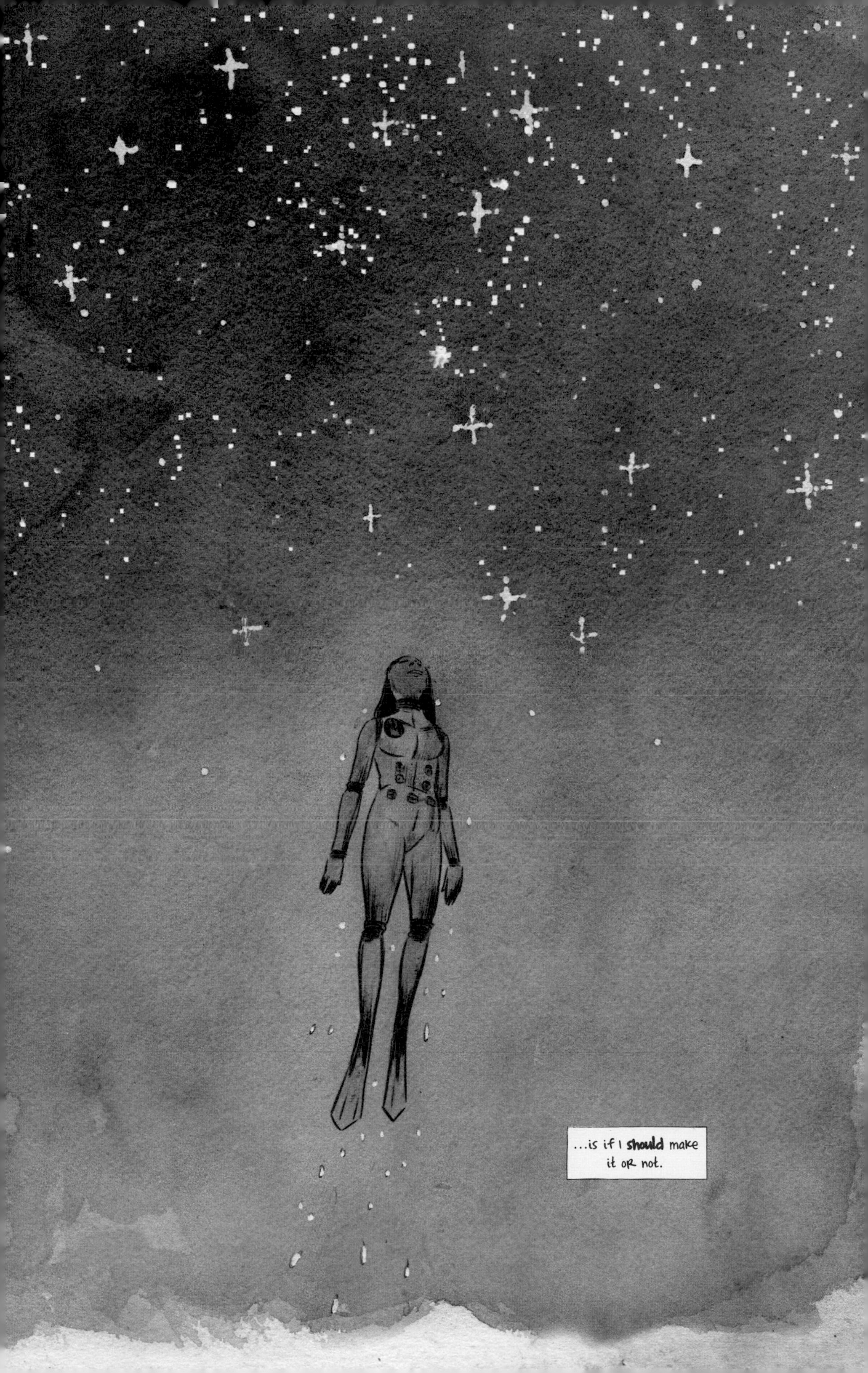
...is if I **should** make it or not.

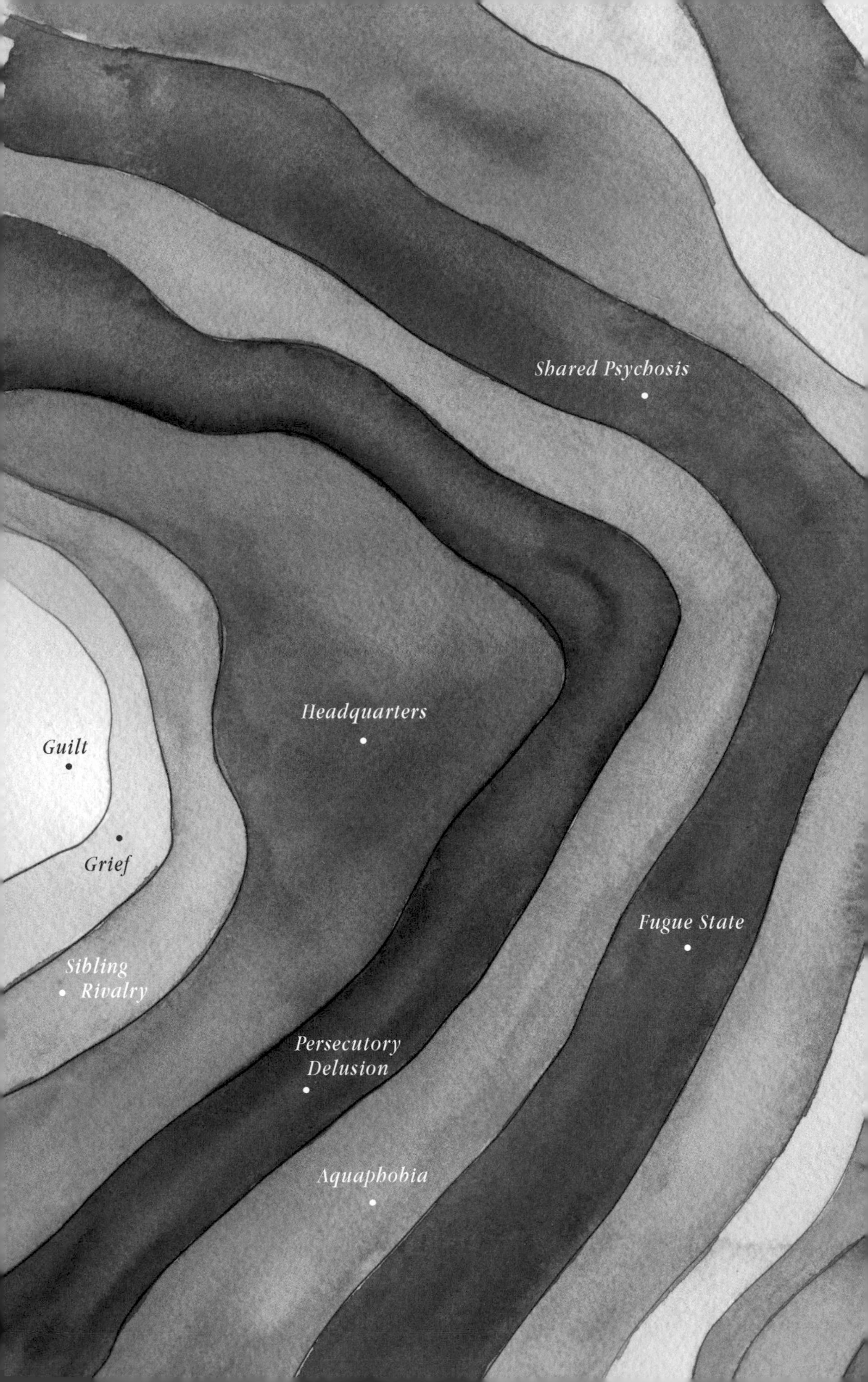
Shared Psychosis
Headquarters
Guilt
Grief
Fugue State
Sibling Rivalry
Persecutory Delusion
Aquaphobia

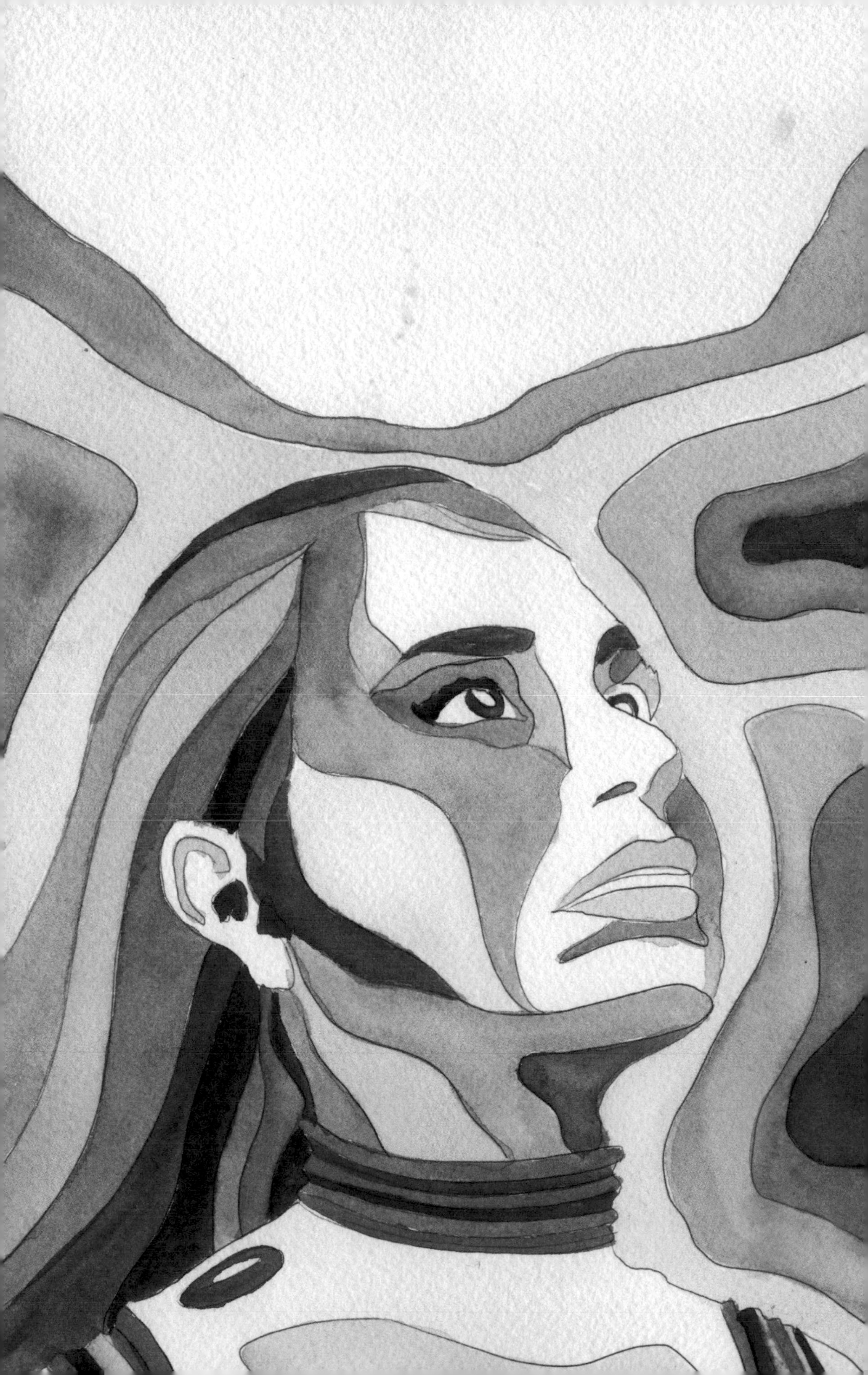

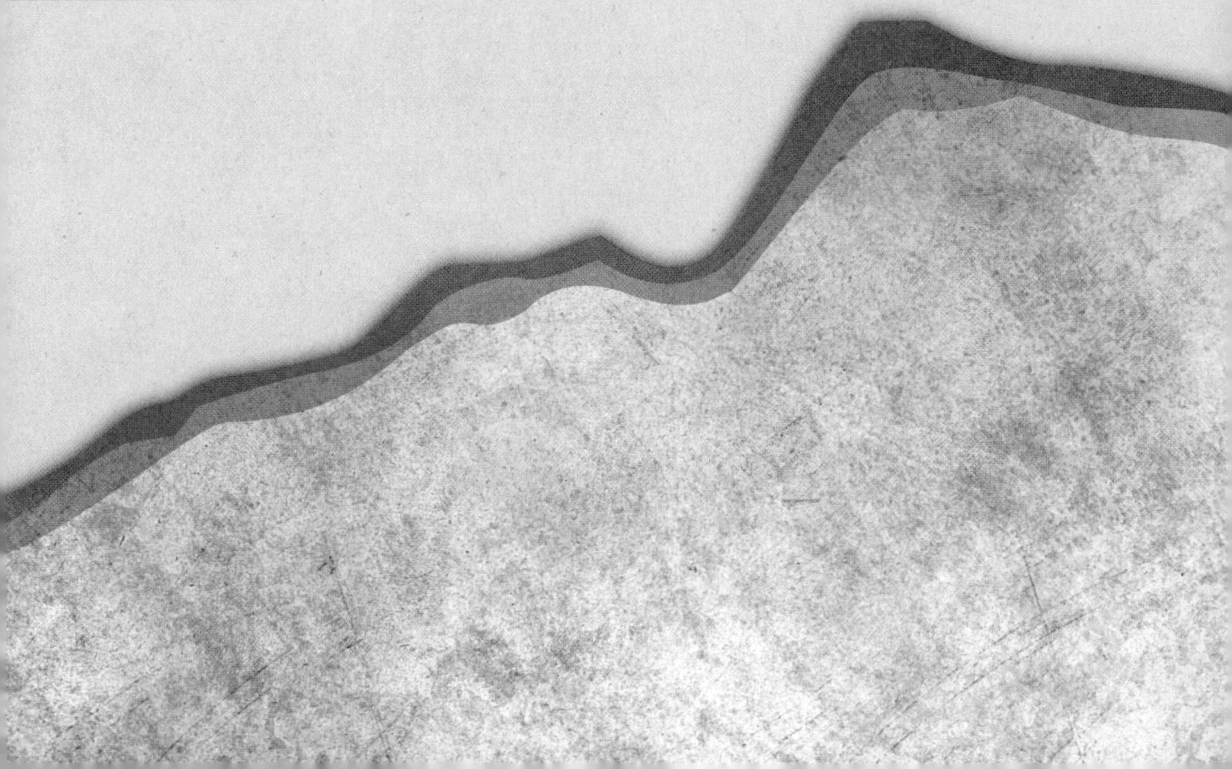

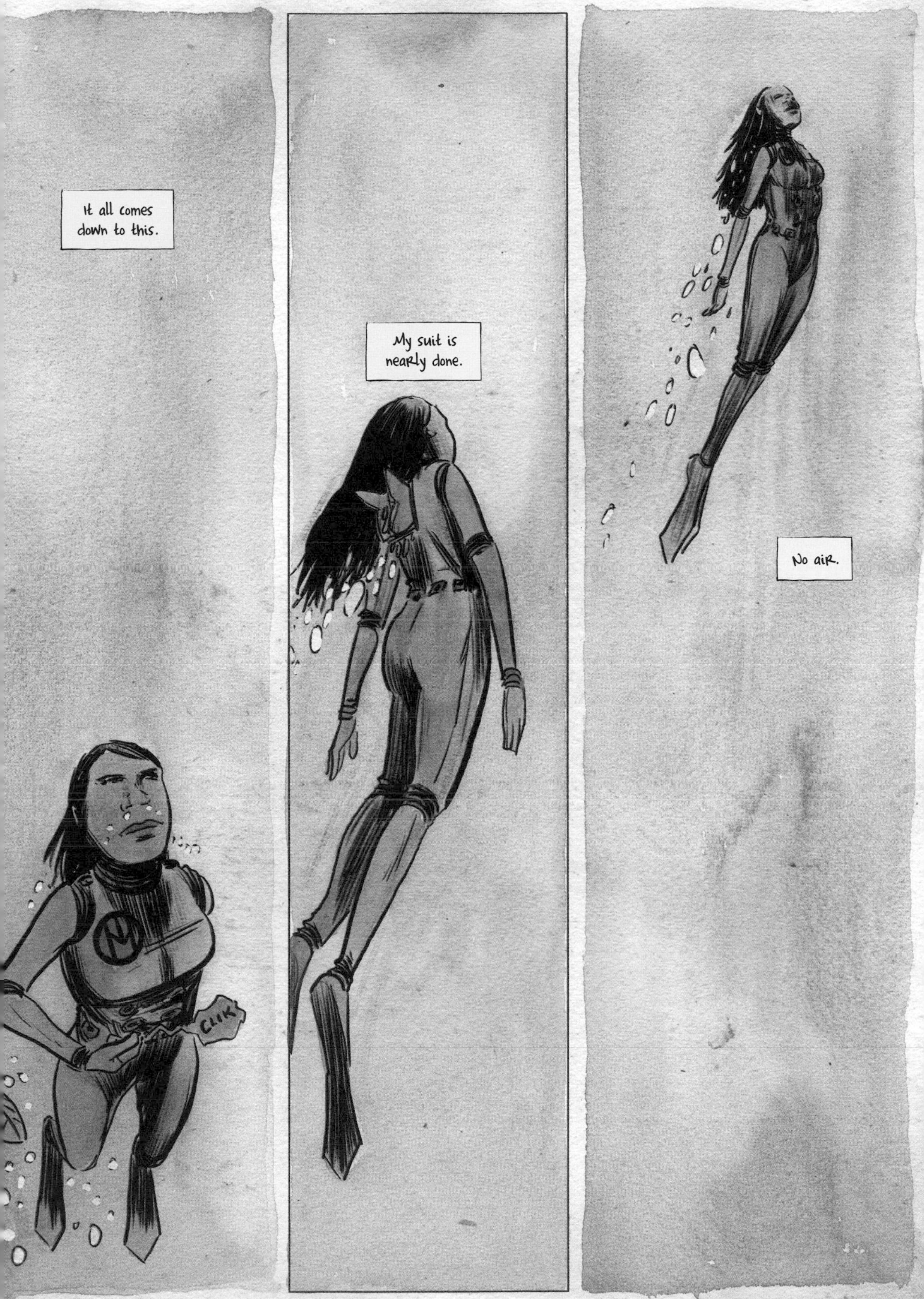
It all comes down to this.
CLIK
My suit is nearly done.
No air.

It will either be enough...

OR it won't.

Just focus...control the air in your lungs.

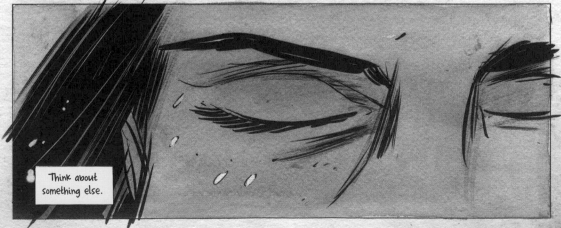

Think about something else.

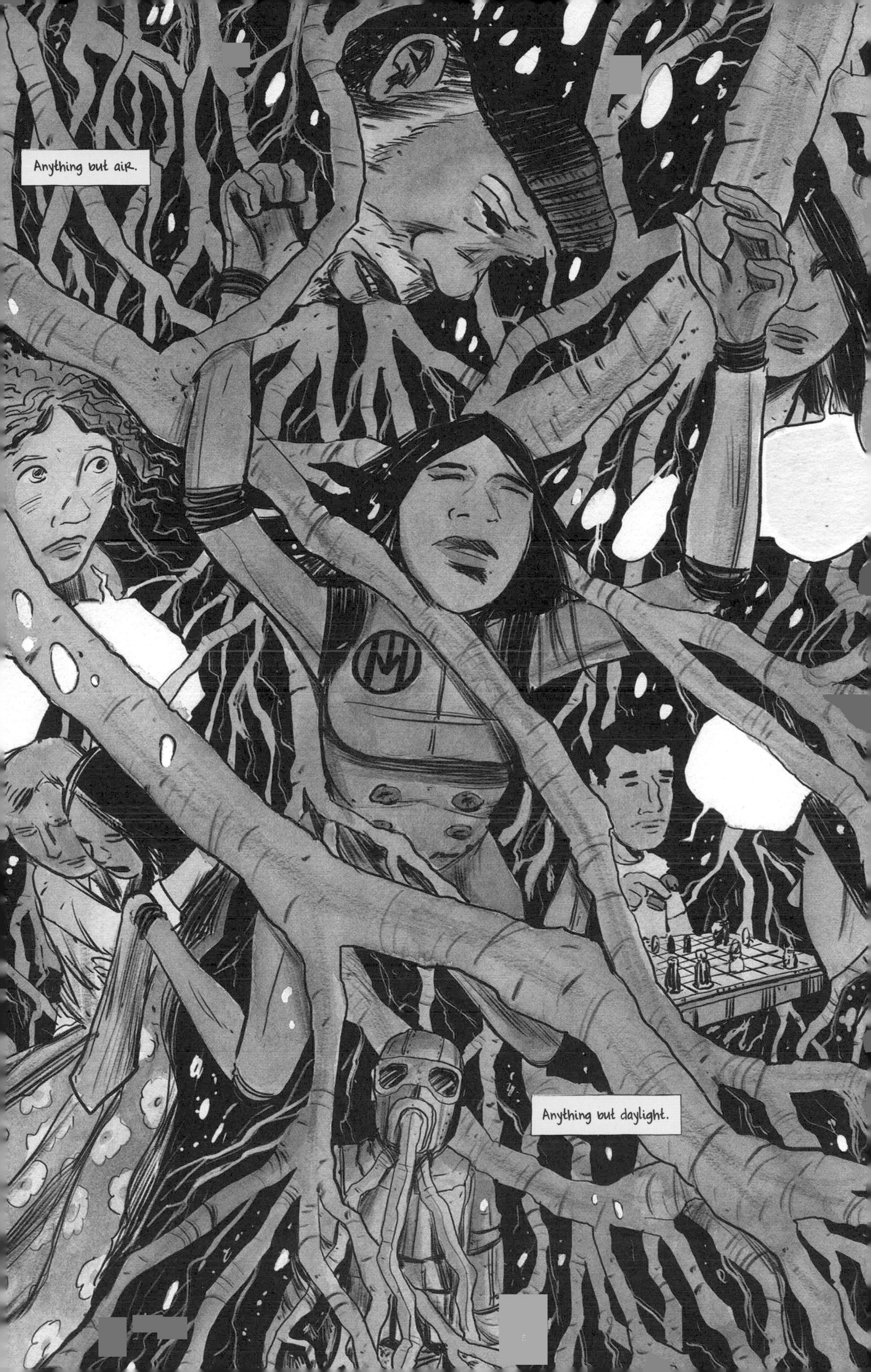
Anything but air.
Anything but daylight.

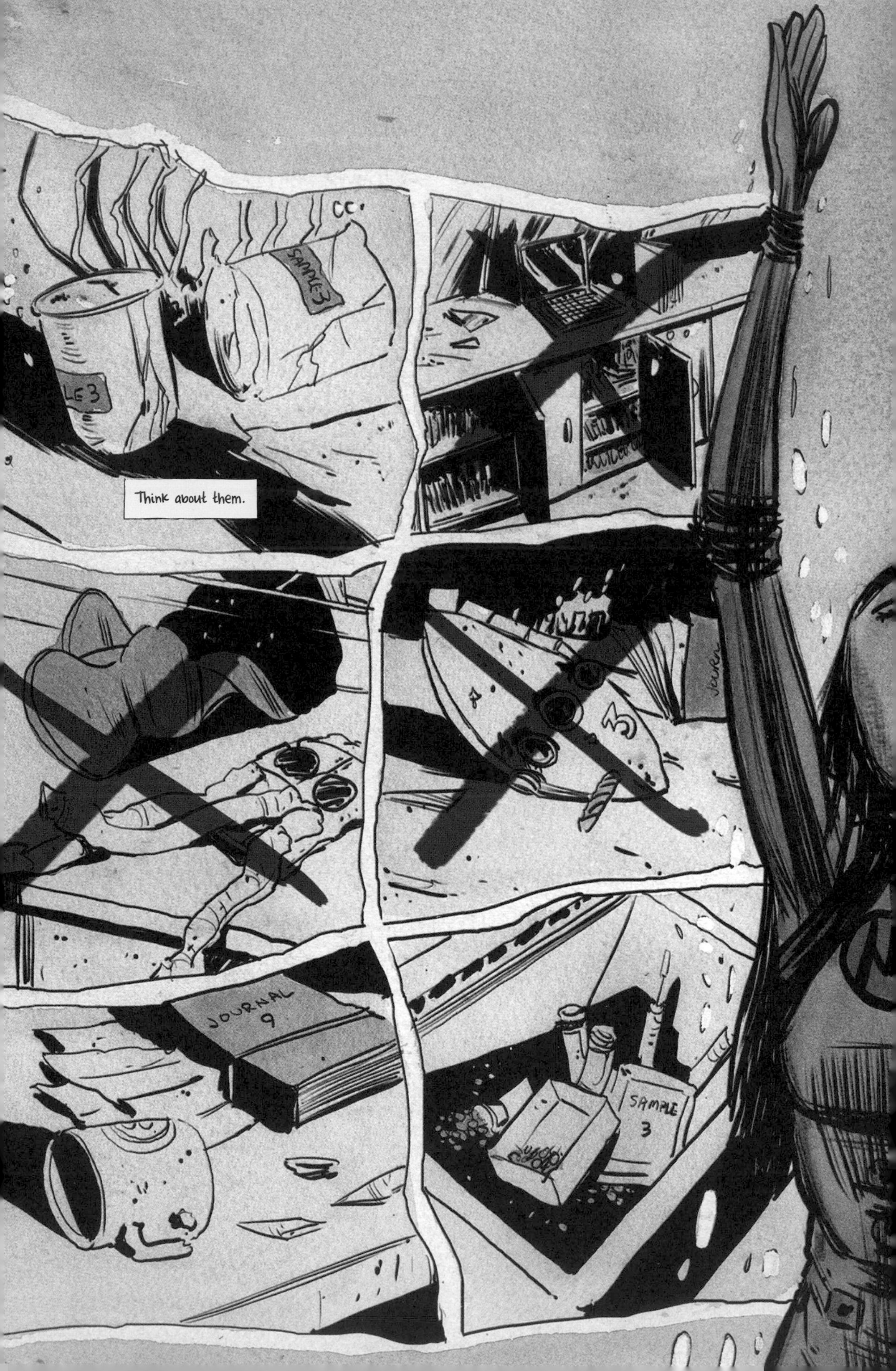
SAMPLE 3
LE 3
Think about them.
3
JOURNAL 9
SAMPLE 3

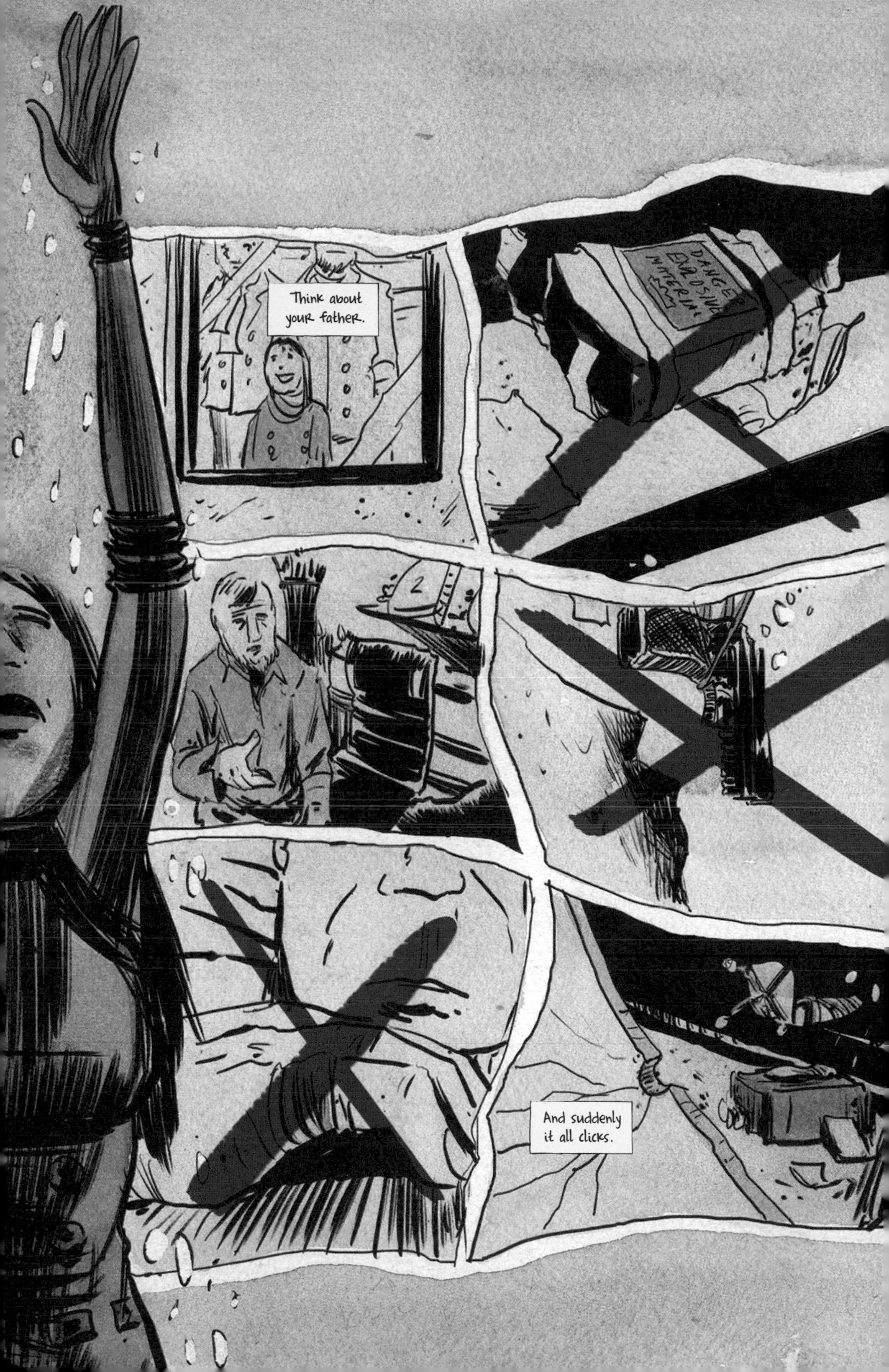
Think about your father.
DANGER EXPLOSIVE MATERIAL
And suddenly it all clicks.

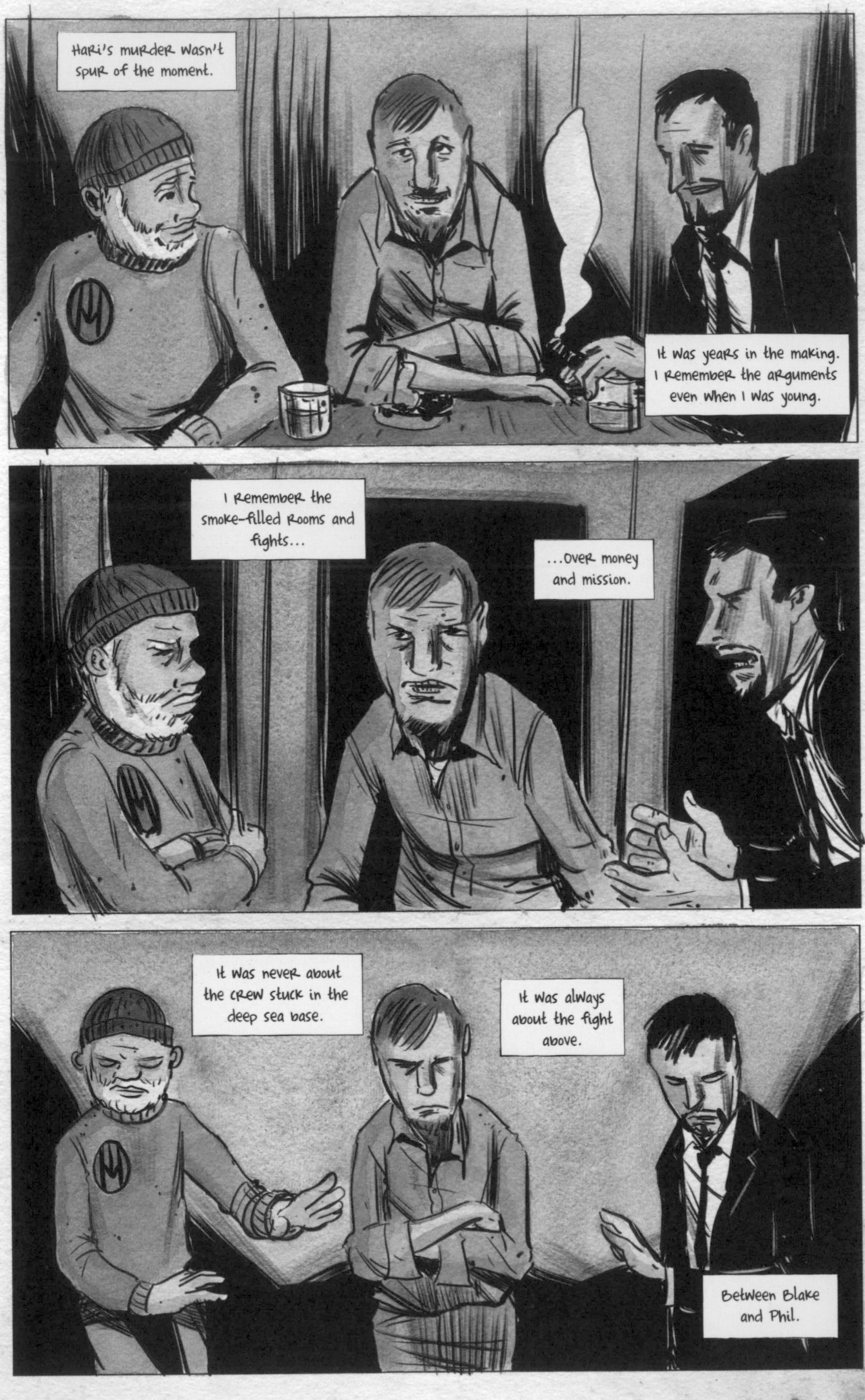
Hari's murder wasn't spur of the moment.
It was years in the making. I remember the arguments even when I was young.
I remember the smoke-filled rooms and fights...
...over money and mission.
It was never about the crew stuck in the deep sea base.
It was always about the fight above.
Between Blake and Phil.

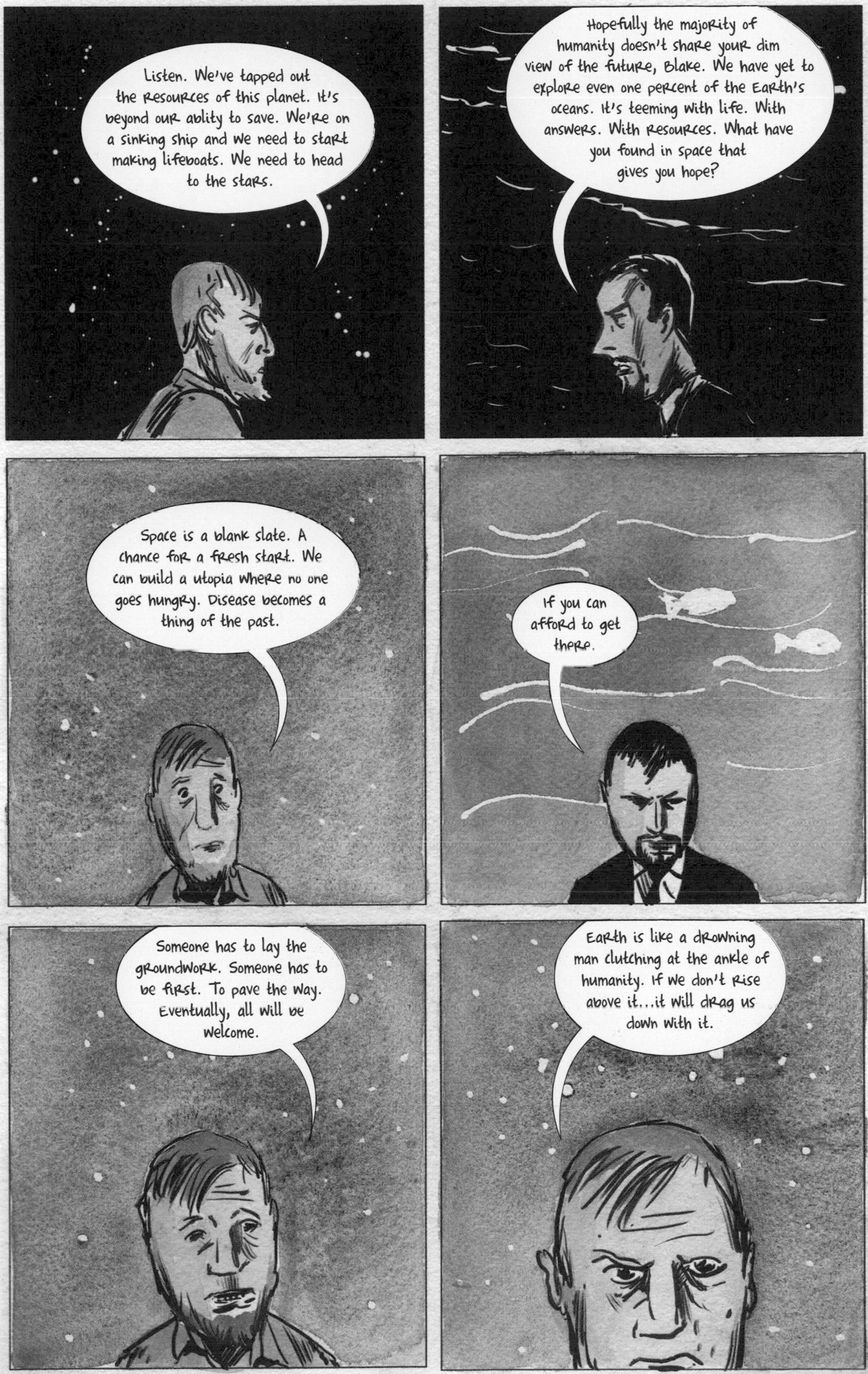
Listen. We've tapped out the resources of this planet. It's beyond our ablity to save. We're on a sinking ship and we need to start making lifeboats. We need to head to the stars.
Hopefully the majority of humanity doesn't share your dim view of the future, Blake. We have yet to explore even one percent of the Earth's oceans. It's teeming with life. With answers. With resources. What have you found in space that gives you hope?
Space is a blank slate. A chance for a fresh start. We can build a utopia where no one goes hungry. Disease becomes a thing of the past.
If you can afford to get there.
Someone has to lay the groundwork. Someone has to be first. To pave the way. Eventually, all will be welcome.
Earth is like a drowning man clutching at the ankle of humanity. If we don't rise above it...it will drag us down with it.

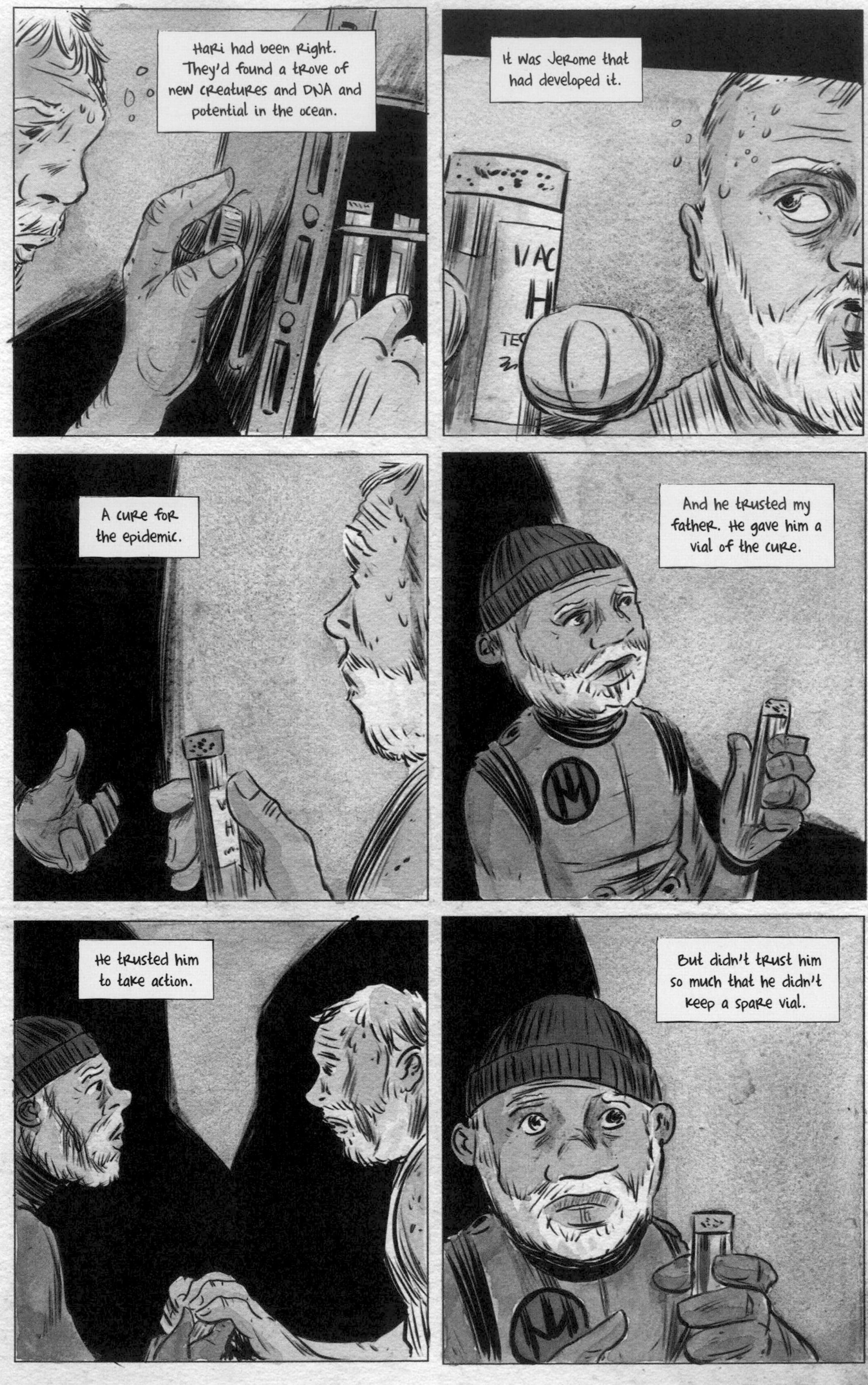
Hari had been right. They'd found a trove of new creatures and DNA and potential in the ocean.
It was Jerome that had developed it.
VAC
H
TE
A cure for the epidemic.
And he trusted my father. He gave him a vial of the cure.
He trusted him to take action.
But didn't trust him so much that he didn't keep a spare vial.

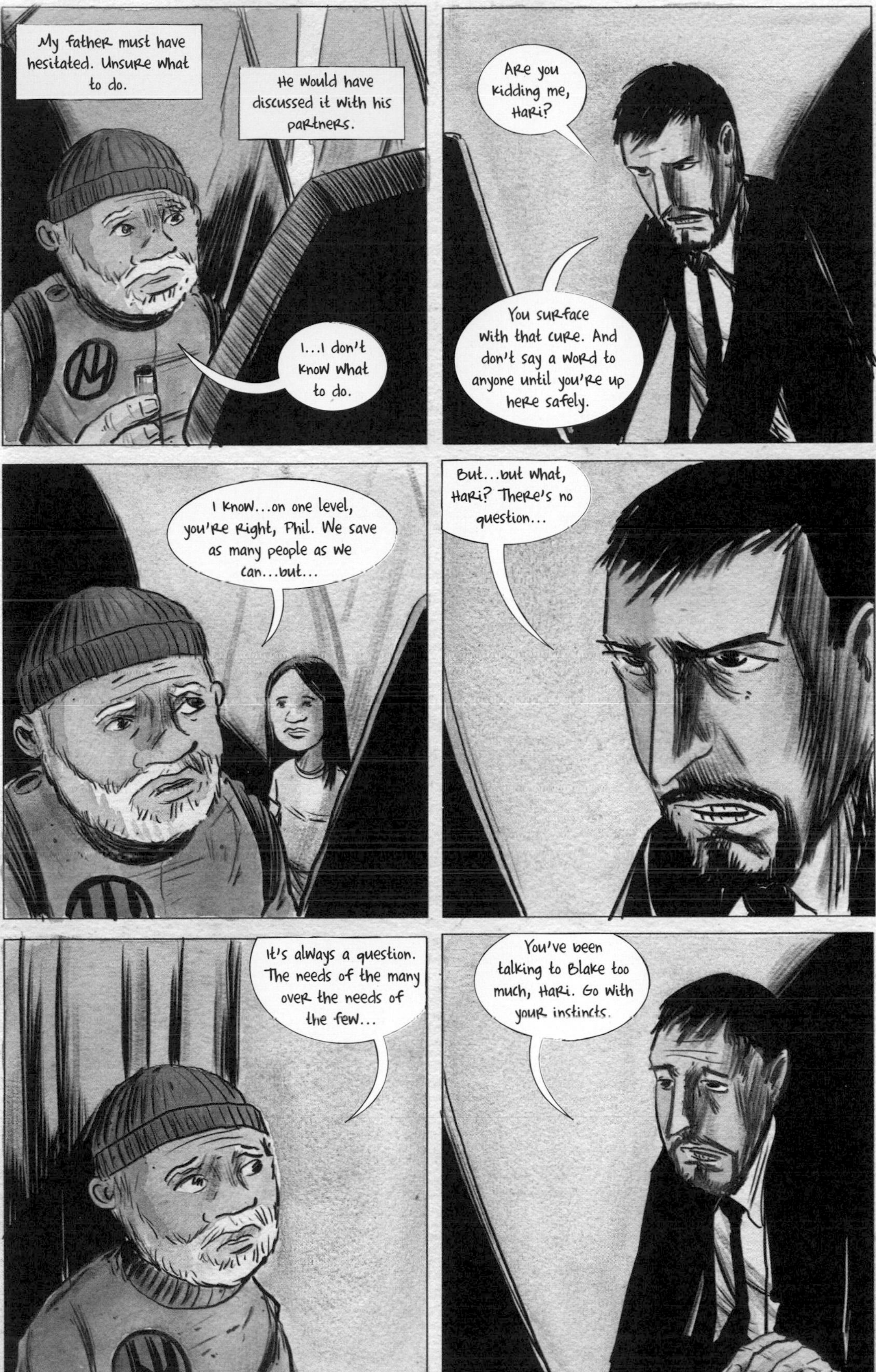
My father must have hesitated. Unsure what to do.
He would have discussed it with his partners.
I...I don't know what to do.
Are you kidding me, Hari?
You surface with that cure. And don't say a word to anyone until you're up here safely.
I know...on one level, you're right, Phil. We save as many people as we can...but...
But...but what, Hari? There's no question...
It's always a question. The needs of the many over the needs of the few...
You've been talking to Blake too much, Hari. Go with your instincts.

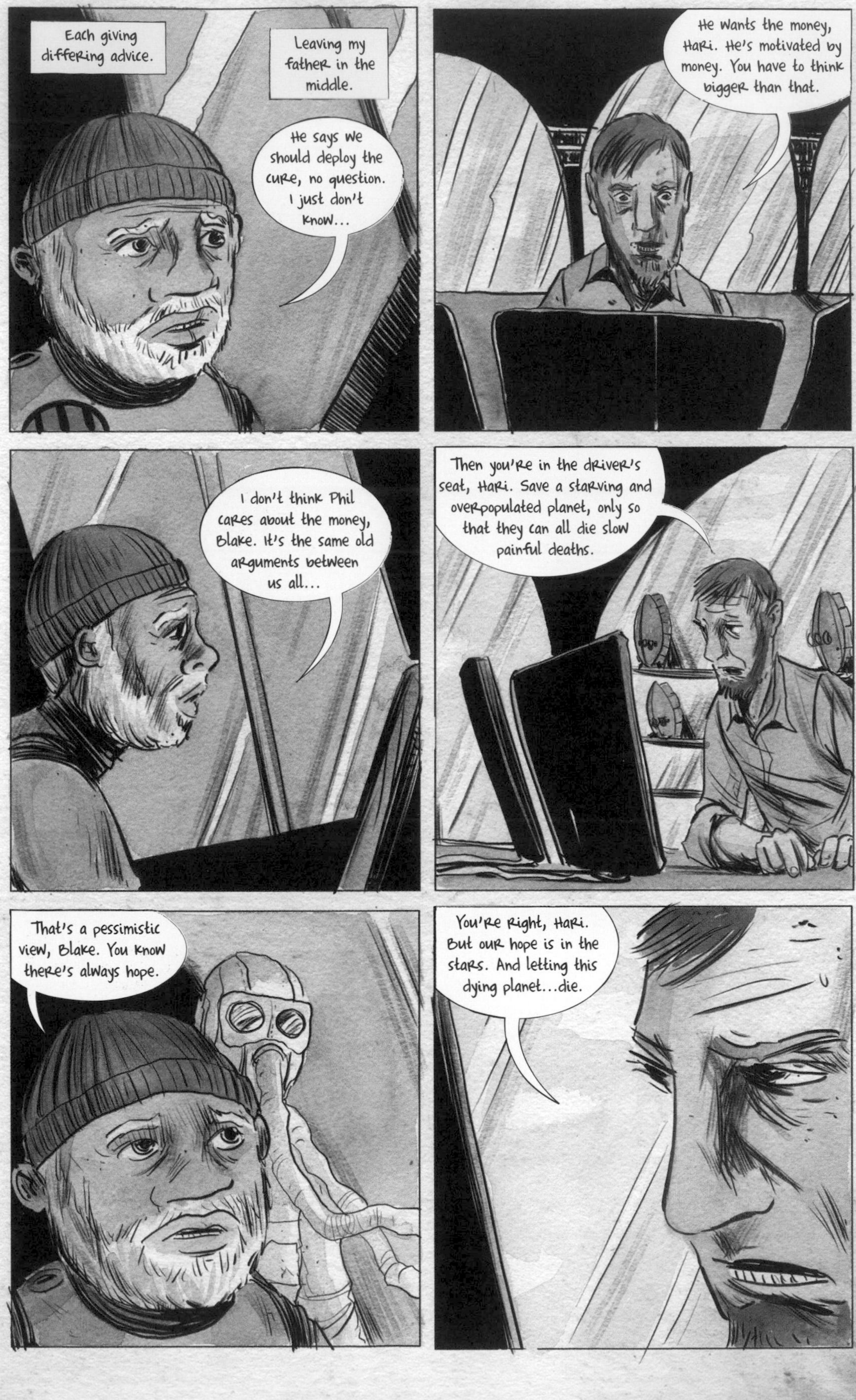
Each giving differing advice.
Leaving my father in the middle.
He says we should deploy the cure, no question. I just don't know...
He wants the money, Hari. He's motivated by money. You have to think bigger than that.
I don't think Phil cares about the money, Blake. It's the same old arguments between us all...
Then you're in the driver's seat, Hari. Save a starving and overpopulated planet, only so that they can all die slow painful deaths.
That's a pessimistic view, Blake. You know there's always hope.
You're right, Hari. But our hope is in the stars. And letting this dying planet...die.

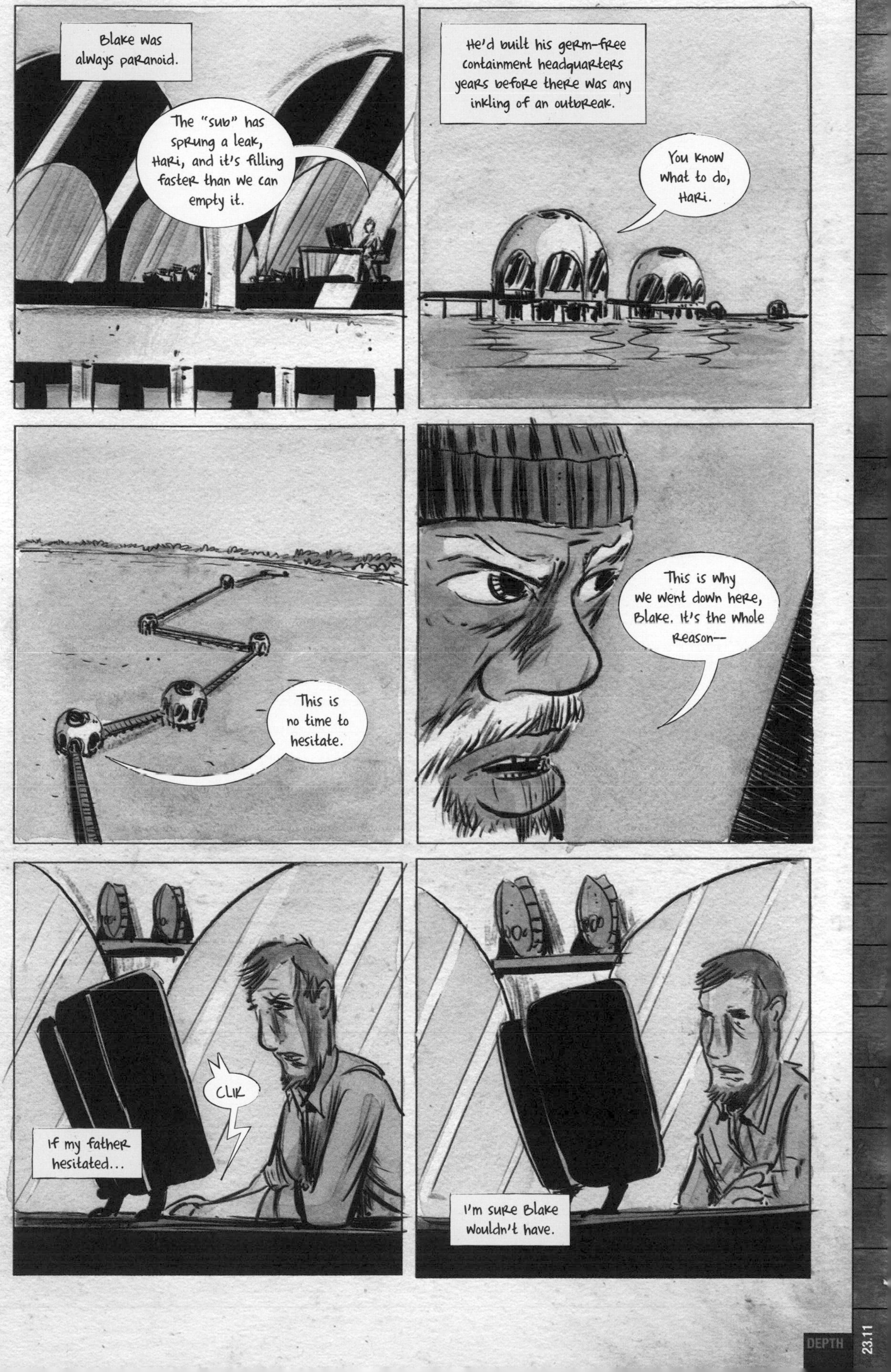
Blake was always paranoid.
The "sub" has sprung a leak, Hari, and it's filling faster than we can empty it.
He'd built his germ-free containment headquarters years before there was any inkling of an outbreak.
You know what to do, Hari.
This is no time to hesitate.
This is why we went down here, Blake. It's the whole reason--
If my father hesitated...
CLIK
I'm sure Blake wouldn't have.

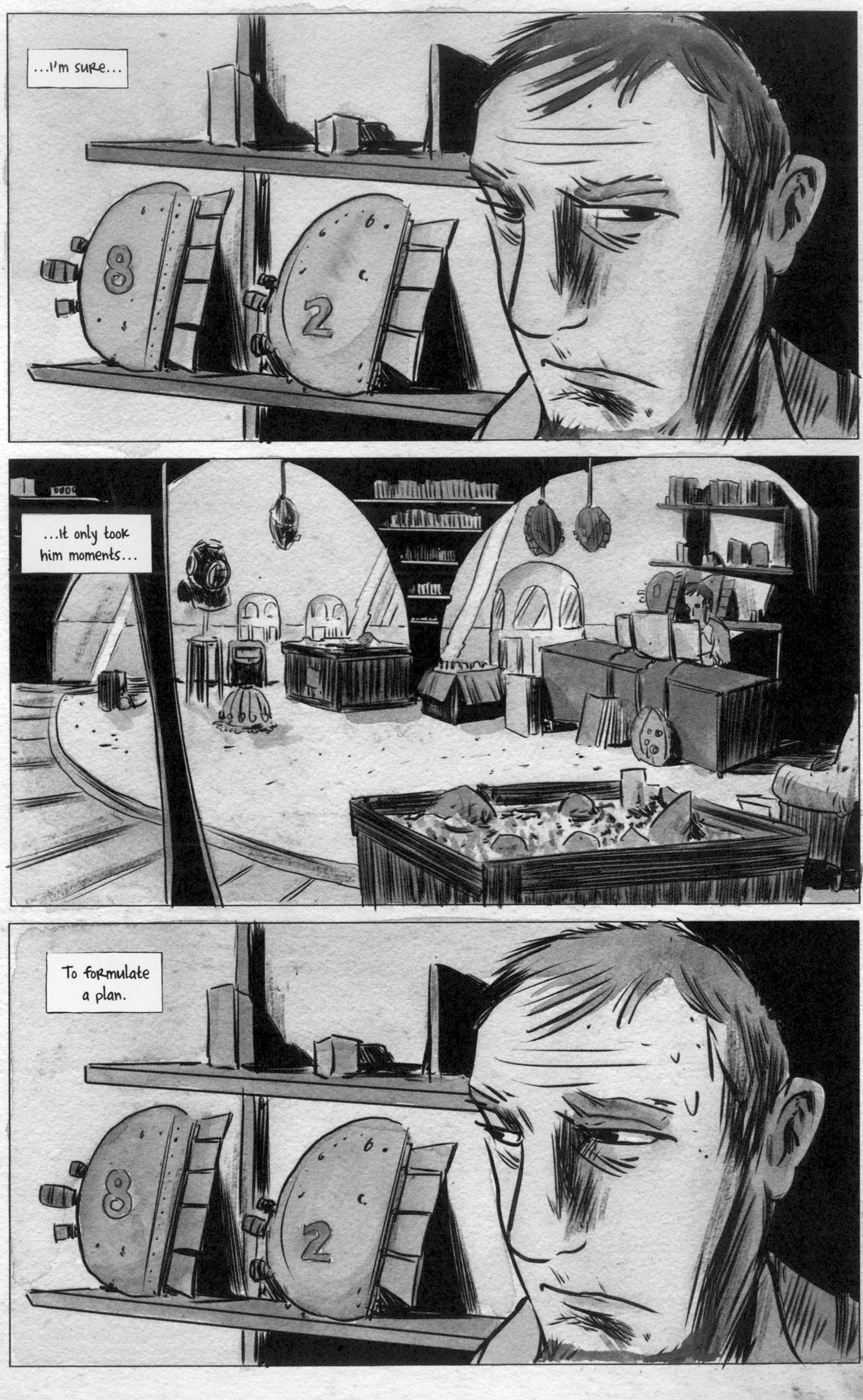
...I'm sure...
...It only took him moments...
To formulate a plan.

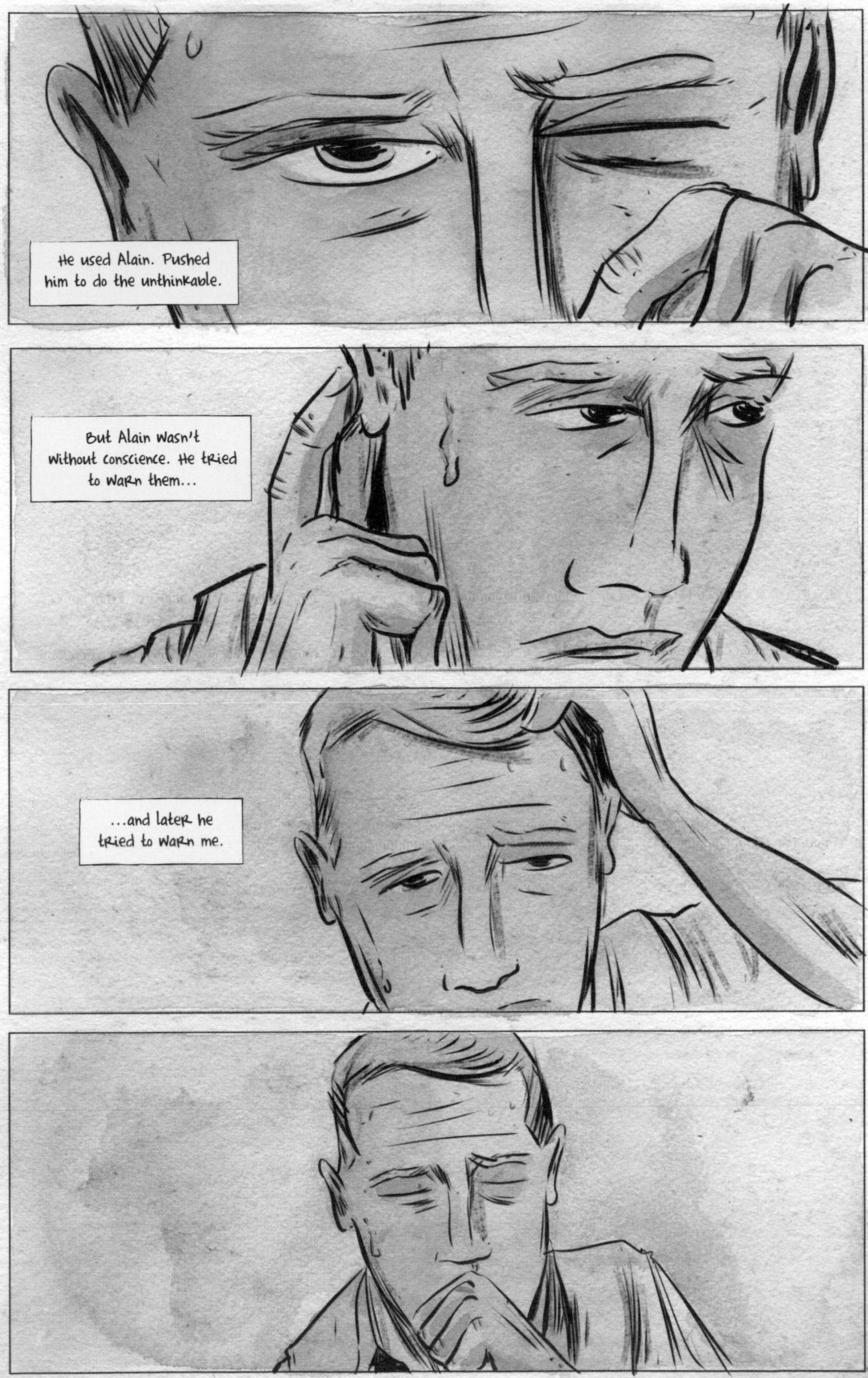
He used Alain. Pushed him to do the unthinkable.
But Alain wasn't without conscience. He tried to warn them...
...and later he tried to warn me.

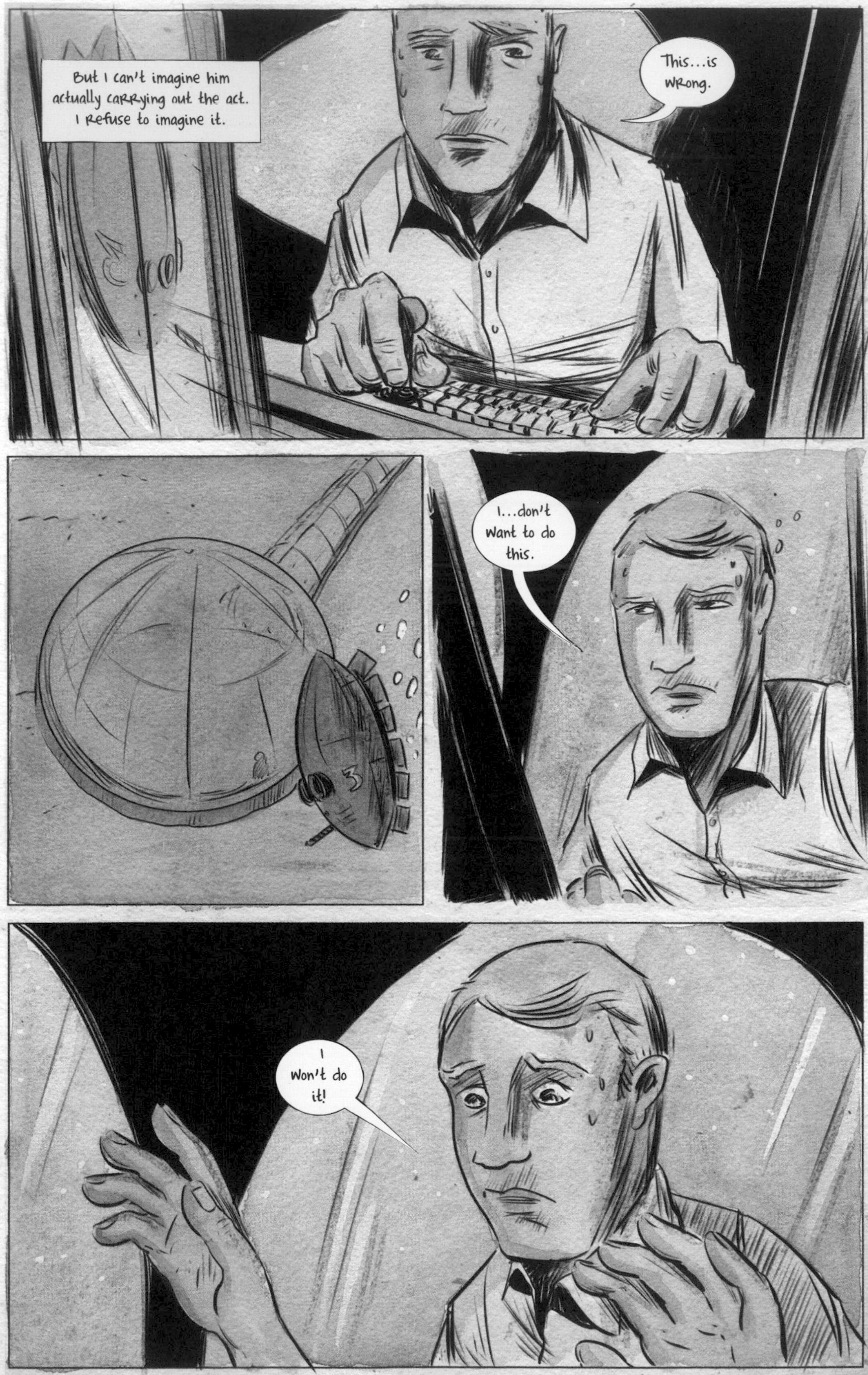
But I can't imagine him actually carrying out the act. I refuse to imagine it.
This...is wrong.
I...don't want to do this.
I won't do it!

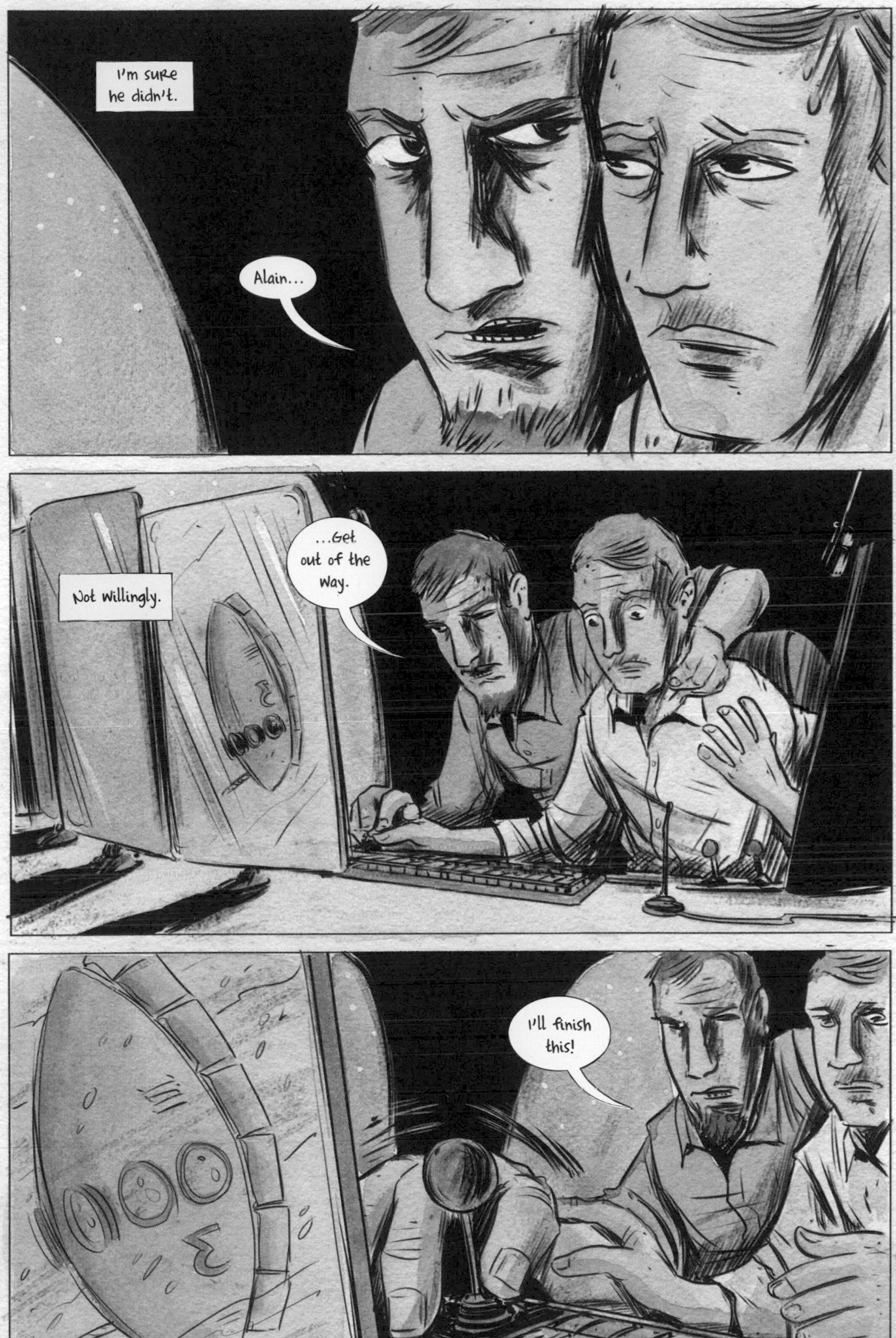

I'm sure he didn't.
Alain...
Not willingly.
...Get out of the way.
I'll finish this!

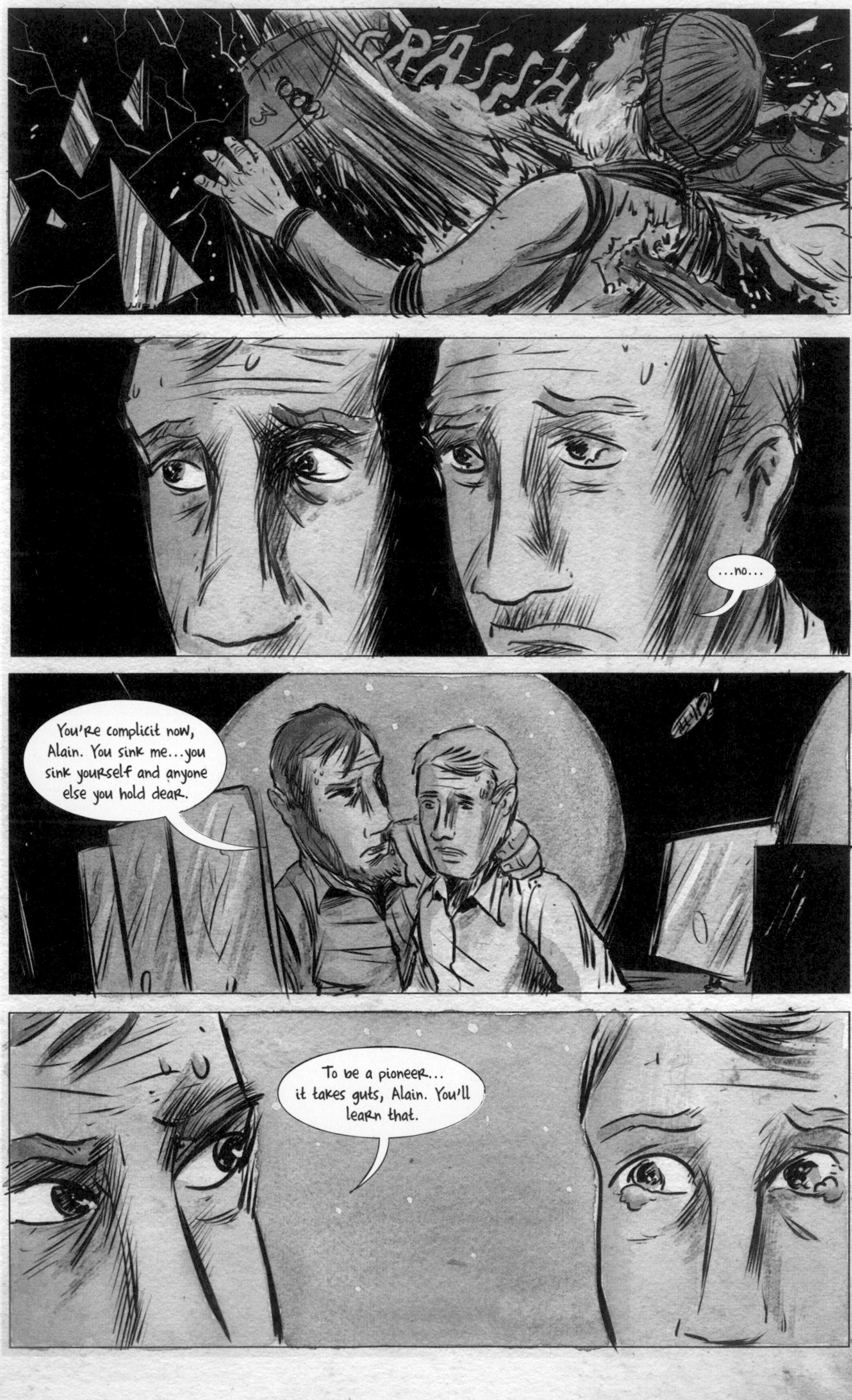
CRASSH
...no...
You're complicit now, Alain. You sink me...you sink yourself and anyone else you hold dear.
To be a pioneer... it takes guts, Alain. You'll learn that.

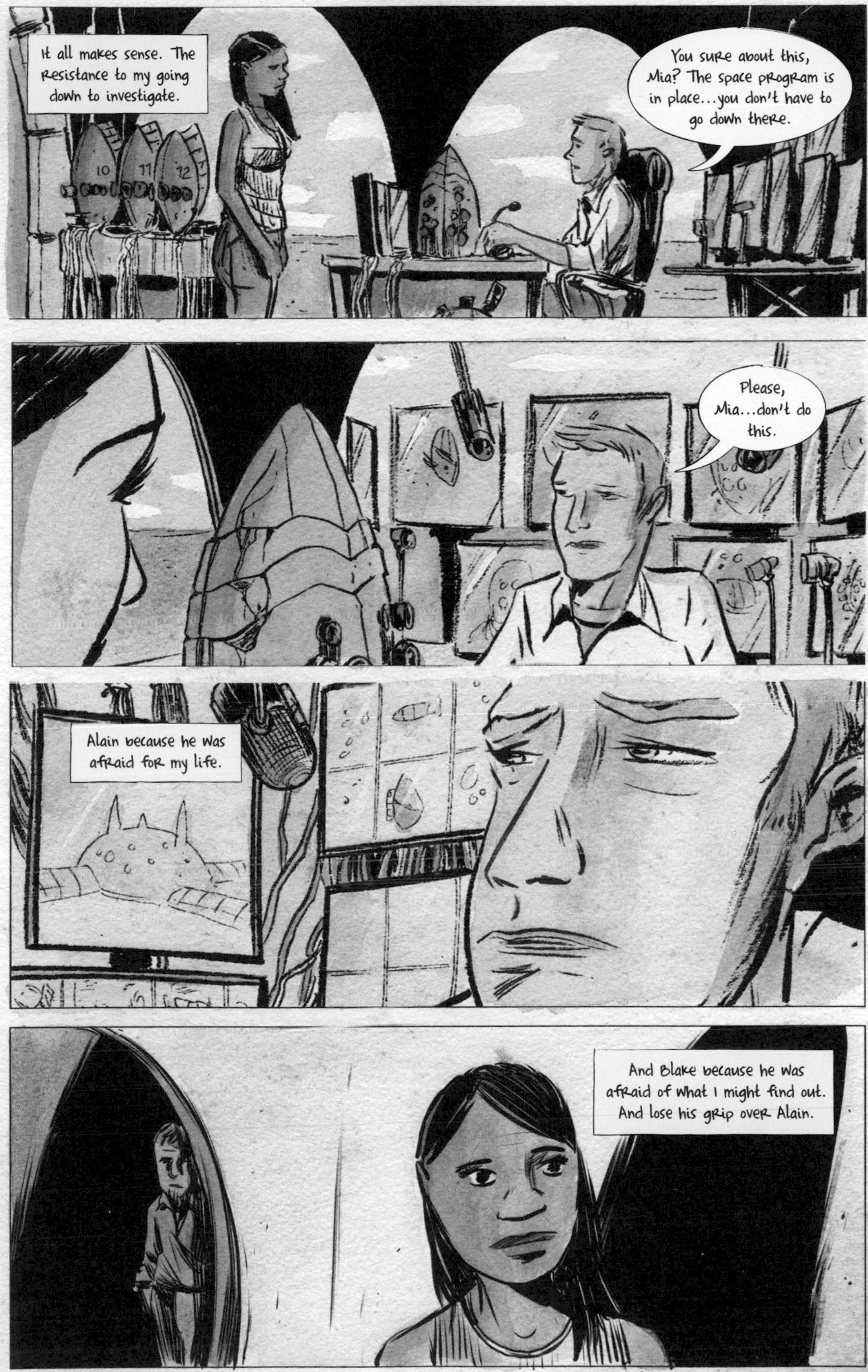

It all makes sense. The Resistance to my going down to investigate.
You sure about this, Mia? The space program is in place...you don't have to go down there.
10
11
12
Please, Mia...don't do this.
Alain because he was afraid for my life.
And Blake because he was afraid of what I might find out. And lose his grip over Alain.

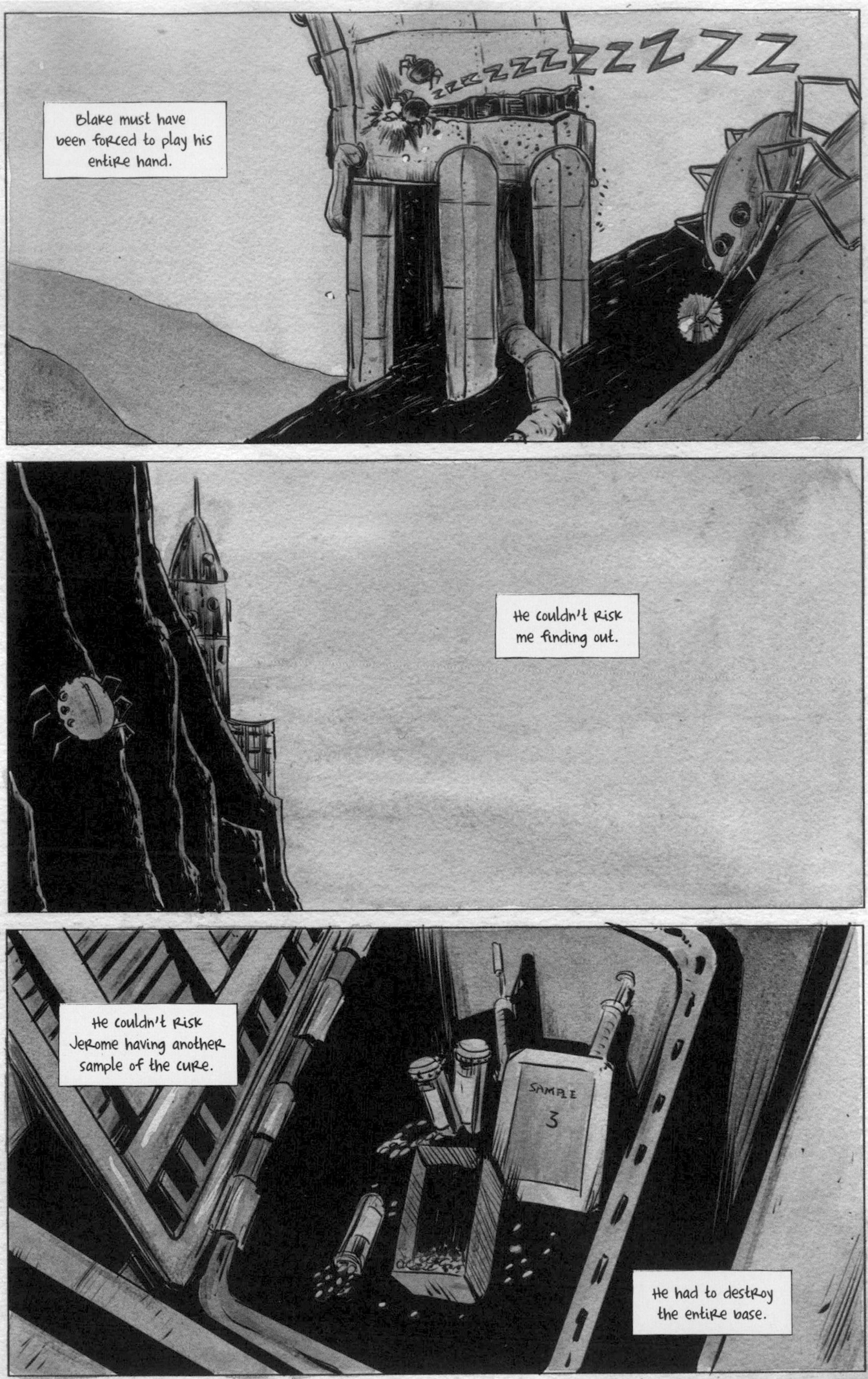
Blake must have been forced to play his entire hand.
ZZZZZZZZZZZZZZ
He couldn't risk me finding out.
He couldn't risk Jerome having another sample of the cure.
SAMPLE 3
He had to destroy the entire base.

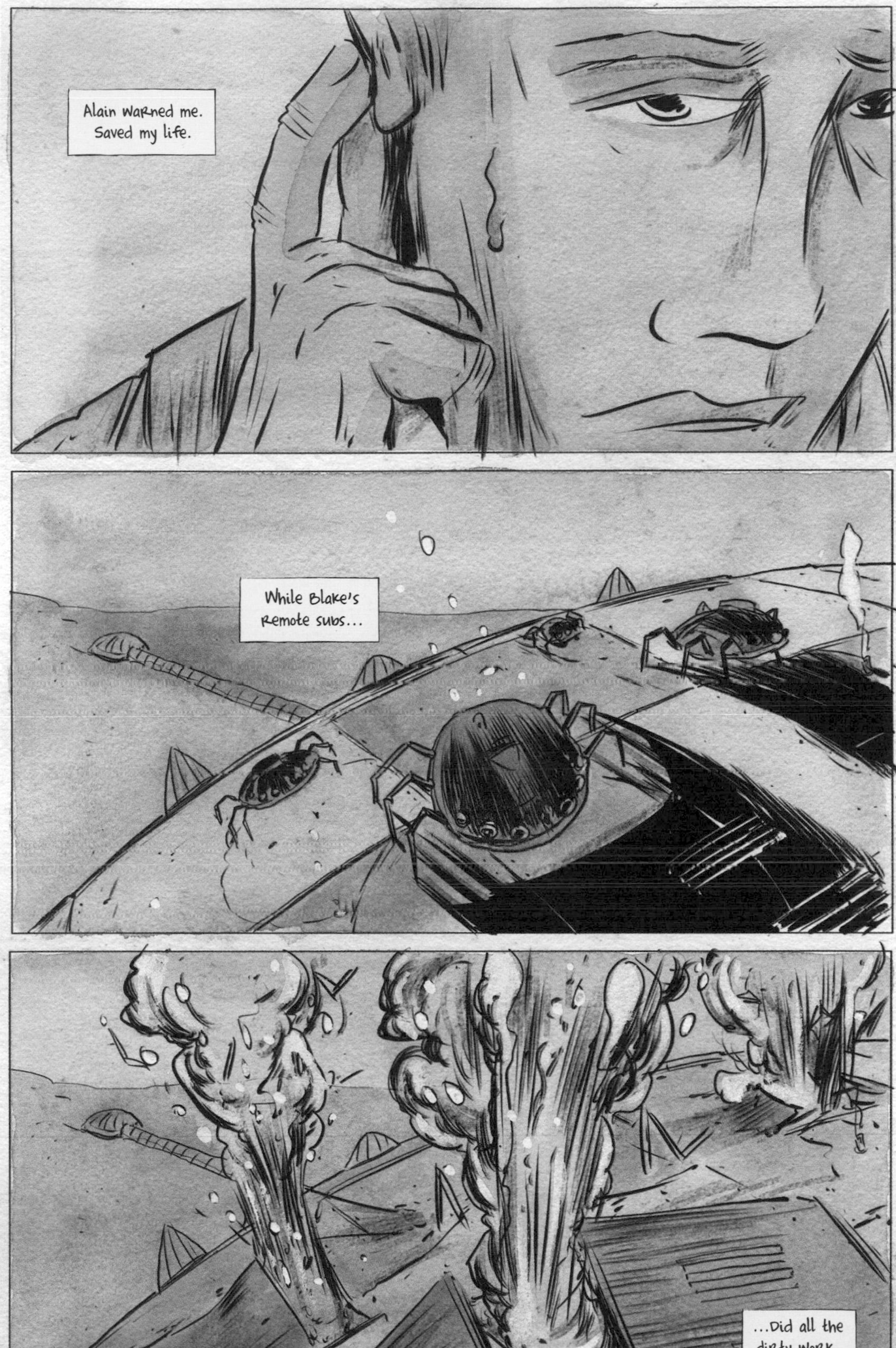
Alain warned me.
Saved my life.
While Blake's
remote subs...
...Did all the
dirty work.

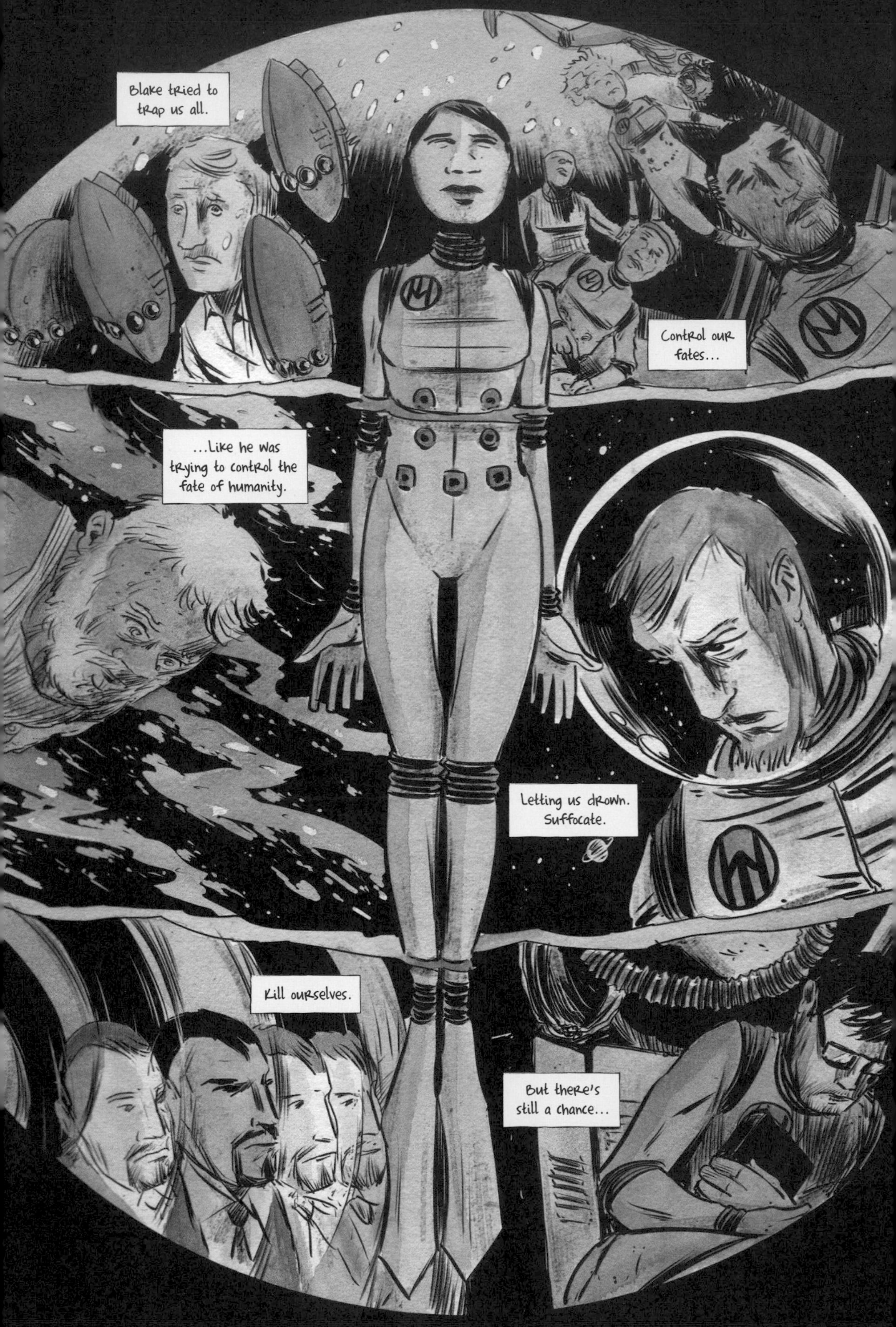
Blake tried to trap us all.
Control our fates...
...Like he was trying to control the fate of humanity.
Letting us drown. Suffocate.
Kill ourselves.
But there's still a chance...

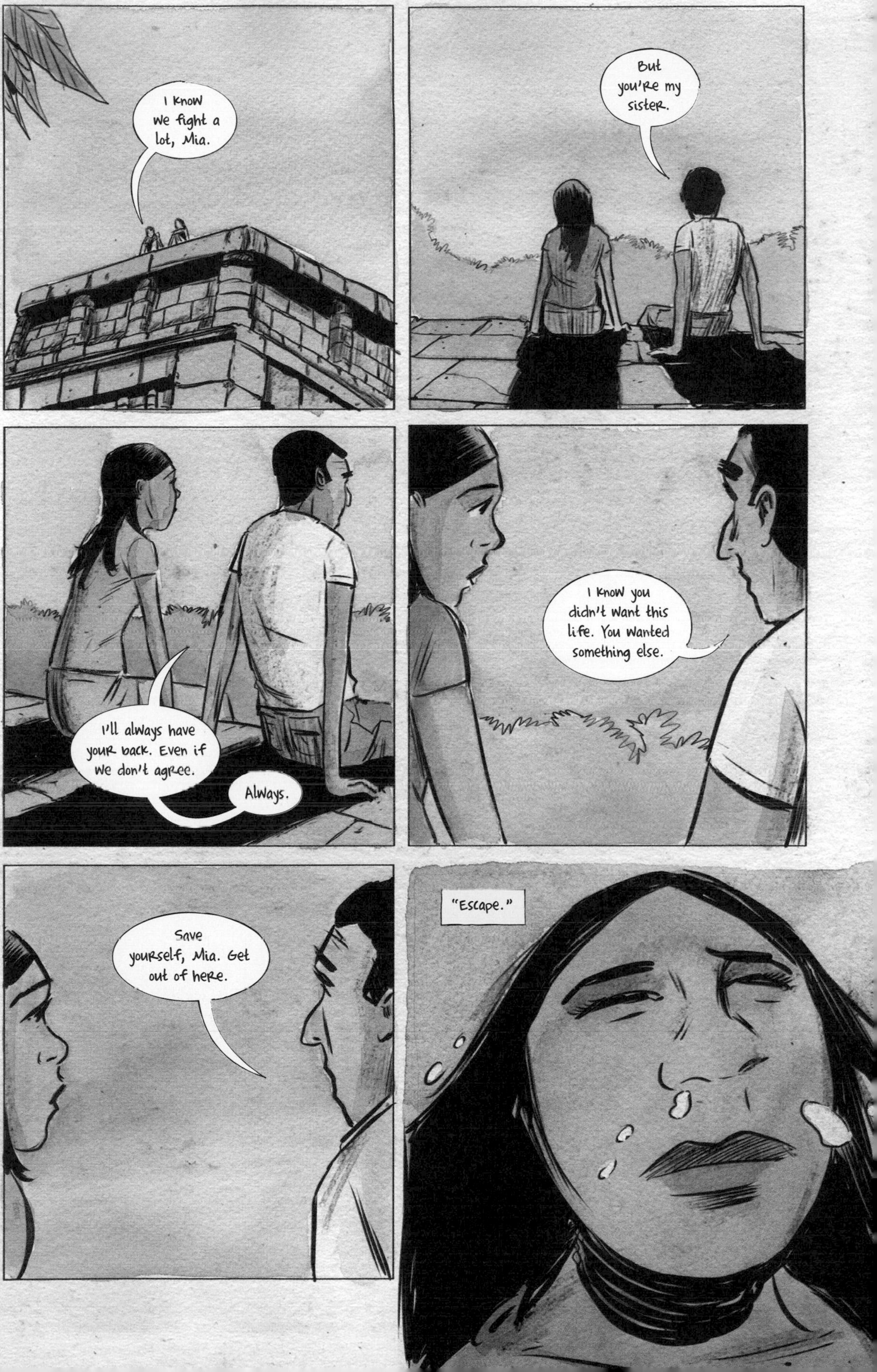
I know we fight a lot, Mia.
But you're my sister.
I'll always have your back. Even if we don't agree.
Always.
I know you didn't want this life. You wanted something else.
Save yourself, Mia. Get out of here.
"Escape."

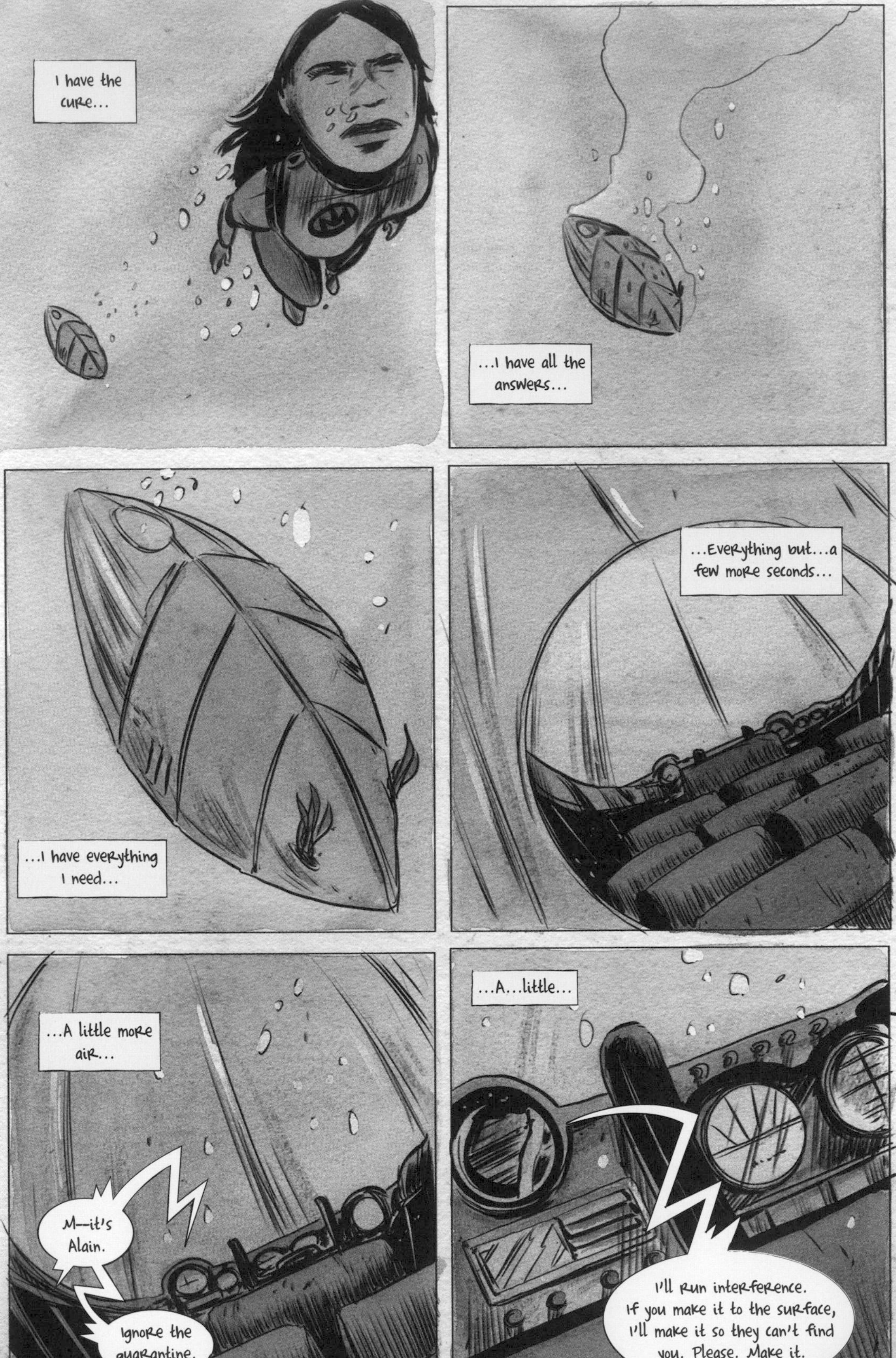
I have the cure...
...I have all the answers...
...I have everything I need...
...Everything but...a few more seconds...
...A little more air...
M--it's Alain.
Ignore the quarantine.
...A...little...
I'll run interference. If you make it to the surface, I'll make it so they can't find you. Please. Make it.

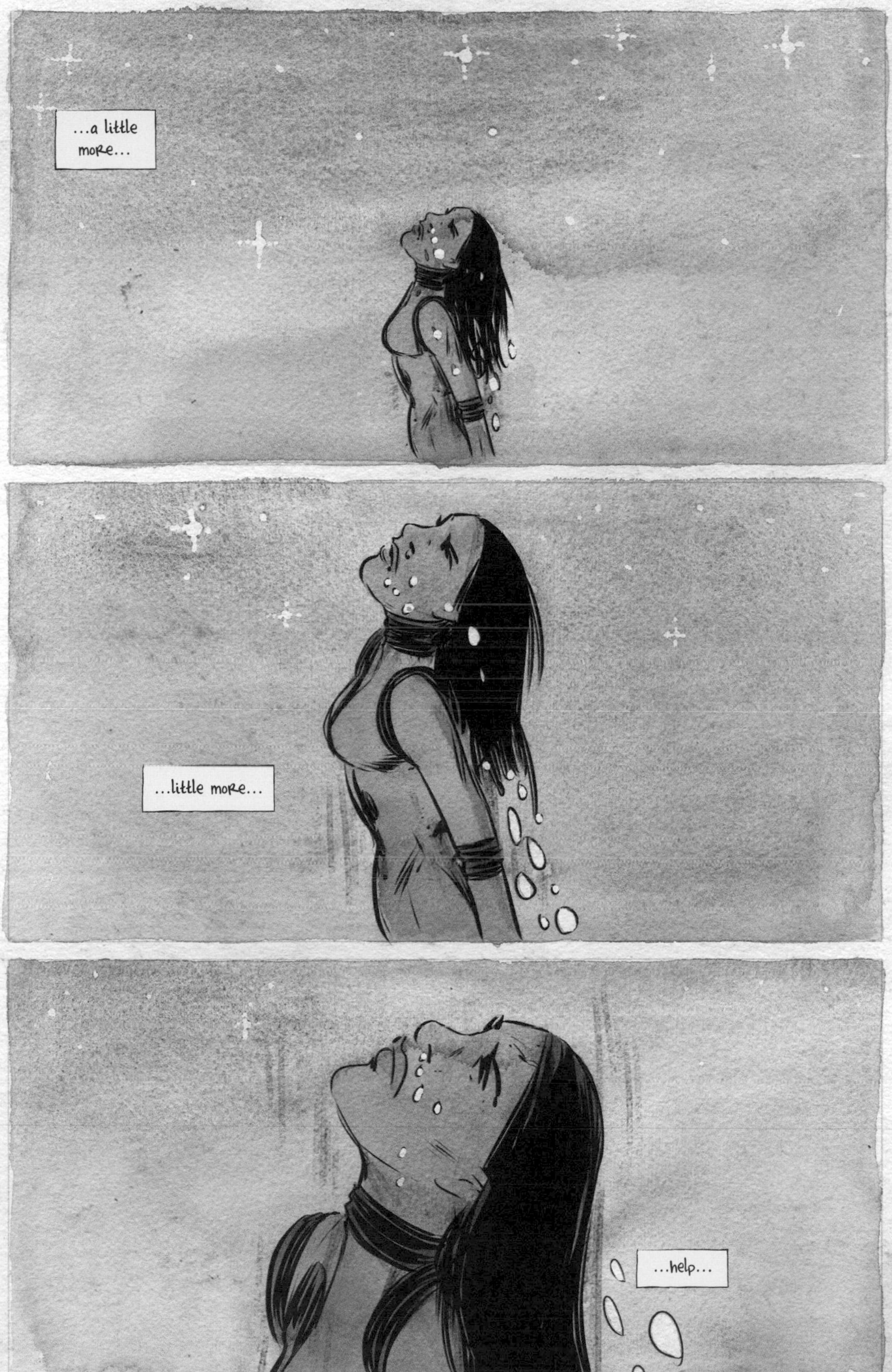
...a little more...
...little more...
...help...

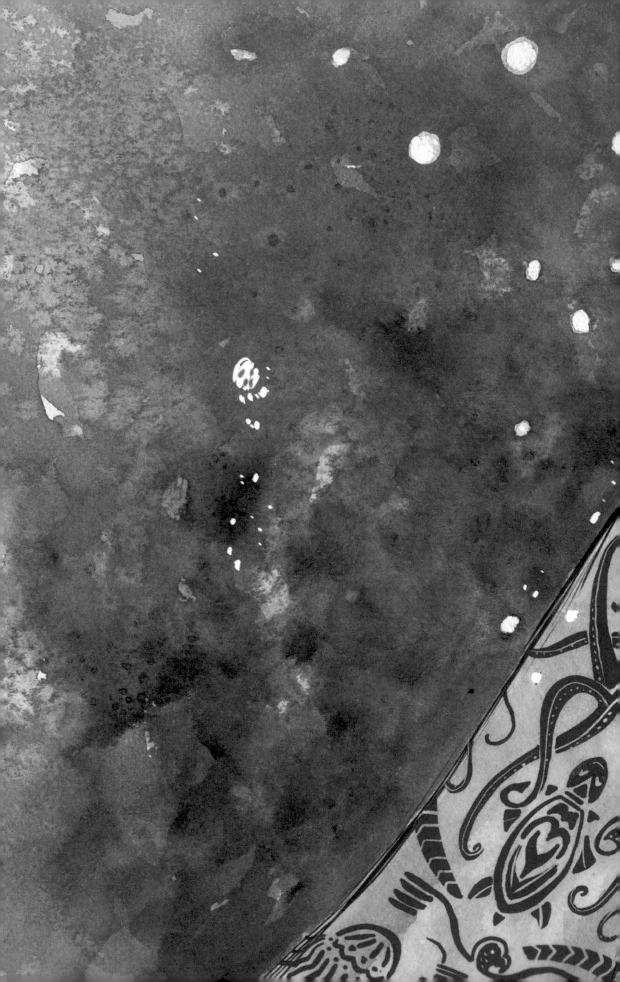

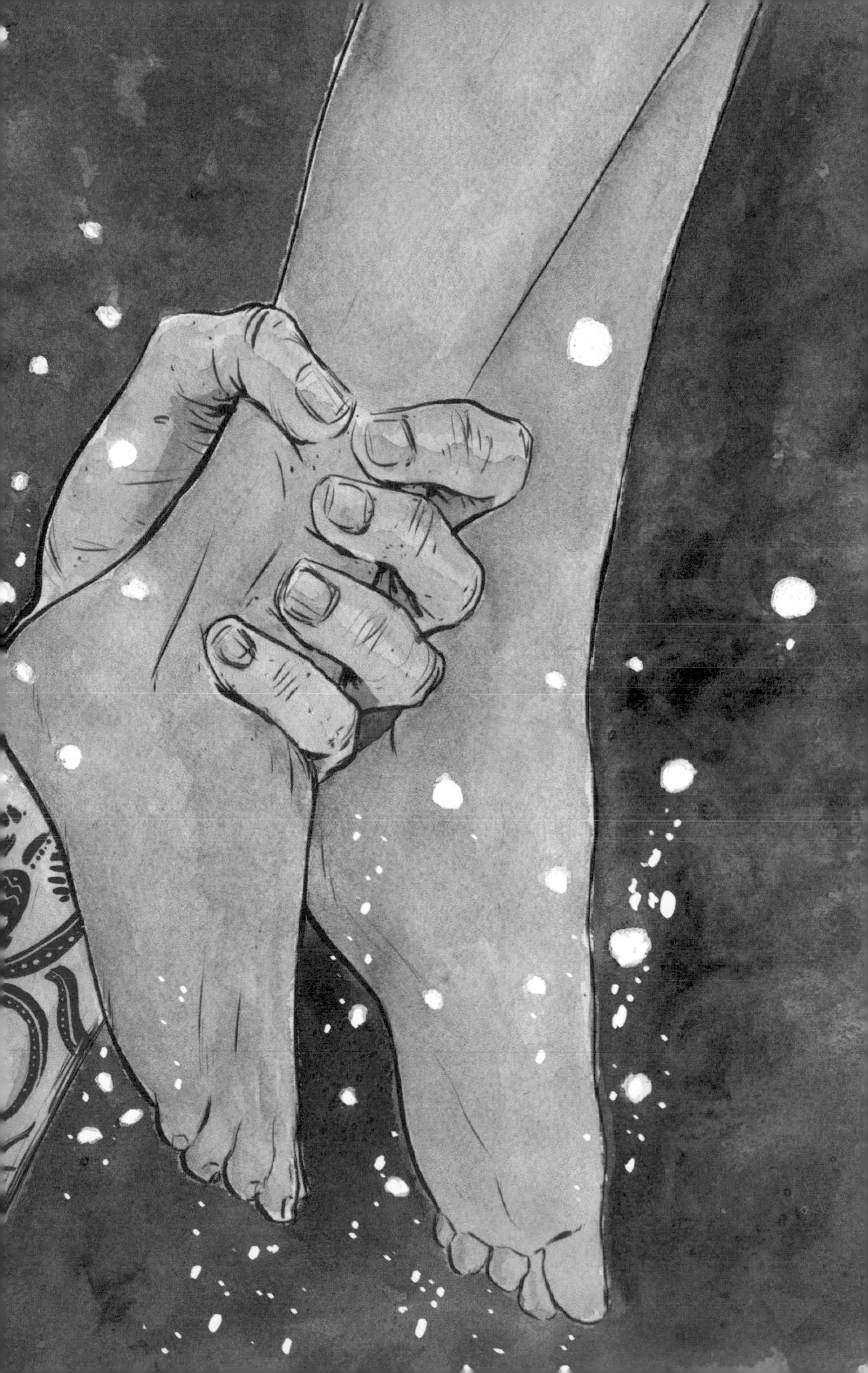

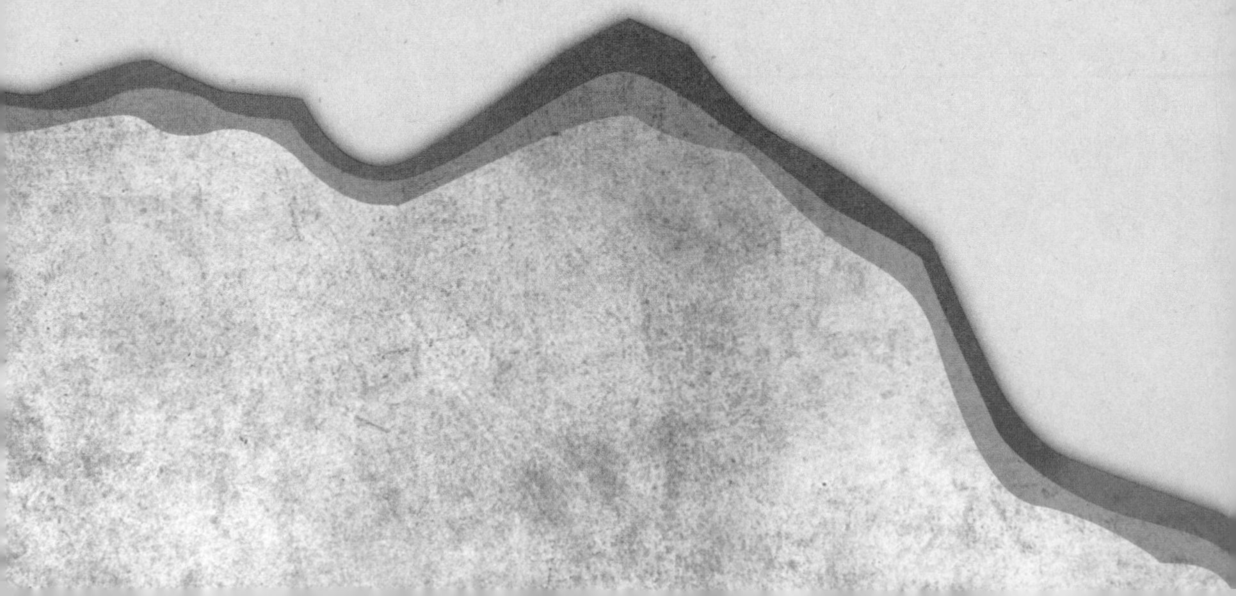

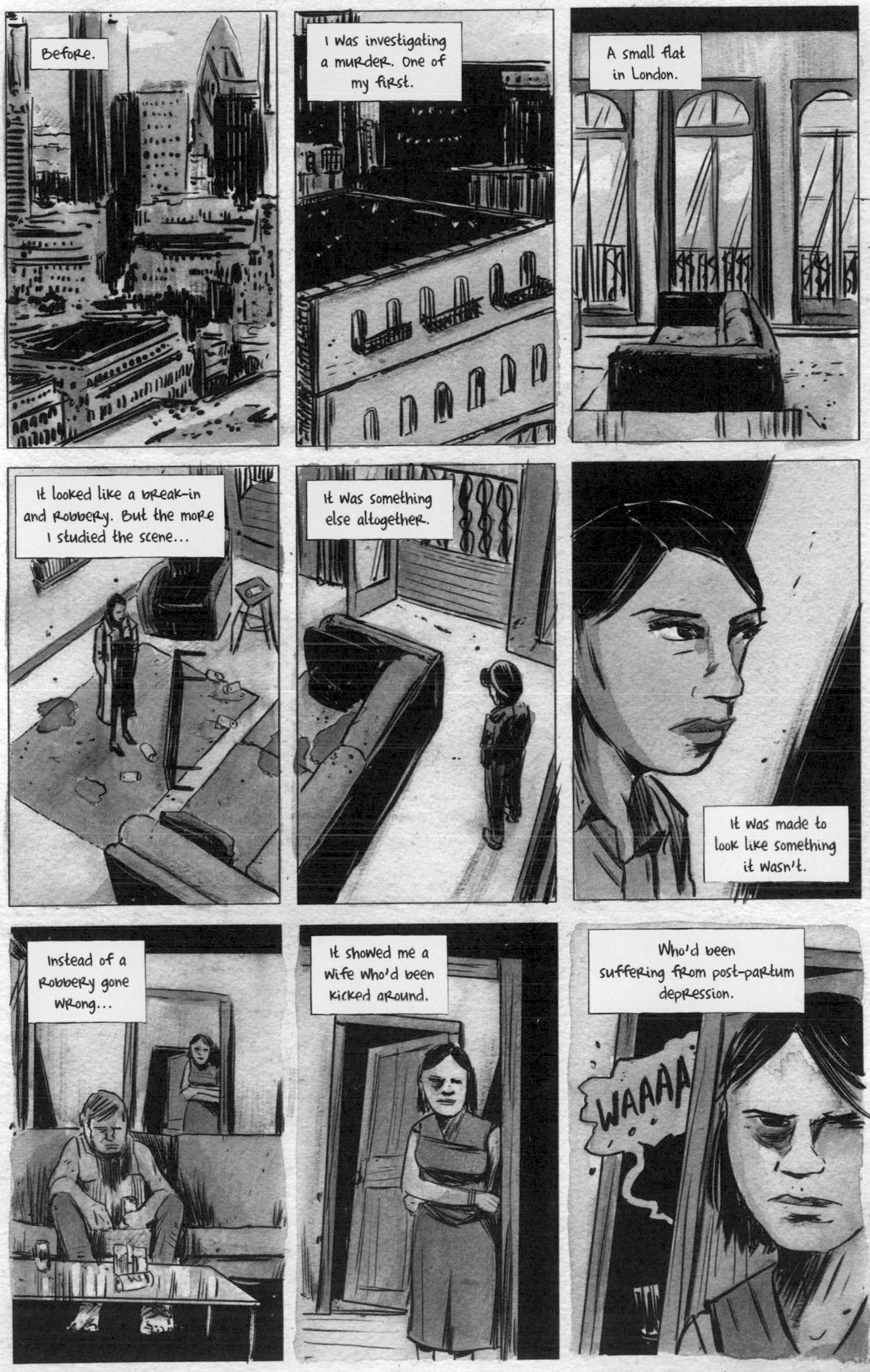
Before.
I was investigating a murder. One of my first.
A small flat in London.
It looked like a break-in and robbery. But the more I studied the scene...
It was something else altogether.
It was made to look like something it wasn't.
Instead of a robbery gone wrong...
It showed me a wife who'd been kicked around.
Who'd been suffering from post-partum depression.
WAAAA

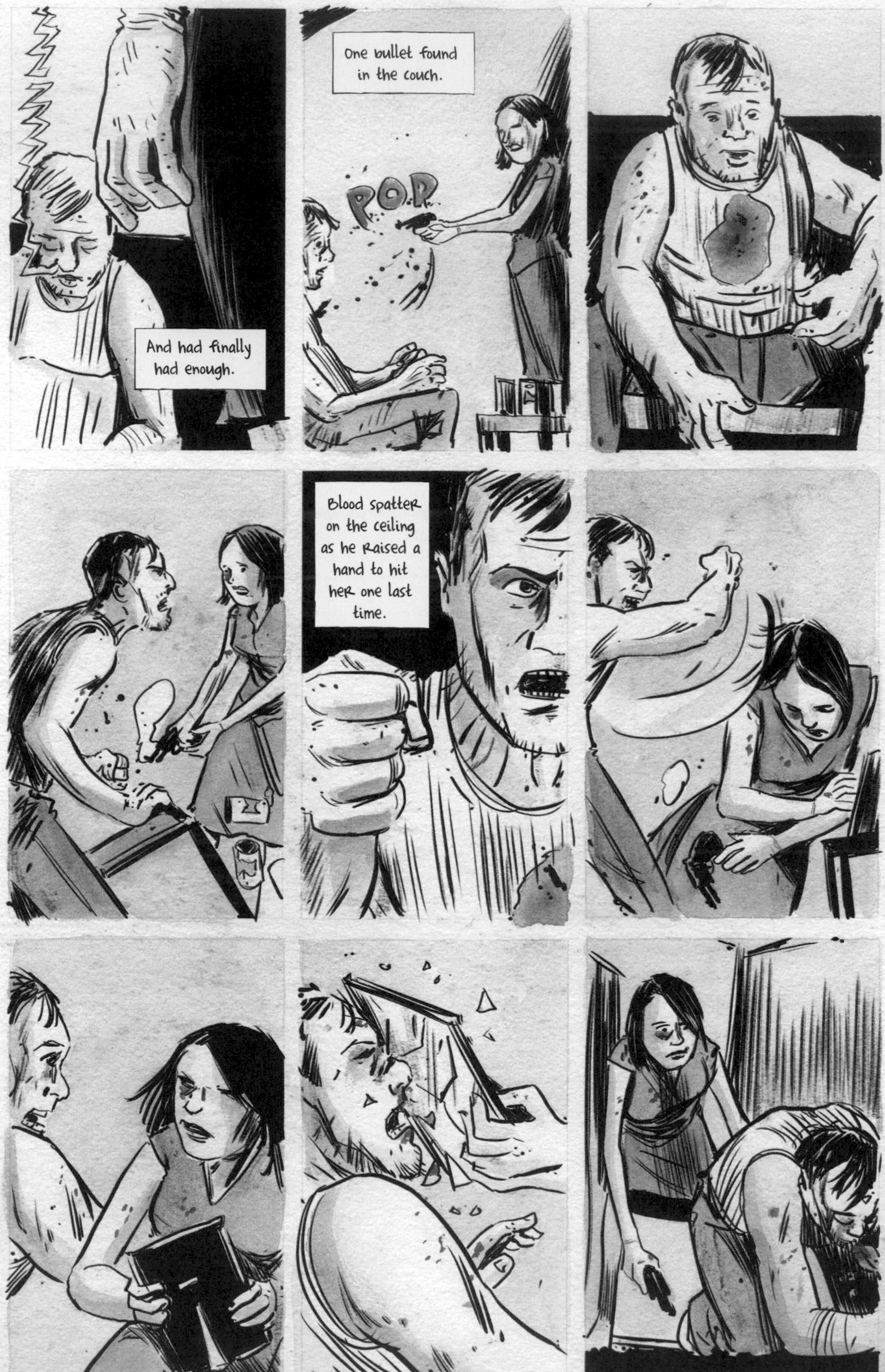
And had finally had enough.
One bullet found in the couch.
POP
Blood spatter on the ceiling as he raised a hand to hit her one last time.

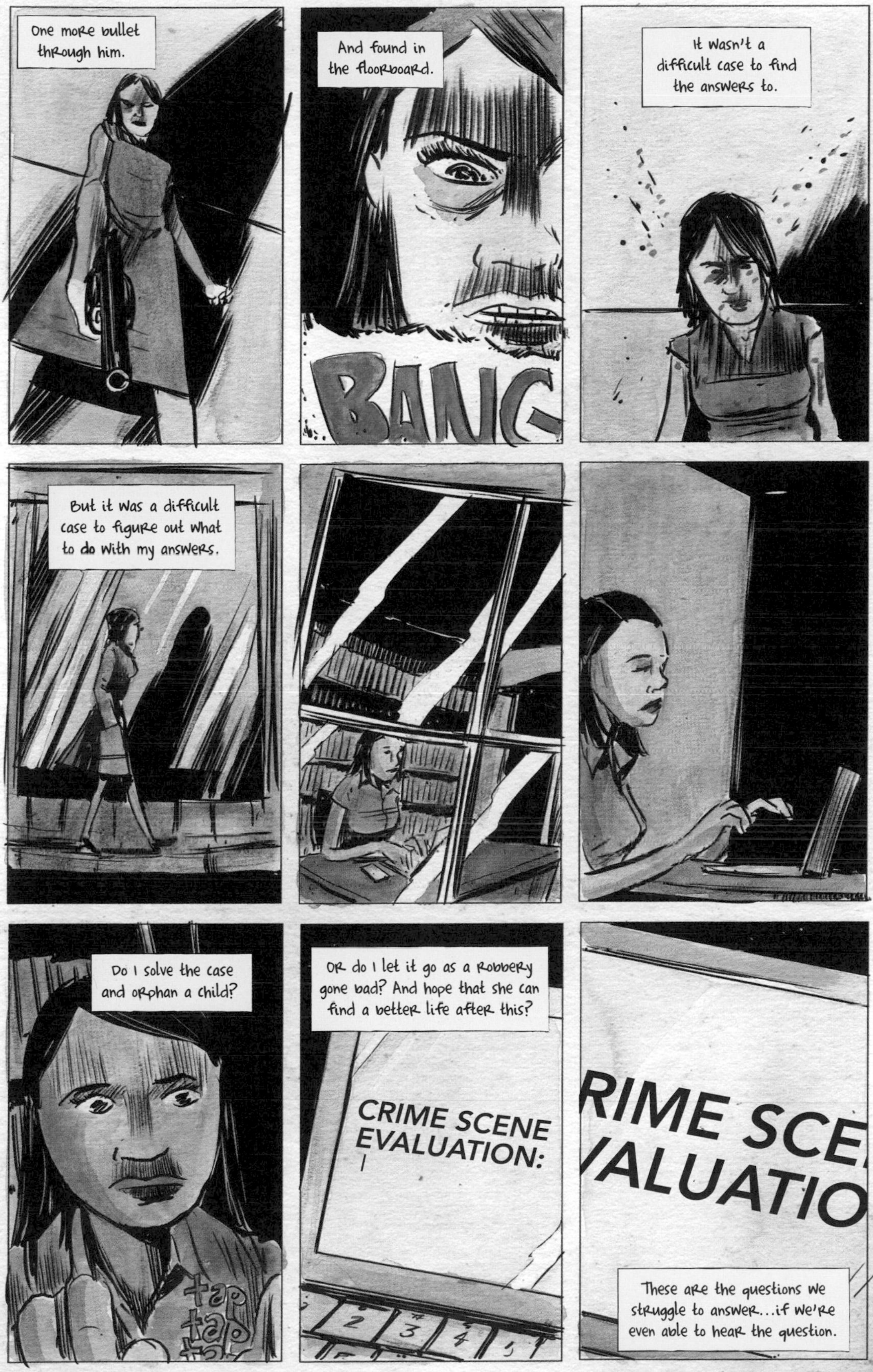
One more bullet through him.
And found in the floorboard.
BANG
It wasn't a difficult case to find the answers to.
But it was a difficult case to figure out what to do with my answers.
Do I solve the case and orphan a child?
tap
tap
Or do I let it go as a robbery gone bad? And hope that she can find a better life after this?
CRIME SCENE EVALUATION:
RIME SCE
VALUATIO
These are the questions we struggle to answer...if we're even able to hear the question.

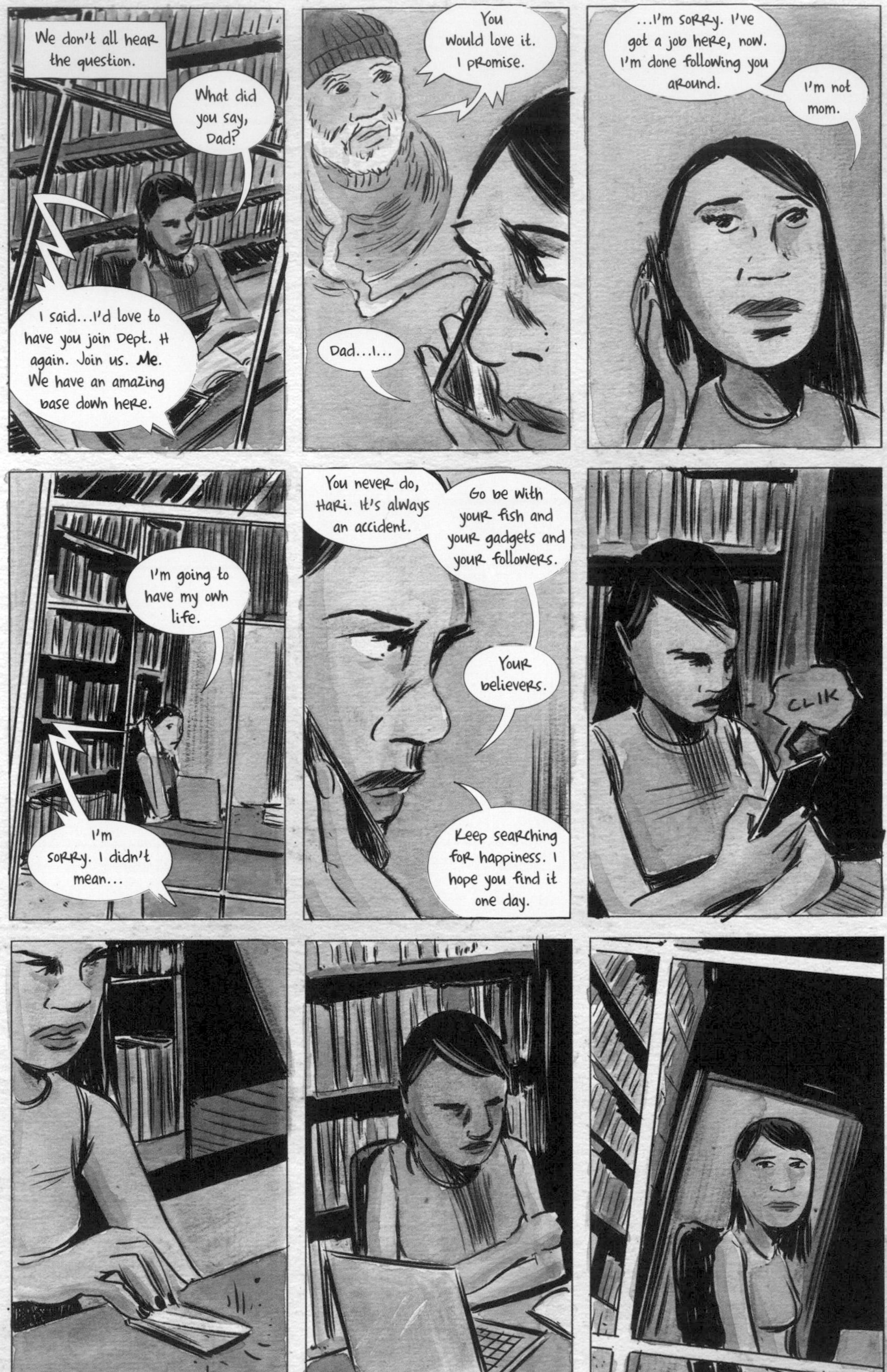
We don't all hear the question.
What did you say, Dad?
I said...I'd love to have you join Dept. H again. Join us. Me. We have an amazing base down here.
You would love it. I promise.
Dad...I...
...I'm sorry. I've got a job here, now. I'm done following you around.
I'm not mom.
I'm going to have my own life.
I'm sorry. I didn't mean...
You never do, Hari. It's always an accident.
Go be with your fish and your gadgets and your followers.
Your believers.
Keep searching for happiness. I hope you find it one day.
CLIK

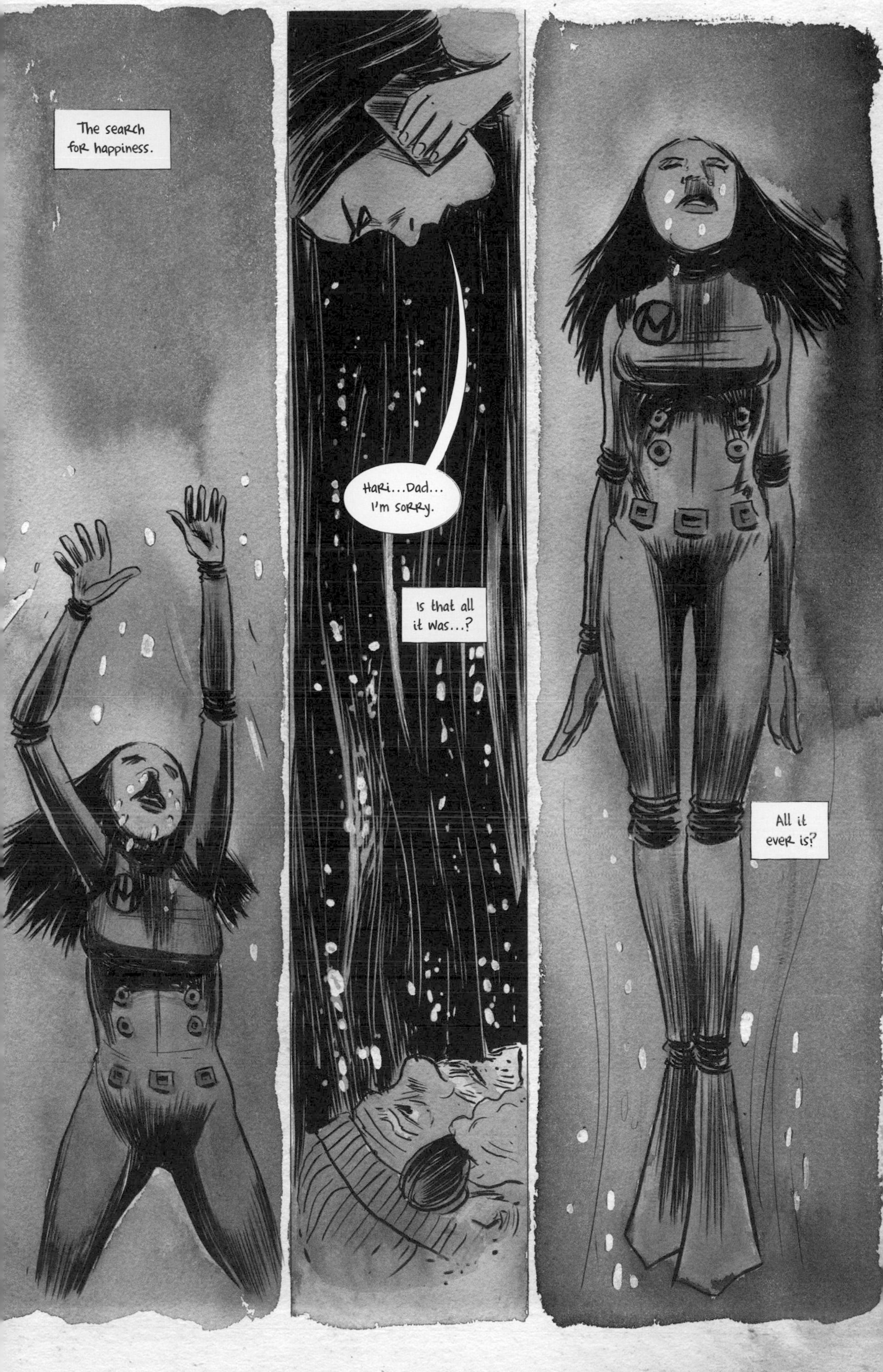
The search for happiness.
Hari...Dad... I'm sorry.
Is that all it was...?
All it ever is?

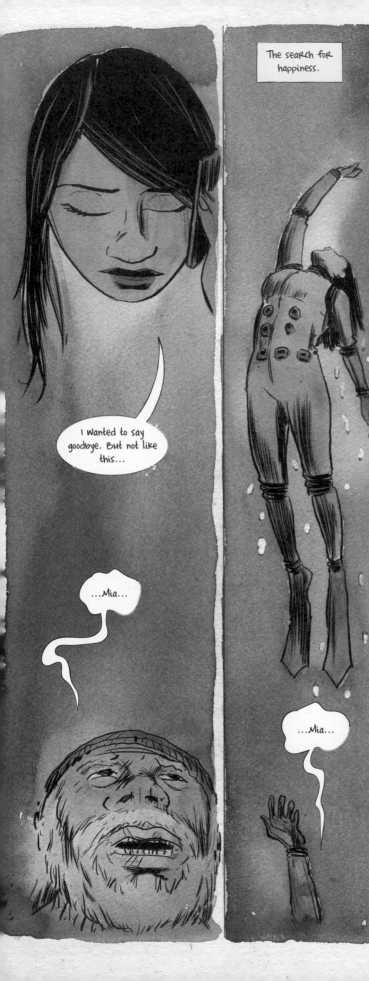

The search for happiness.

I wanted to say goodbye. But not like this...

...Mia...

...Mia...

Does anyone ever find it?

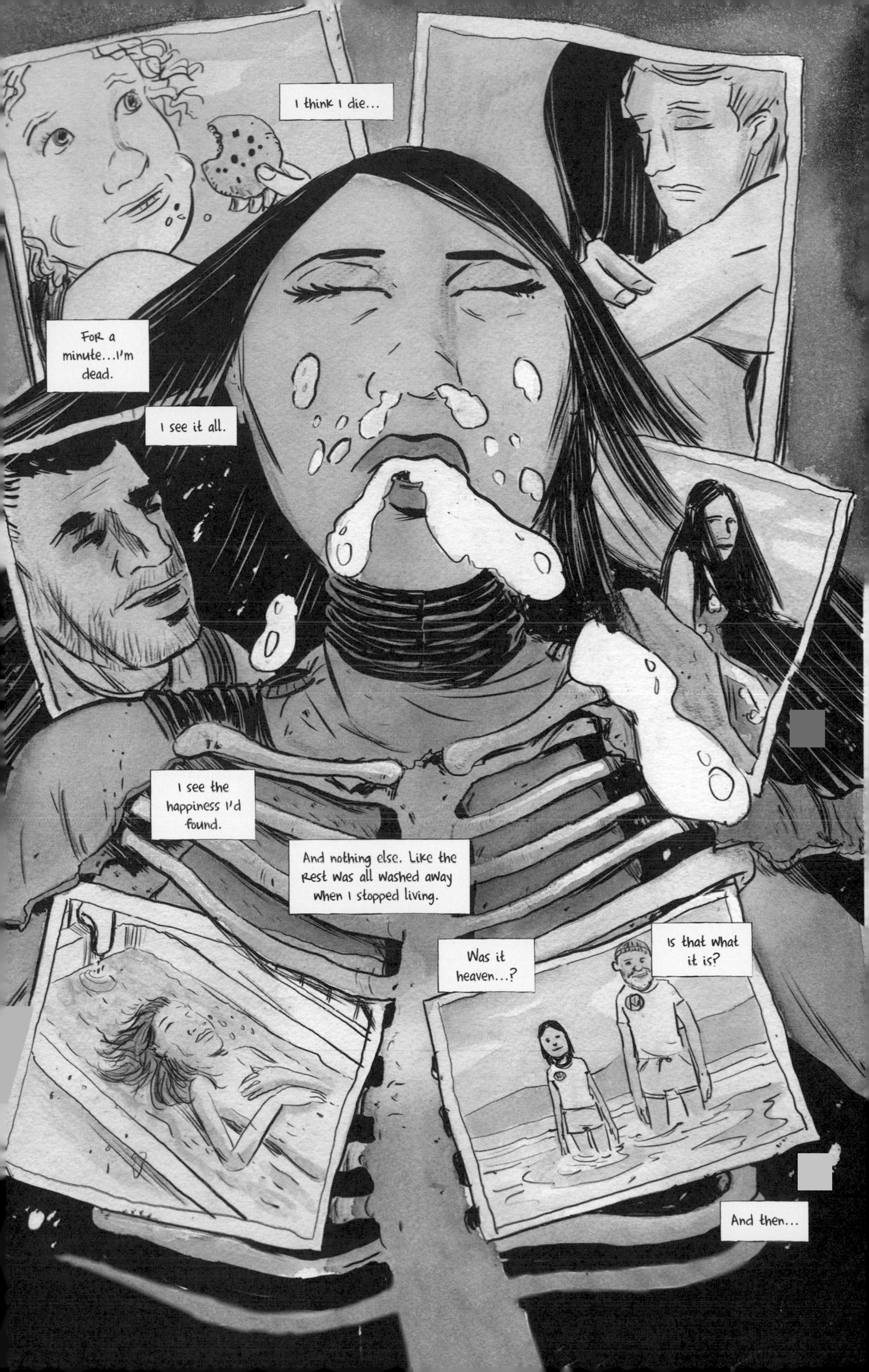
I think I die...
For a minute...I'm dead.
I see it all.
I see the happiness I'd found.
And nothing else. Like the rest was all washed away when I stopped living.
Was it heaven...?
Is that what it is?
And then...

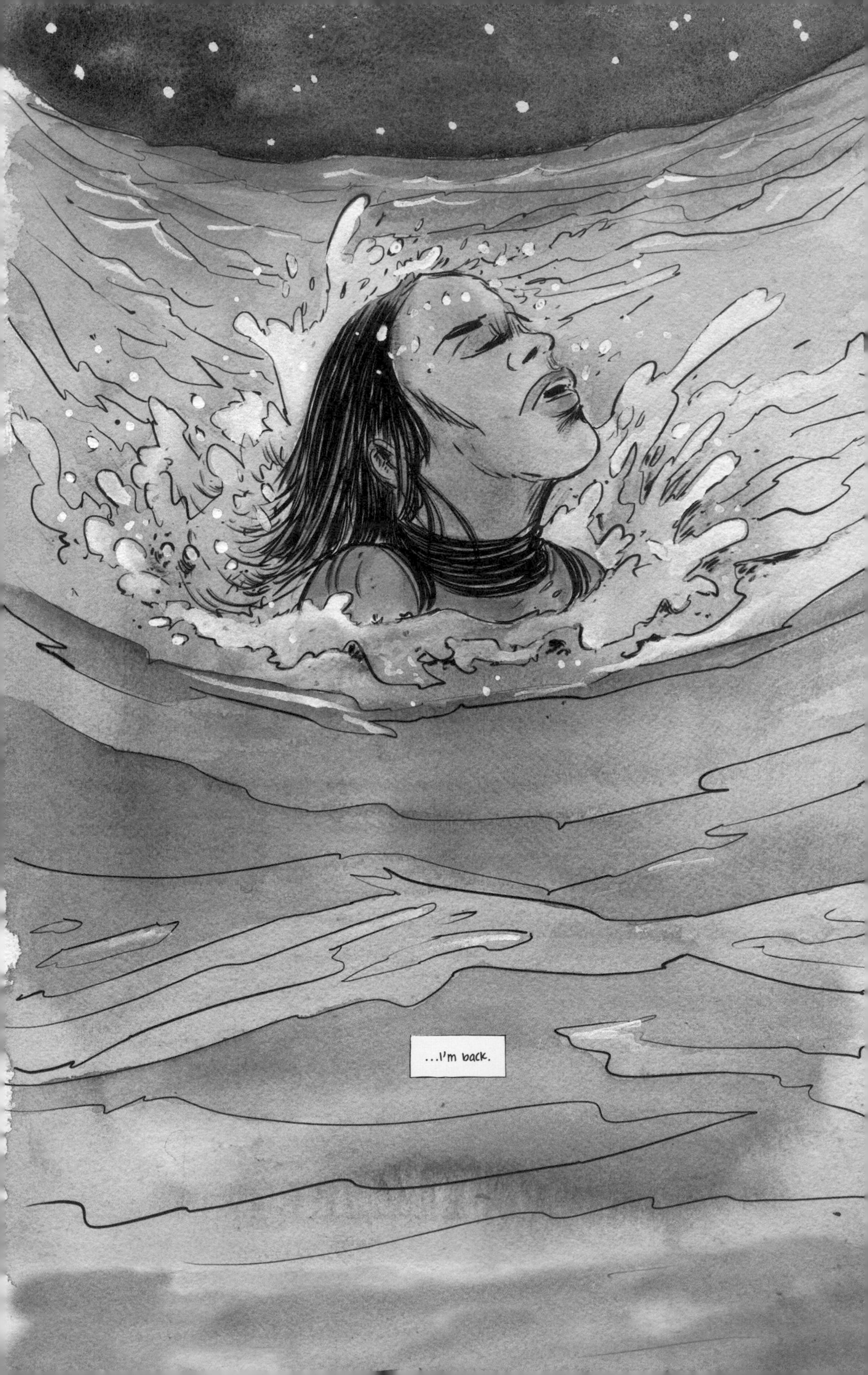
...I'm back.

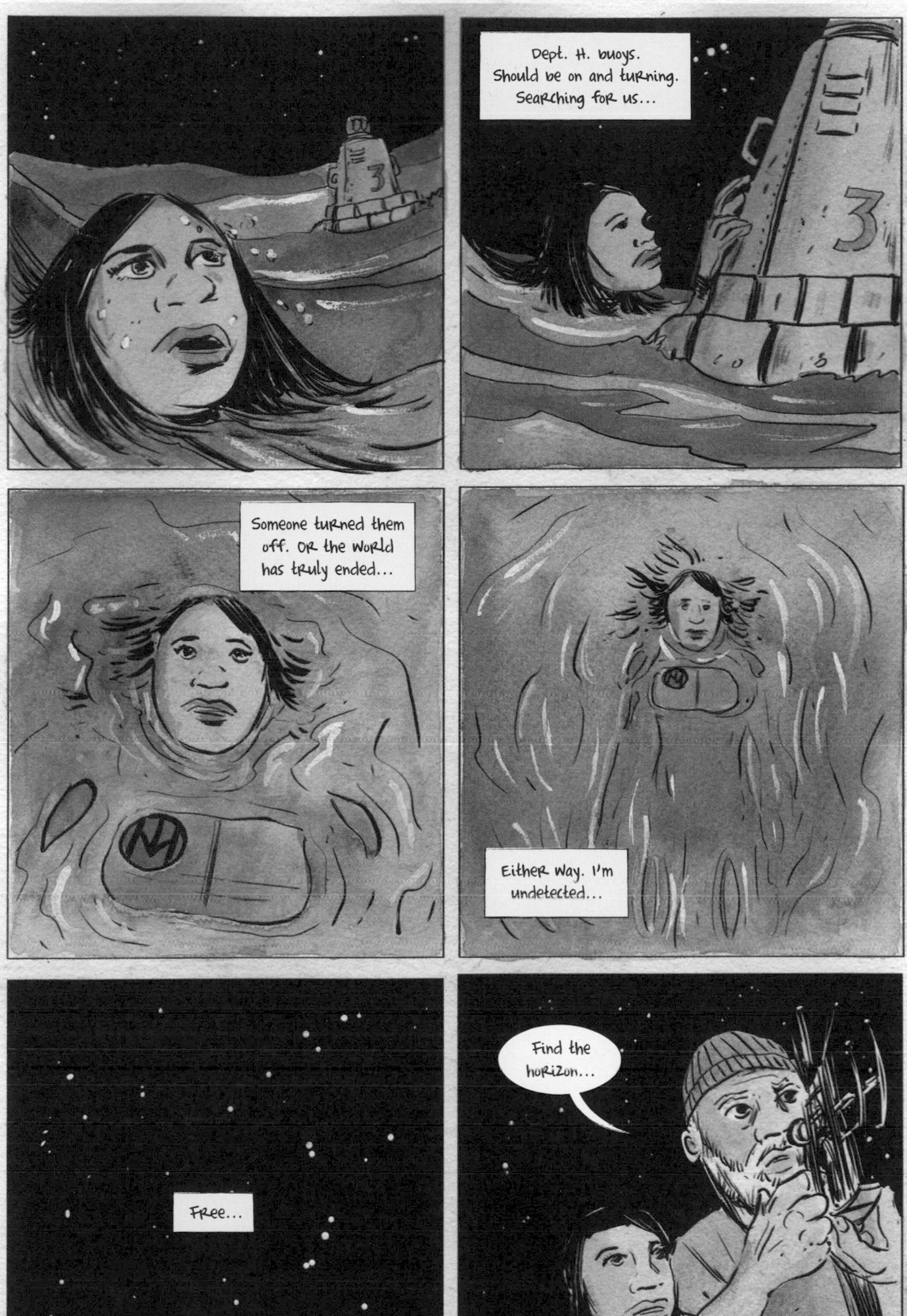
Dept. H. buoys.
Should be on and turning.
Searching for us...
Someone turned them off. Or the world has truly ended...
Either way. I'm undetected...
Free...
Find the horizon...

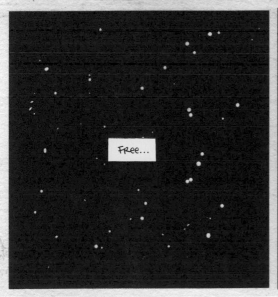

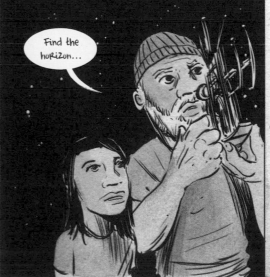

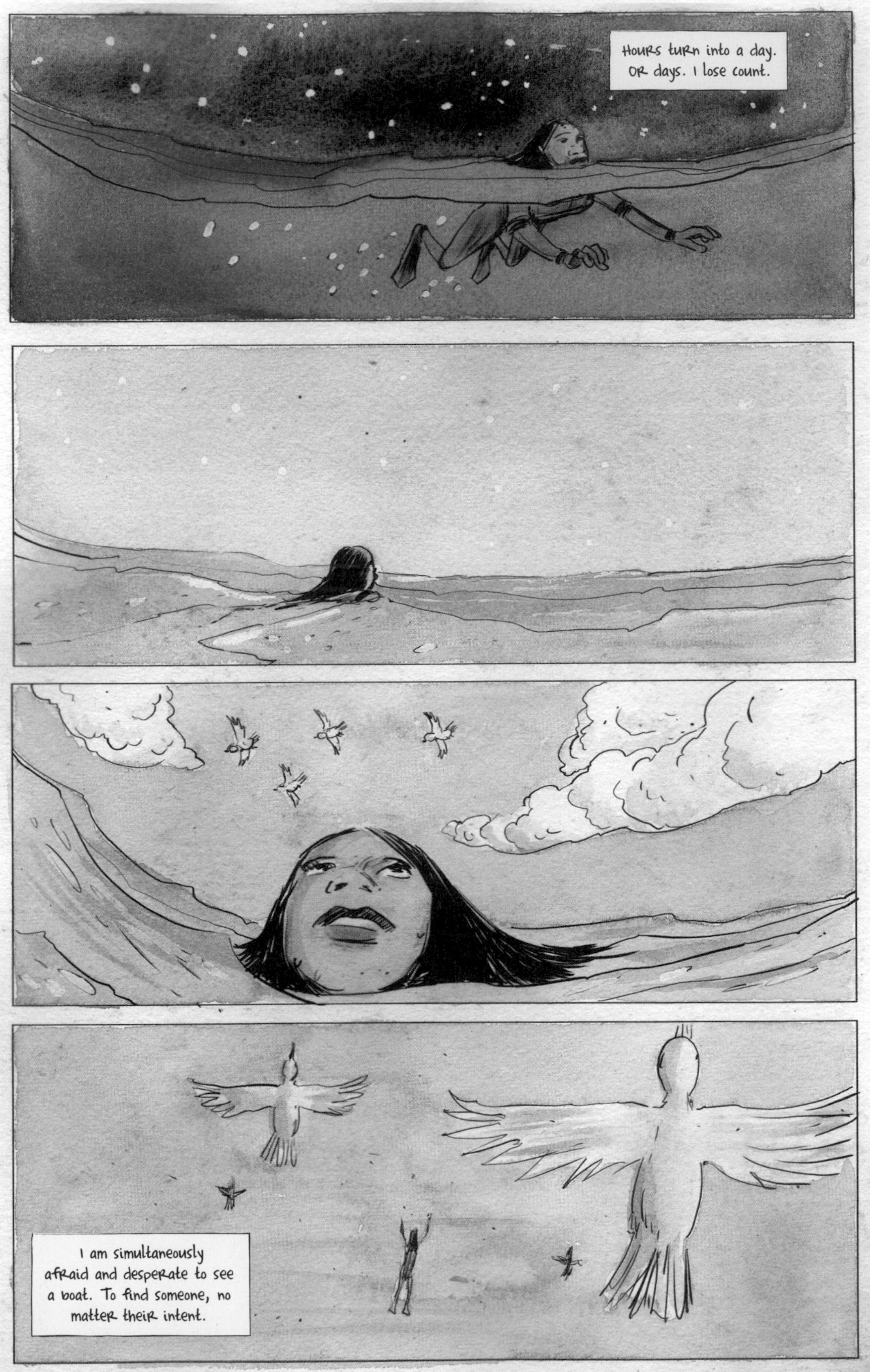

Hours turn into a day. Or days. I lose count.
I am simultaneously afraid and desperate to see a boat. To find someone, no matter their intent.

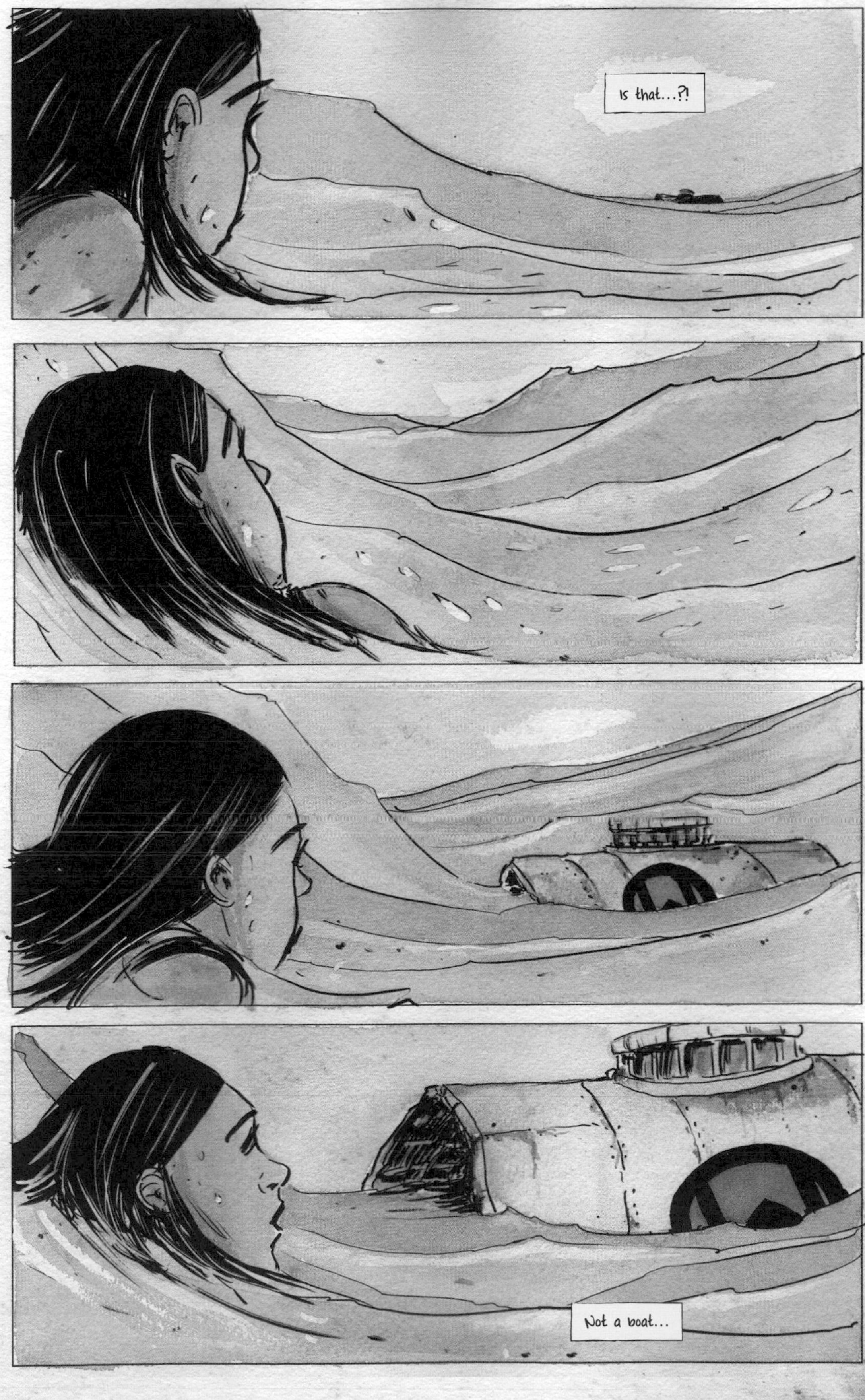
Is that...?!
Not a boat...

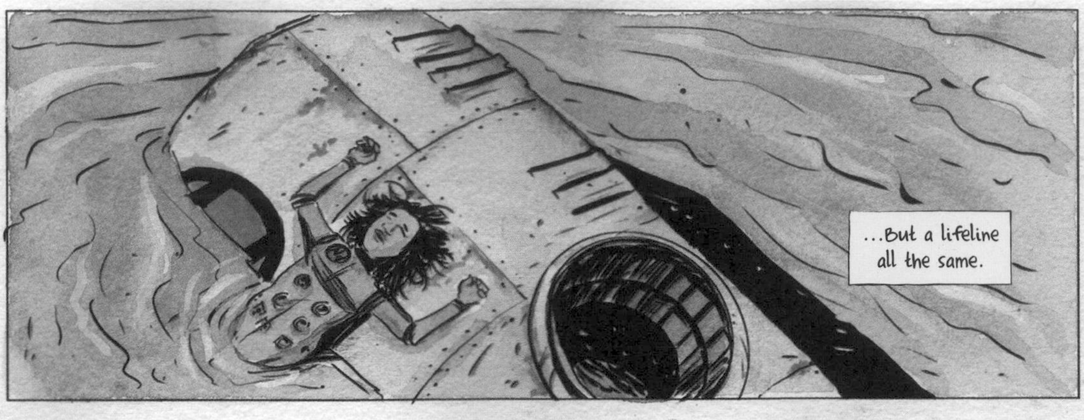
...But a lifeline
all the same.

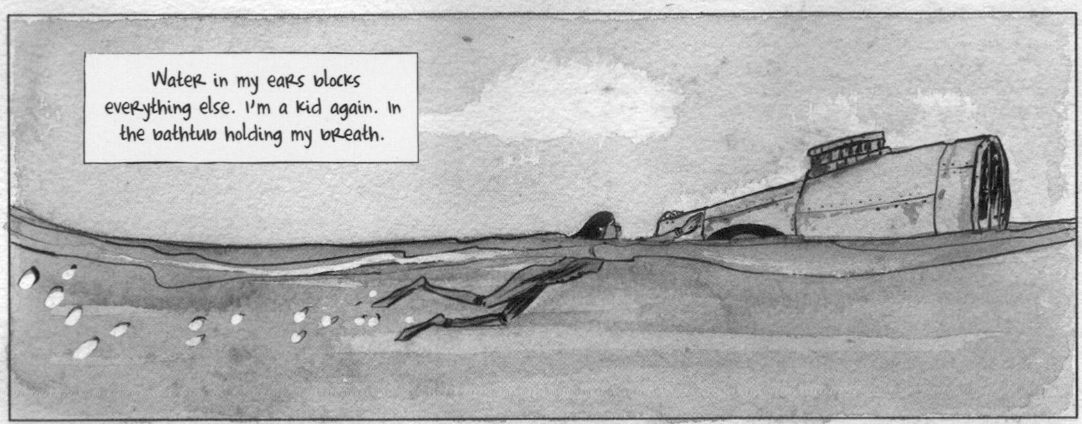
Water in my ears blocks
everything else. I'm a kid again. In
the bathtub holding my breath.

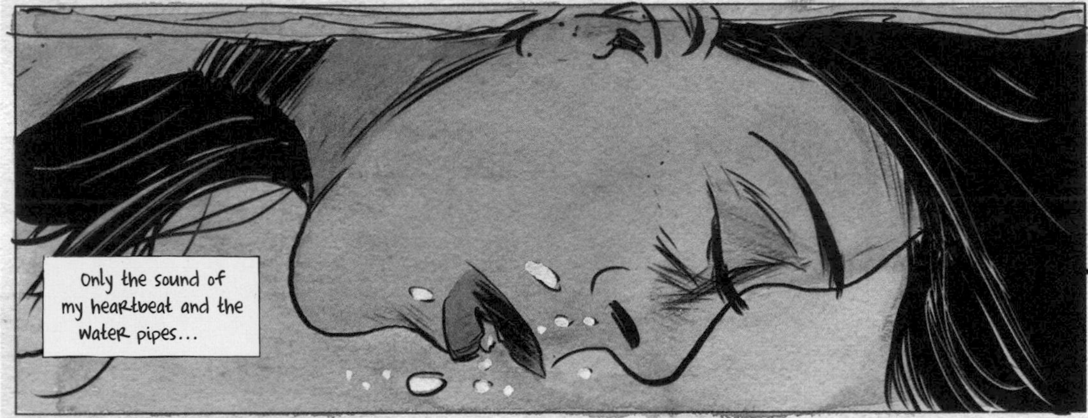
Only the sound of
my heartbeat and the
water pipes...

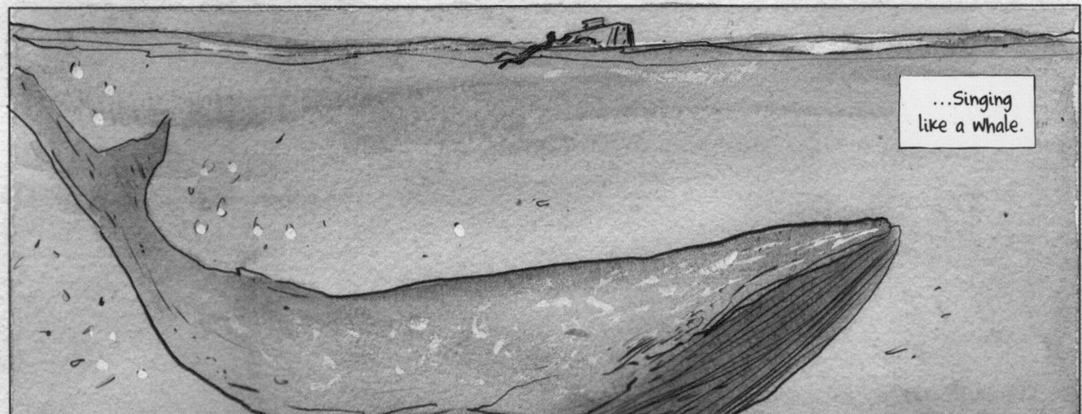
...Singing
like a whale.

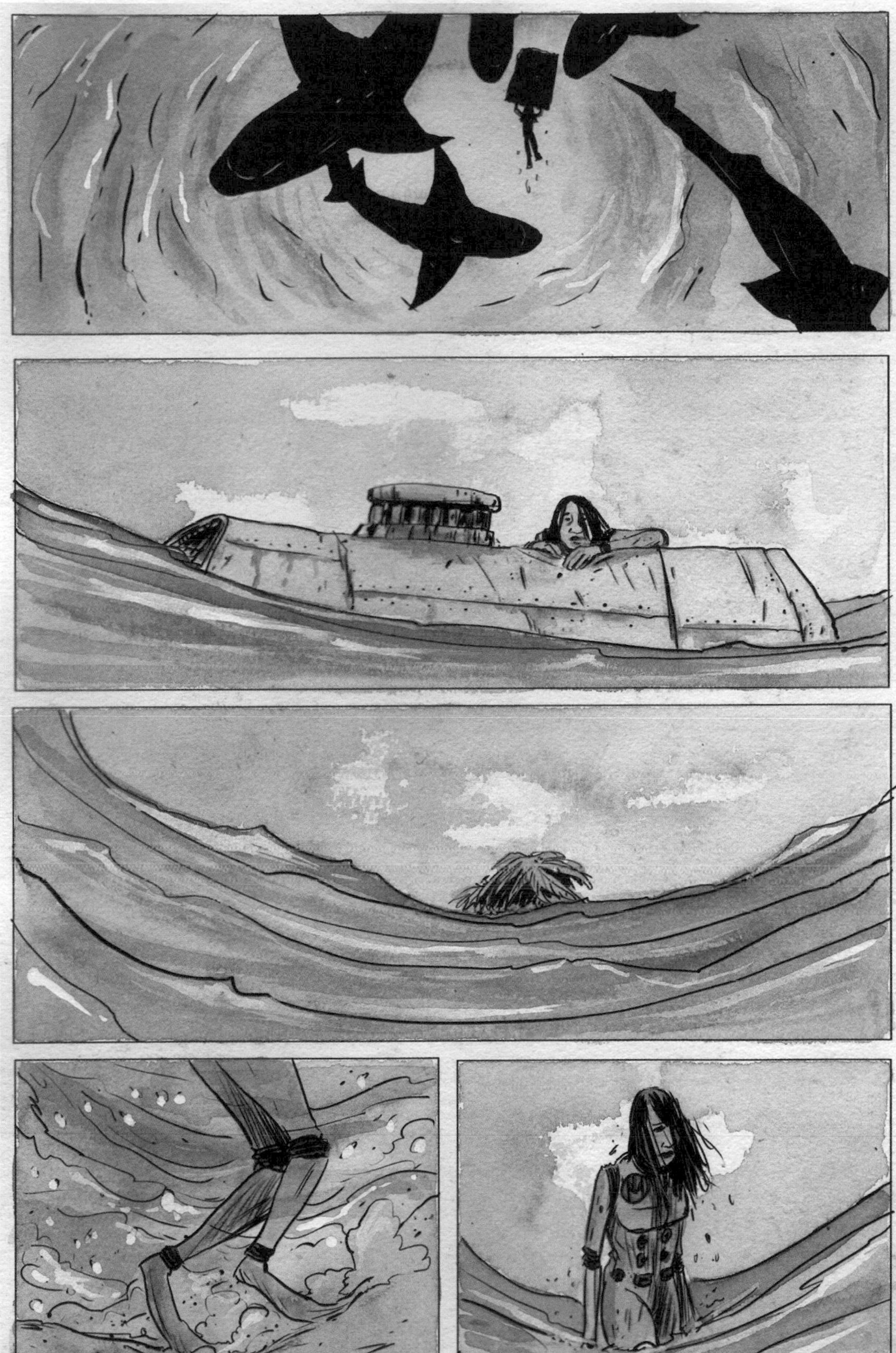

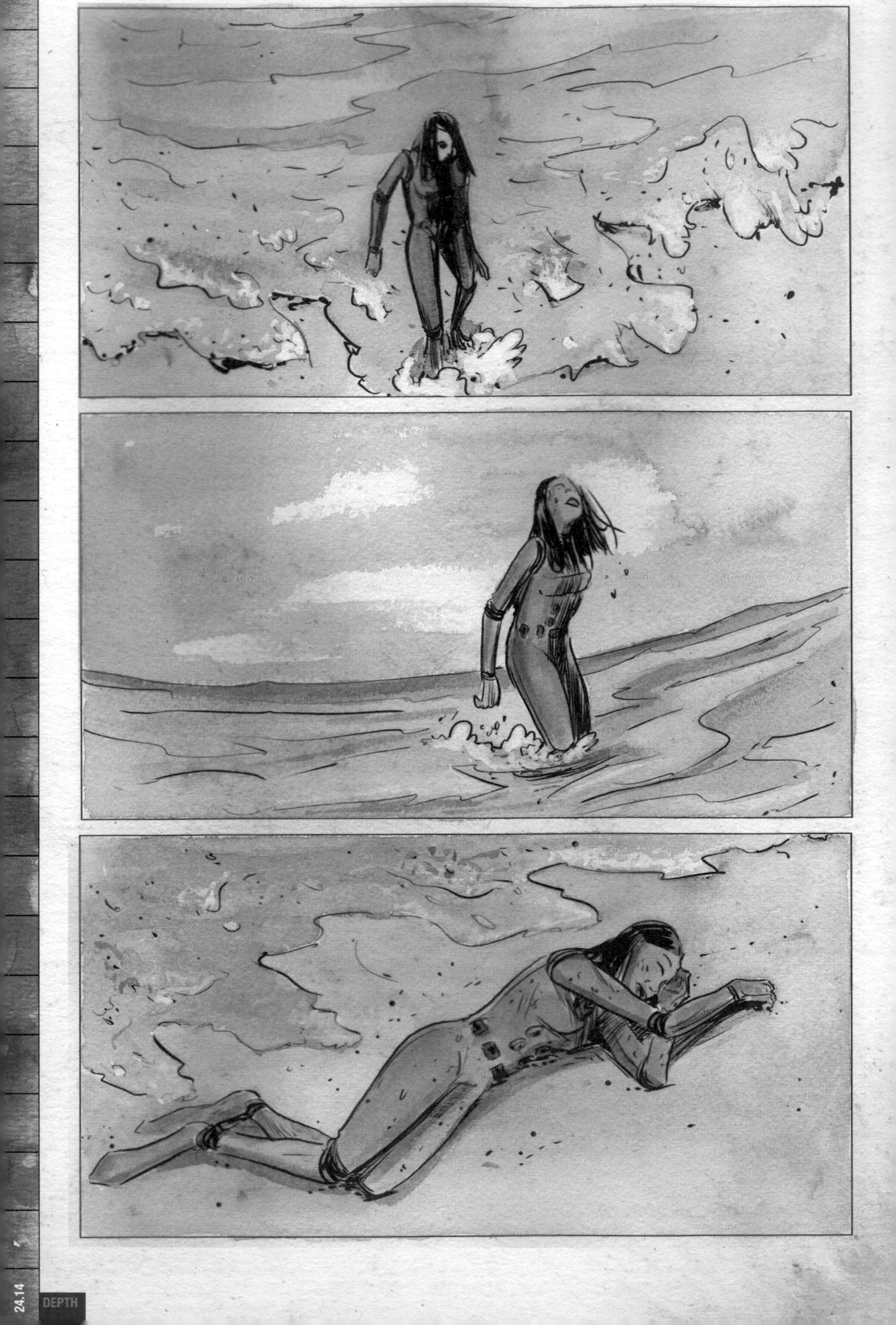

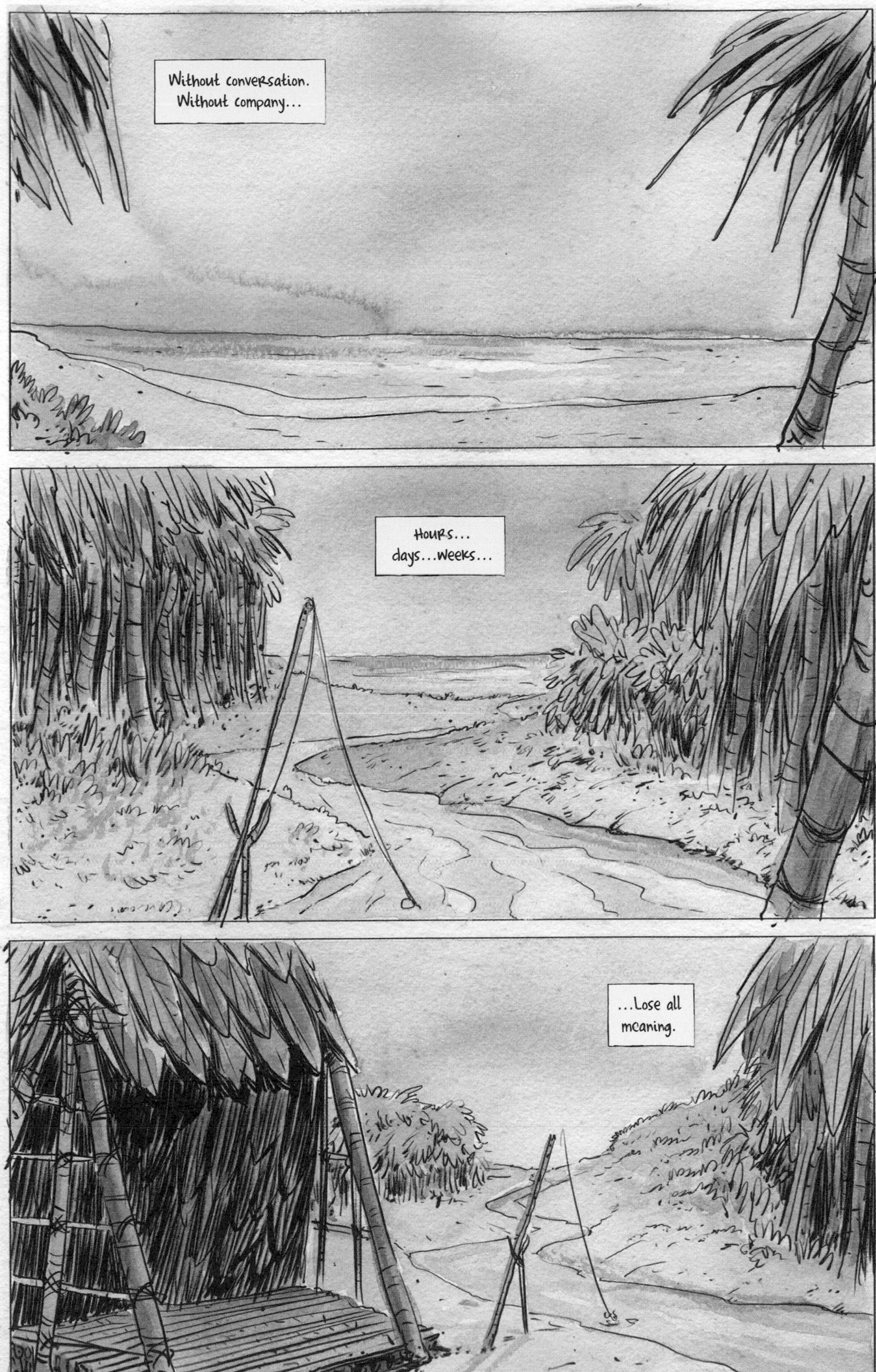
Without conversation. Without company...
Hours... days...weeks...
...Lose all meaning.

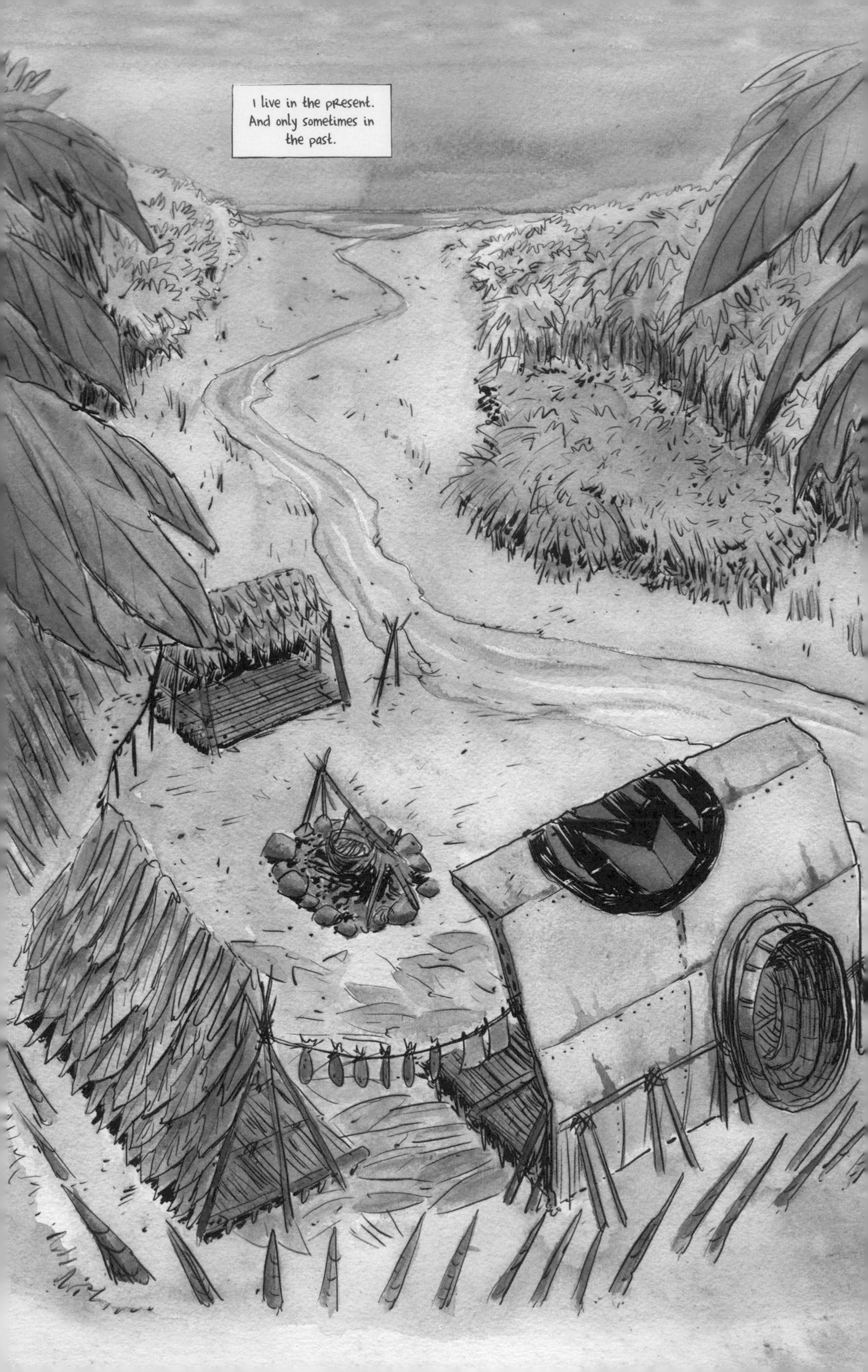
I live in the present. And only sometimes in the past.

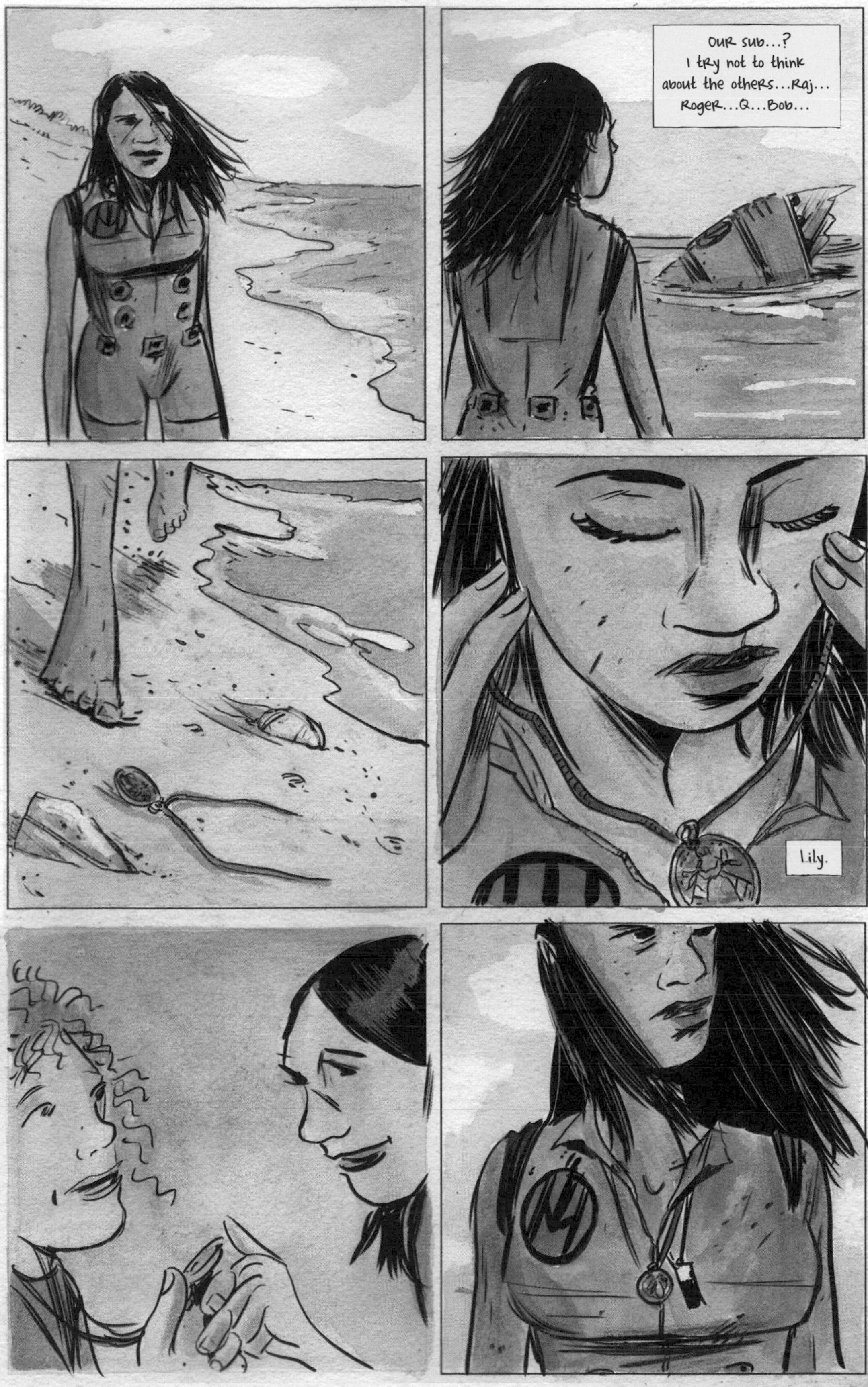
OUR SUB…?
I try not to think about the others…Raj…Roger…Q…Bob…
Lily.

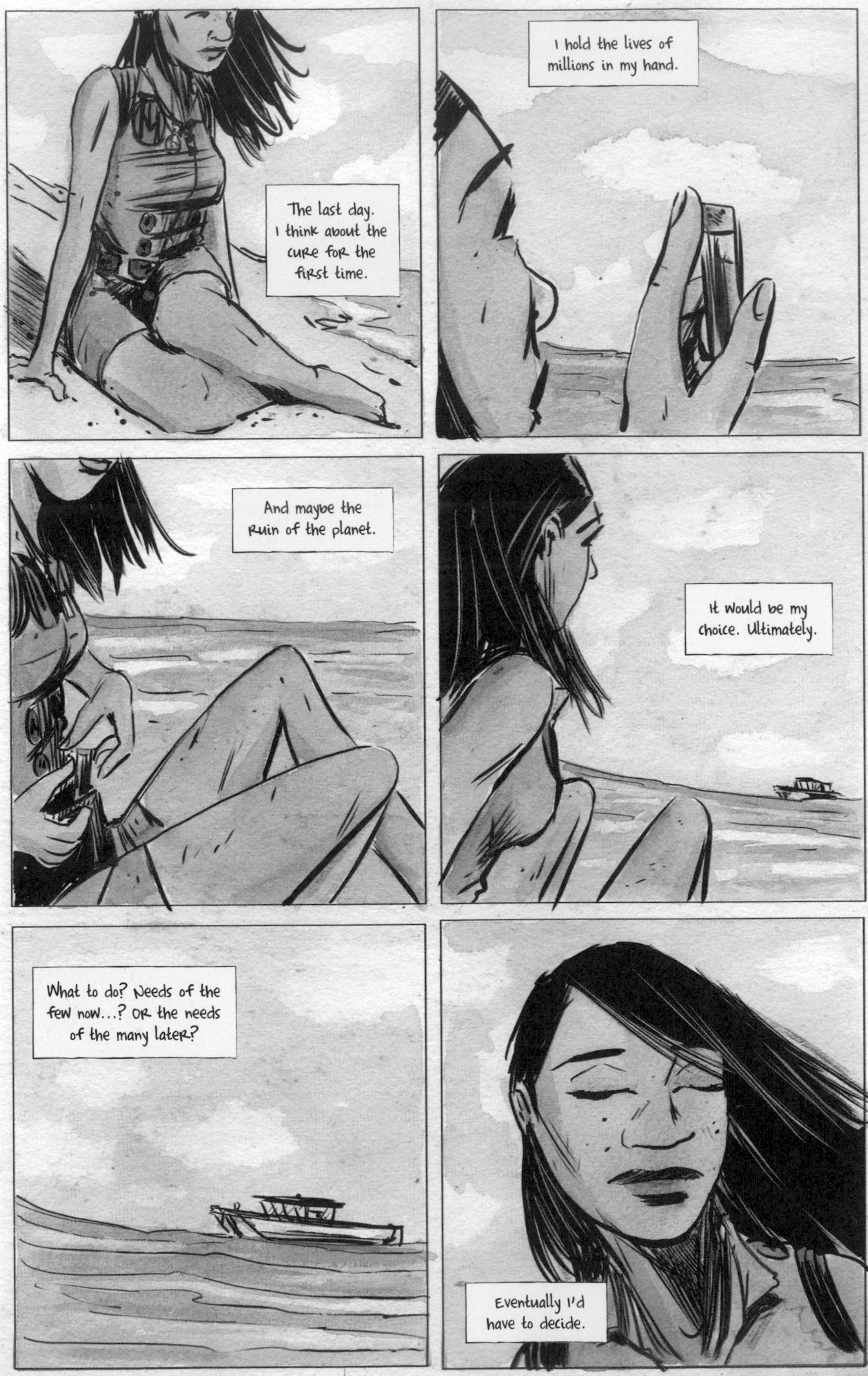
The last day. I think about the cure for the first time.
I hold the lives of millions in my hand.
And maybe the ruin of the planet.
It would be my choice. Ultimately.
What to do? Needs of the few now...? Or the needs of the many later?
Eventually I'd have to decide.

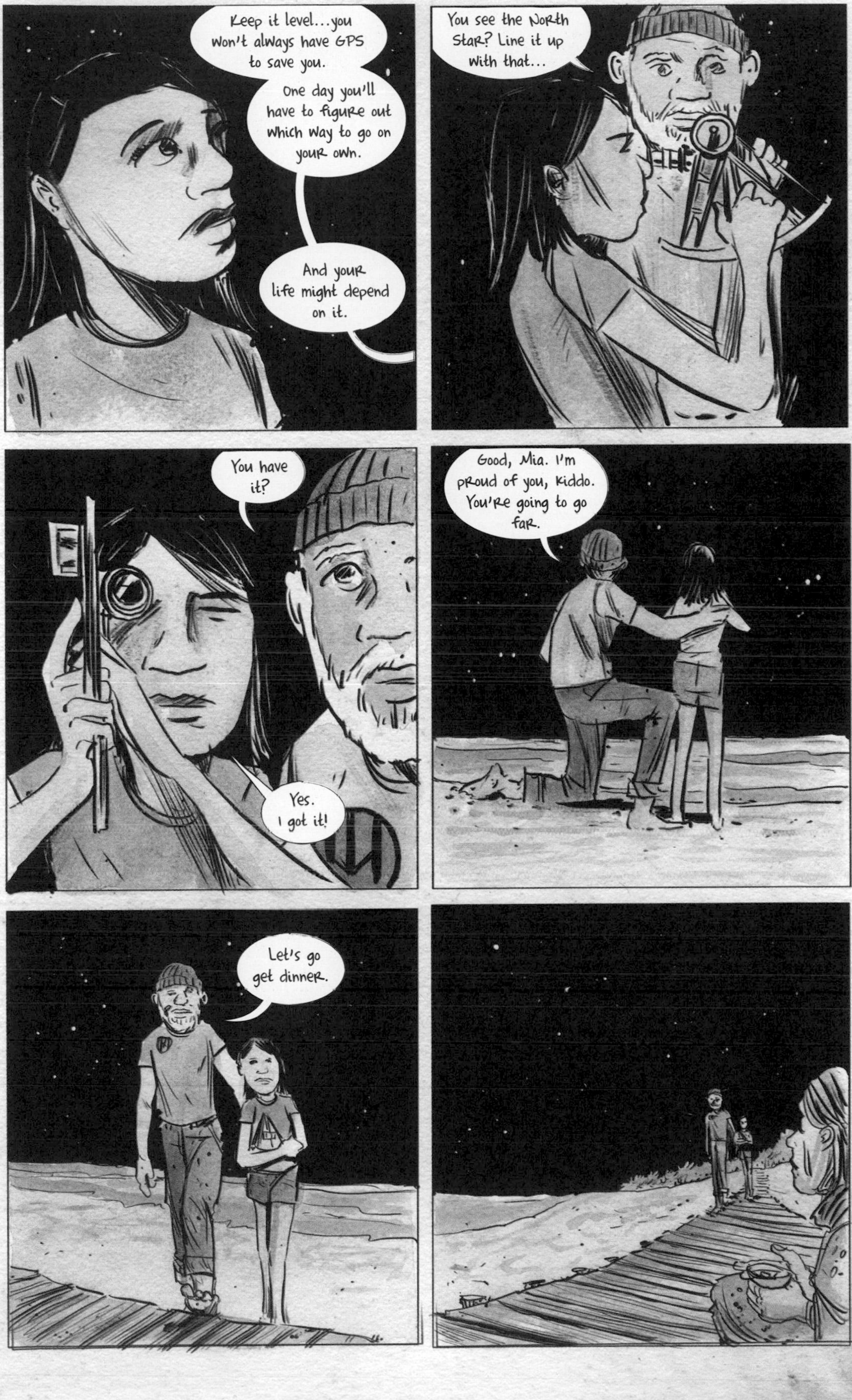
Keep it level...you won't always have GPS to save you.
One day you'll have to figure out which way to go on your own.
And your life might depend on it.
You see the North Star? Line it up with that...
You have it?
Yes. I got it!
Good, Mia. I'm proud of you, kiddo. You're going to go far.
Let's go get dinner.

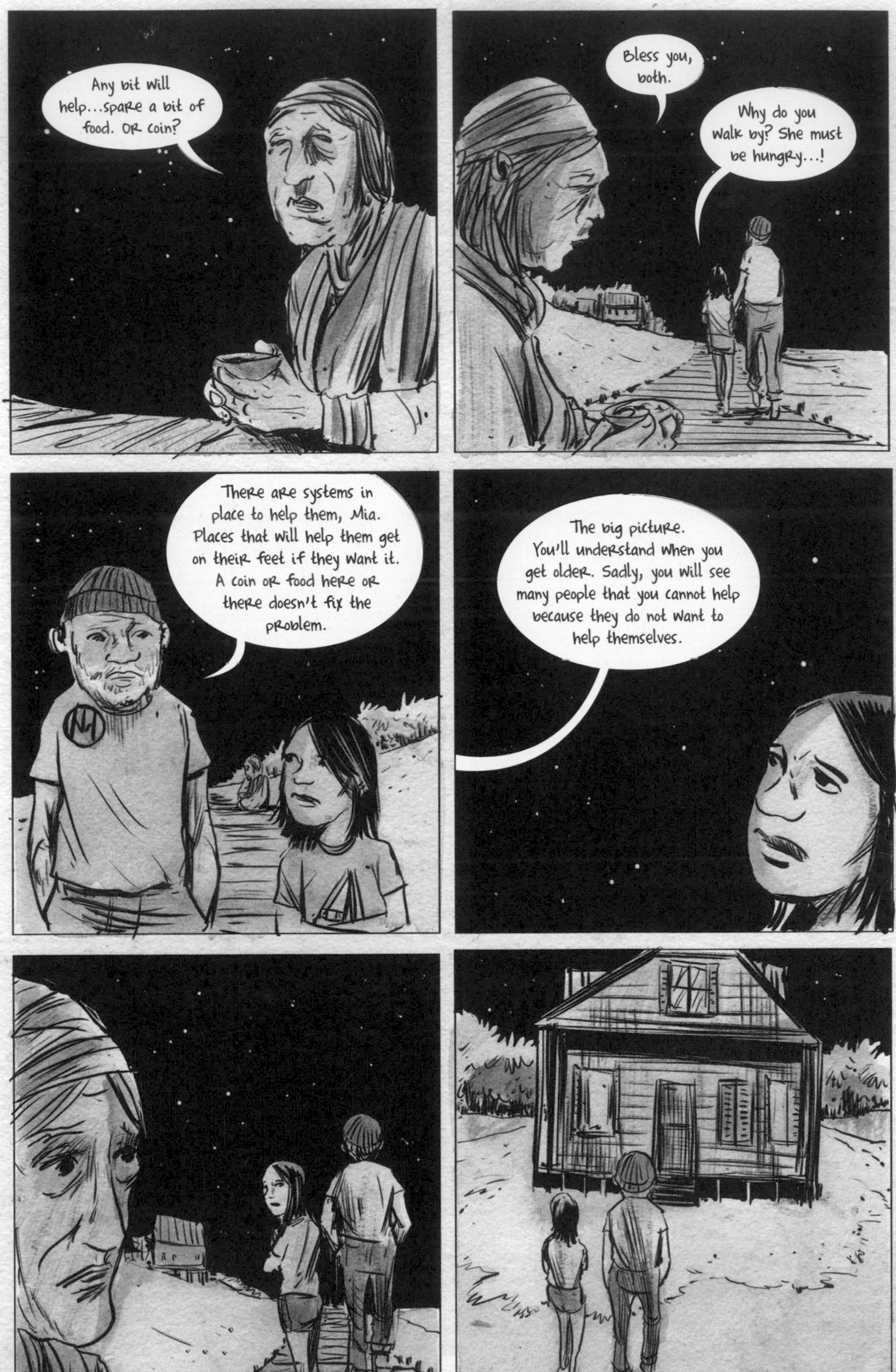
Any bit will help...spare a bit of food. Or coin?
Bless you, both.
Why do you walk by? She must be hungry...!
There are systems in place to help them, Mia. Places that will help them get on their feet if they want it. A coin or food here or there doesn't fix the problem.
The big picture. You'll understand when you get older. Sadly, you will see many people that you cannot help because they do not want to help themselves.

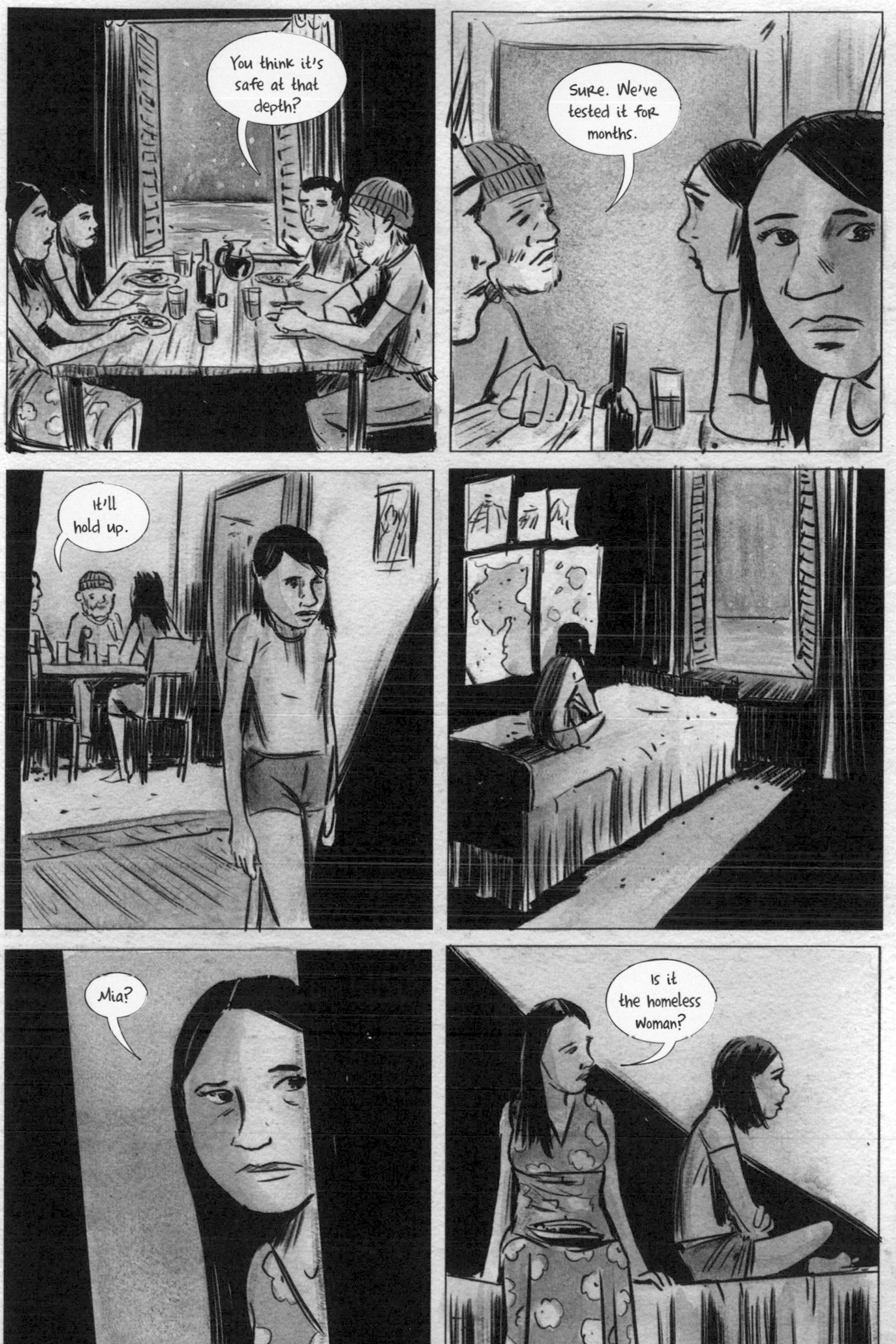
You think it's safe at that depth?
Sure. We've tested it for months.
It'll hold up.
Mia?
Is it the homeless woman?

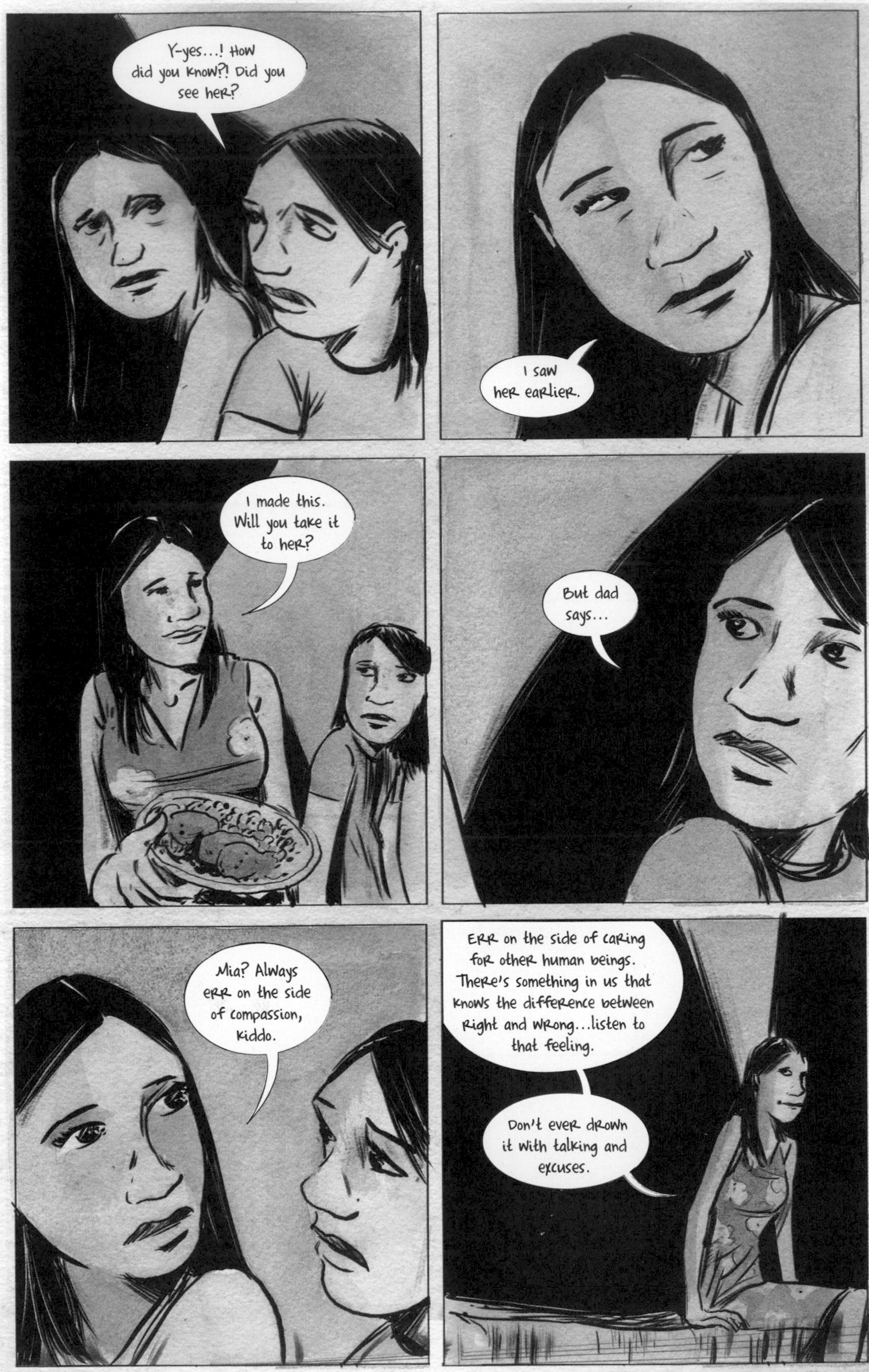
Y-yes...! How did you know?! Did you see her?
I saw her earlier.
I made this. Will you take it to her?
But dad says...
Mia? Always err on the side of compassion, kiddo.
Err on the side of caring for other human beings. There's something in us that knows the difference between right and wrong...listen to that feeling.
Don't ever drown it with talking and excuses.

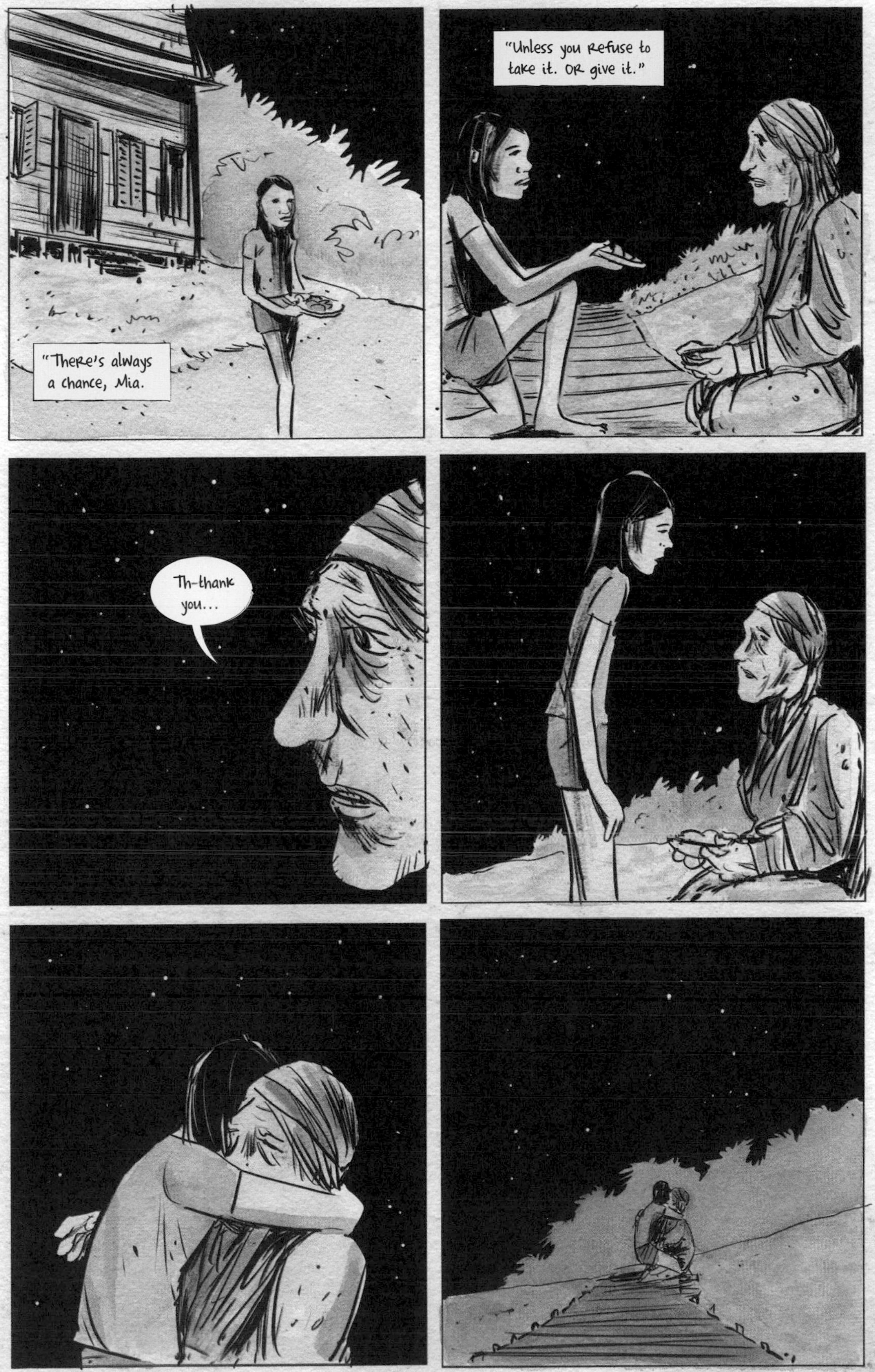
"There's always a chance, Mia.
"Unless you refuse to take it. OR give it."
Th-thank you...

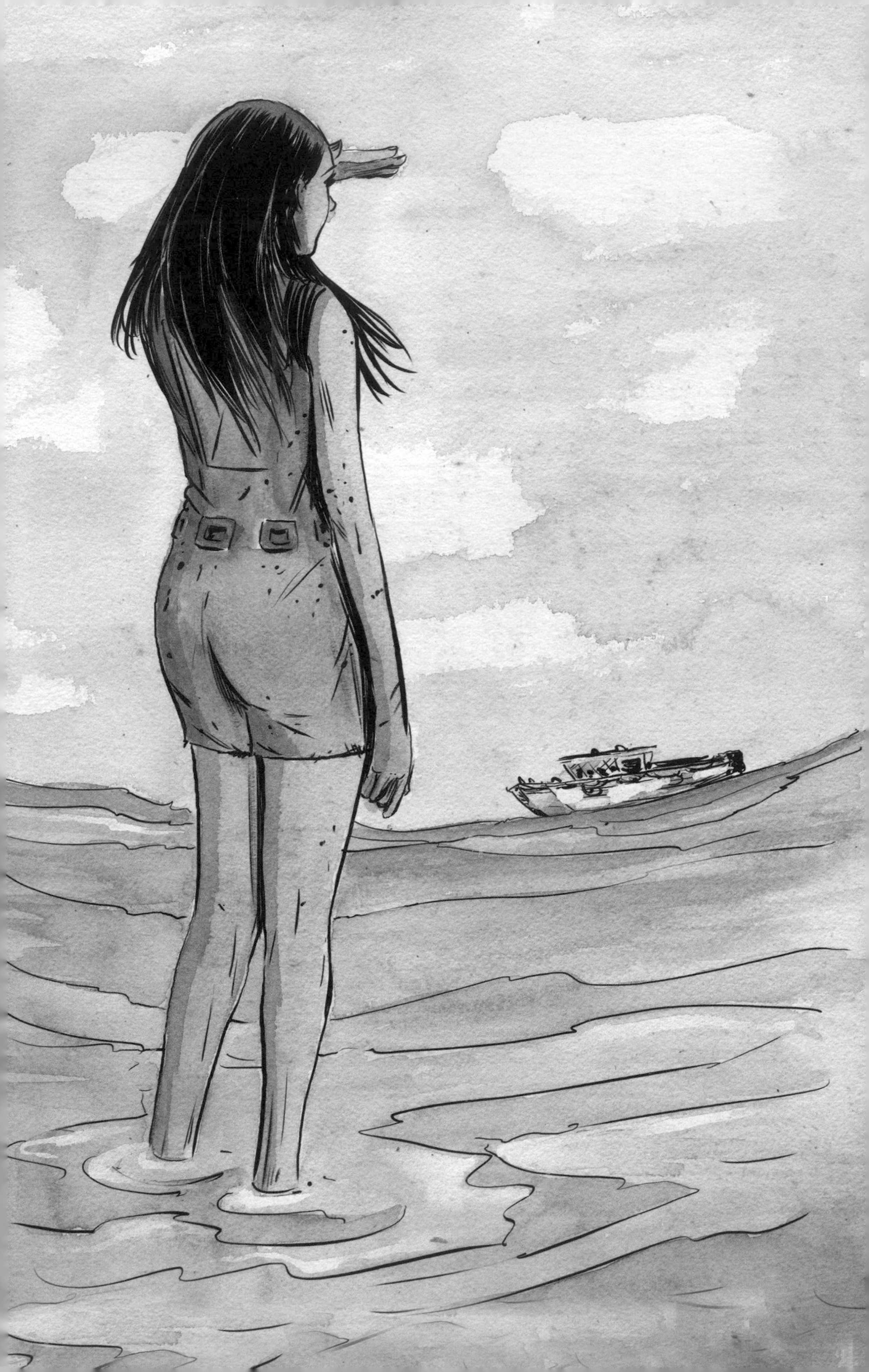

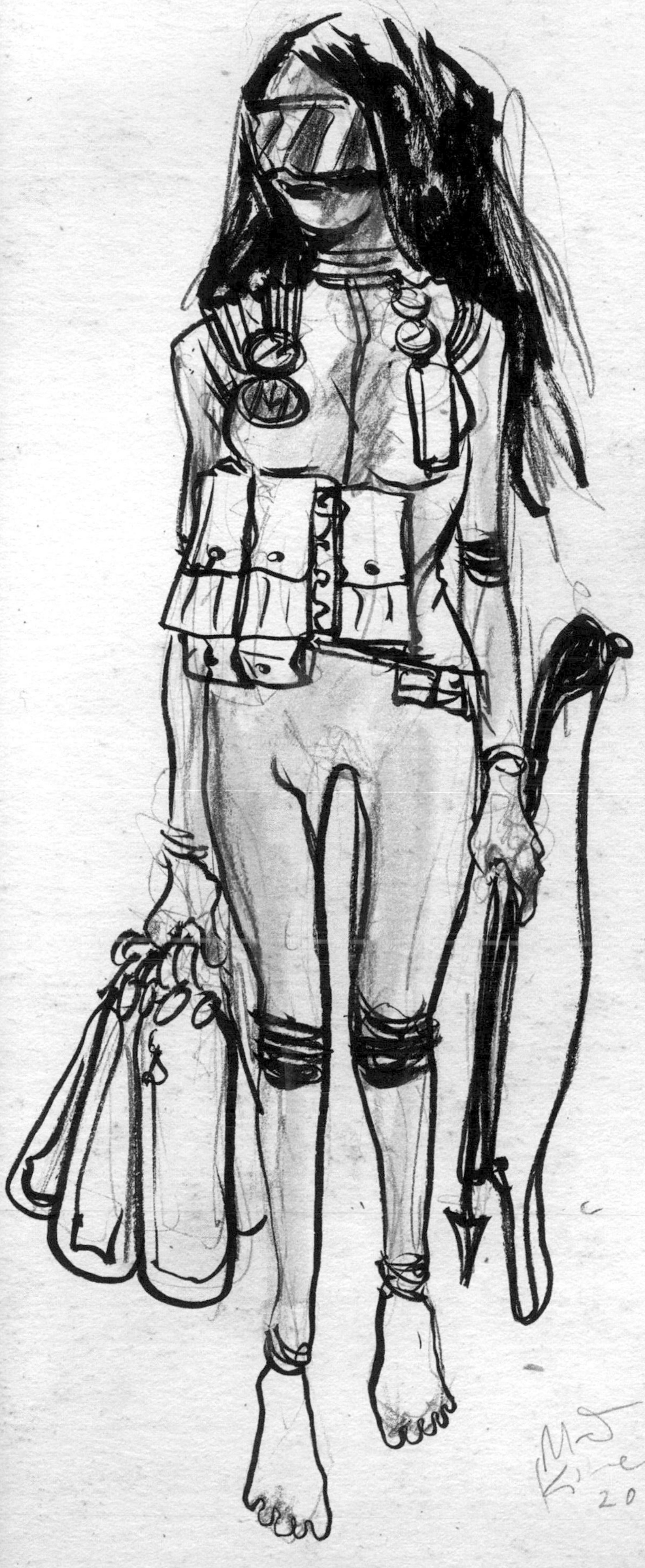

To safely ascend from a deep scuba diving session, divers must remain at each particular depth until sufficient gas has been eliminated from the body. Each of these is called a decompression stop.

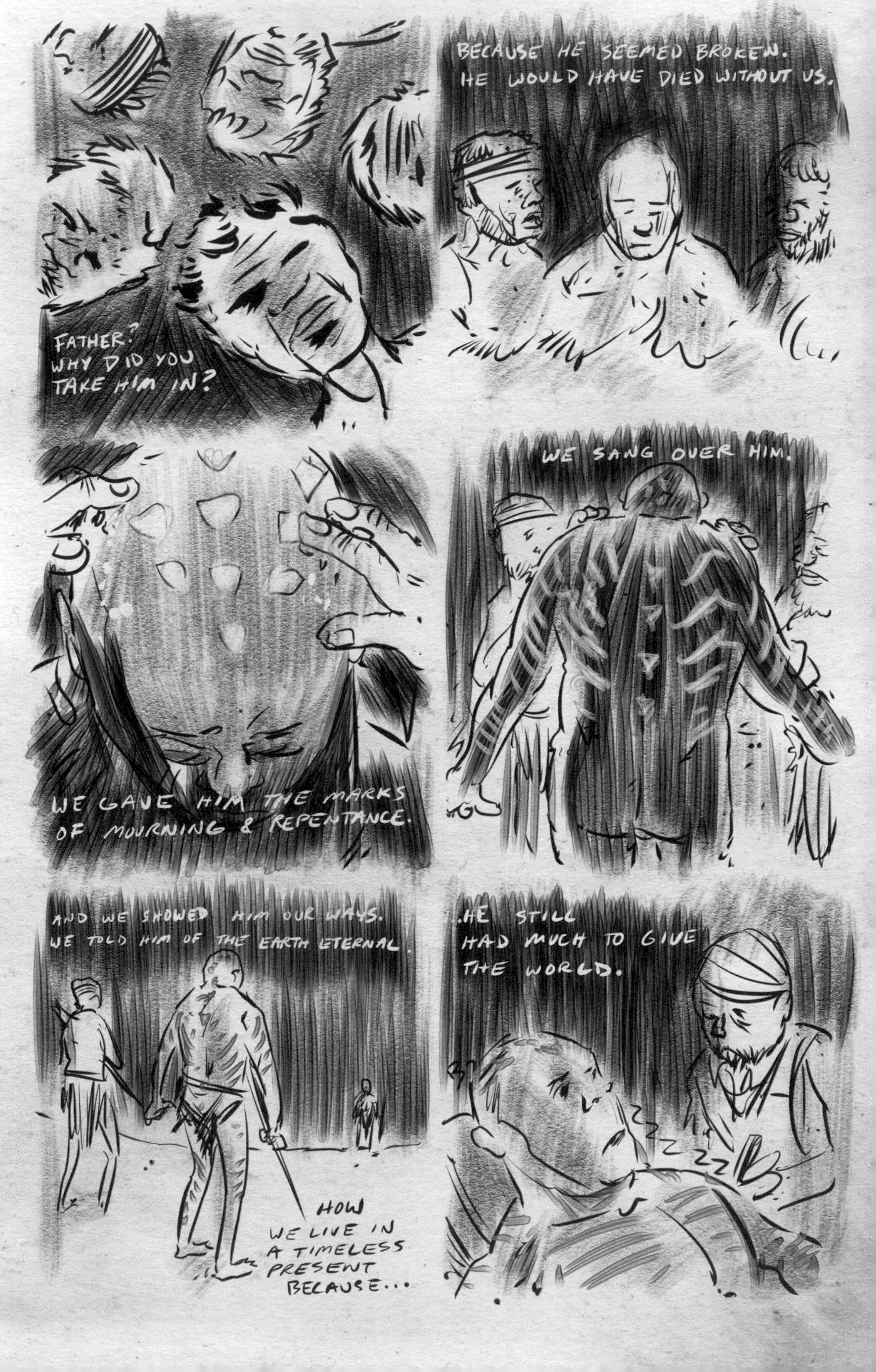
FATHER?
WHY DID YOU
TAKE HIM IN?
BECAUSE HE SEEMED BROKEN.
HE WOULD HAVE DIED WITHOUT US.
WE GAVE HIM THE MARKS
OF MOURNING & REPENTANCE.
WE SANG OVER HIM.
AND WE SHOWED HIM OUR WAYS.
WE TOLD HIM OF THE EARTH ETERNAL.
HOW
WE LIVE IN
A TIMELESS
PRESENT
BECAUSE...
HE STILL
HAD MUCH TO GIVE
THE WORLD.

The DIVERS' CHOICE

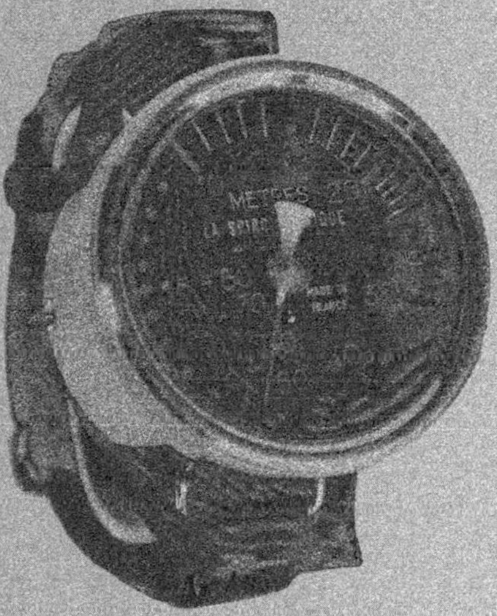

Model #PV-0604

Peavy offers deep sea diving instruments to meet the most demanding diving needs. They provide a vital measure of safety while adding interest and fun to diving.

Our Model #PV-0604 Combination Depth Gauge and Compass tells you at a glance exactly how deep you're getting and where you're headed, with a range of 0 to 80 metres in 5 metre increments.

This distinctive device sports a large, luminous dial and bullet-proof crystal with a handy glass-cutting insert. The PV-0604 also features a fully magnetized body which encases a gelignite charge with adjustable timer guaranteed to make a powerful impression.

And should you encounter a seriously challenging situation, extricate yourself by deploying our patented retractable Razor-tooth™ cable saw that also serves double duty as a garrote.

See this and other fine Peavy Survival Instruments at discerning marine supply houses & adventure outfitters world-wide. Guaranteed for the life of the wearer.

Peavy Survival Instrument Companies, Zanzibar, Vienna & Antikythera.

Peavy Survival Instruments

"For the Life Lived with Èlan & Verve"

Jeff Ryals

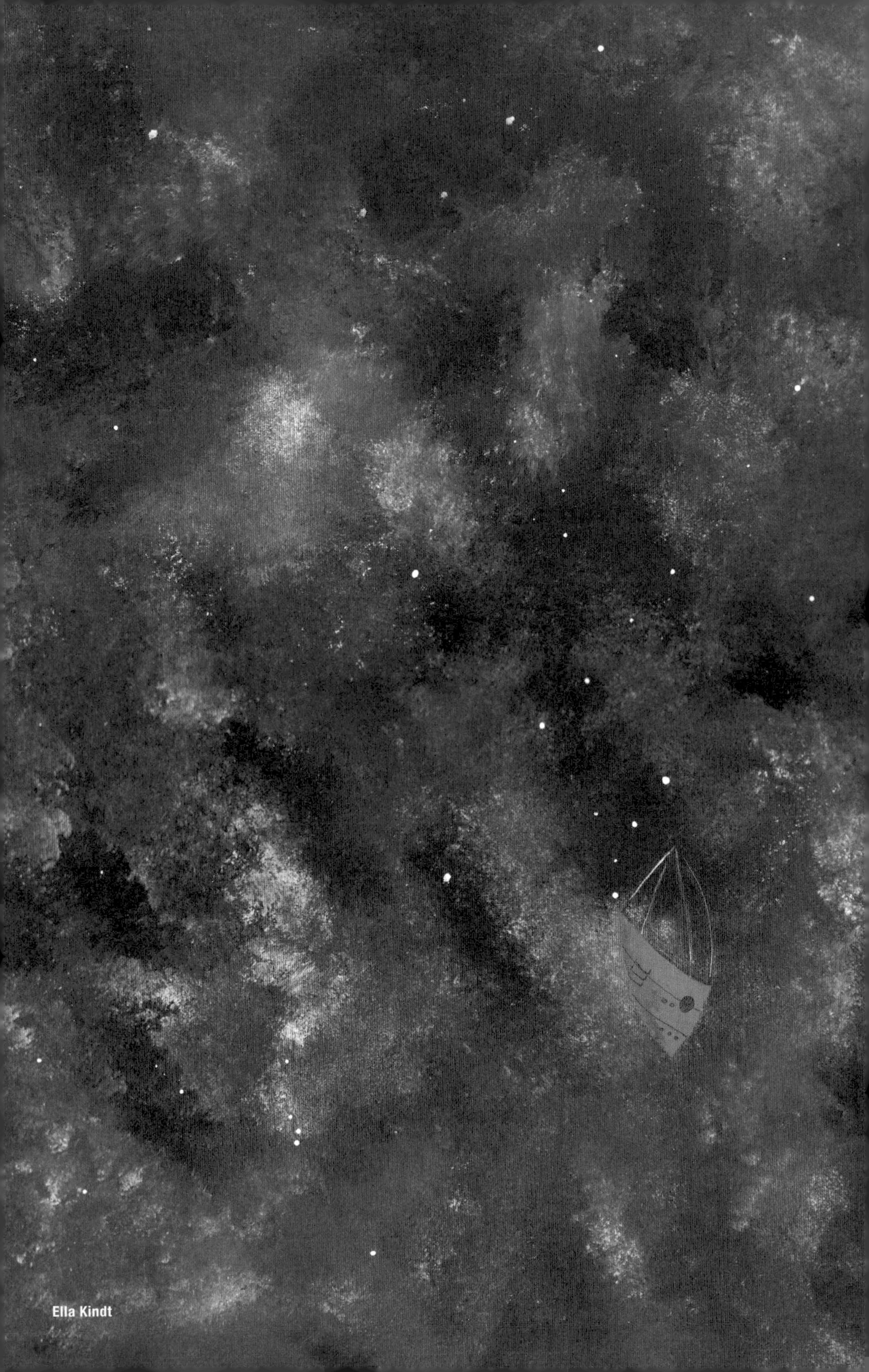
Ella Kindt

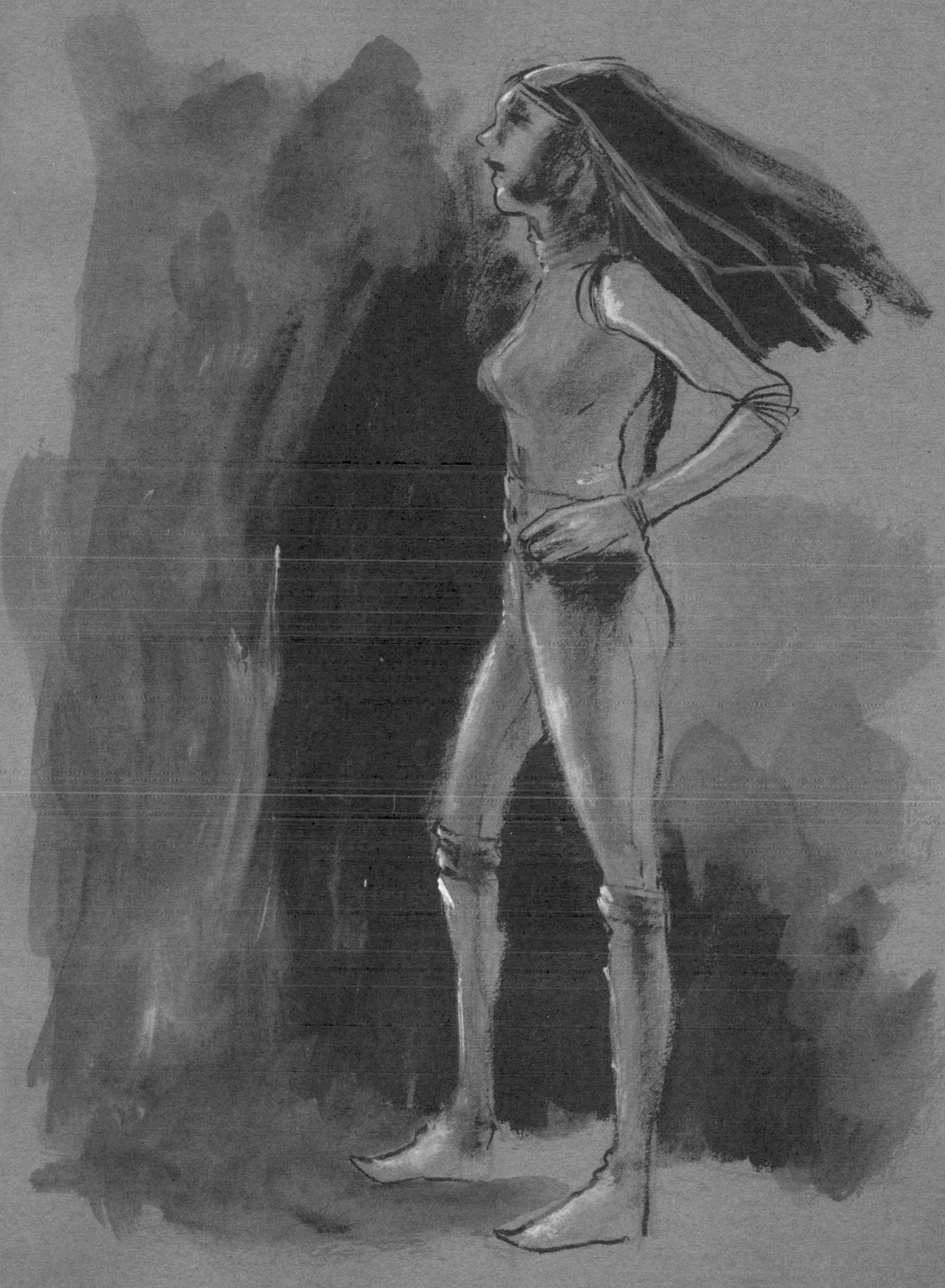

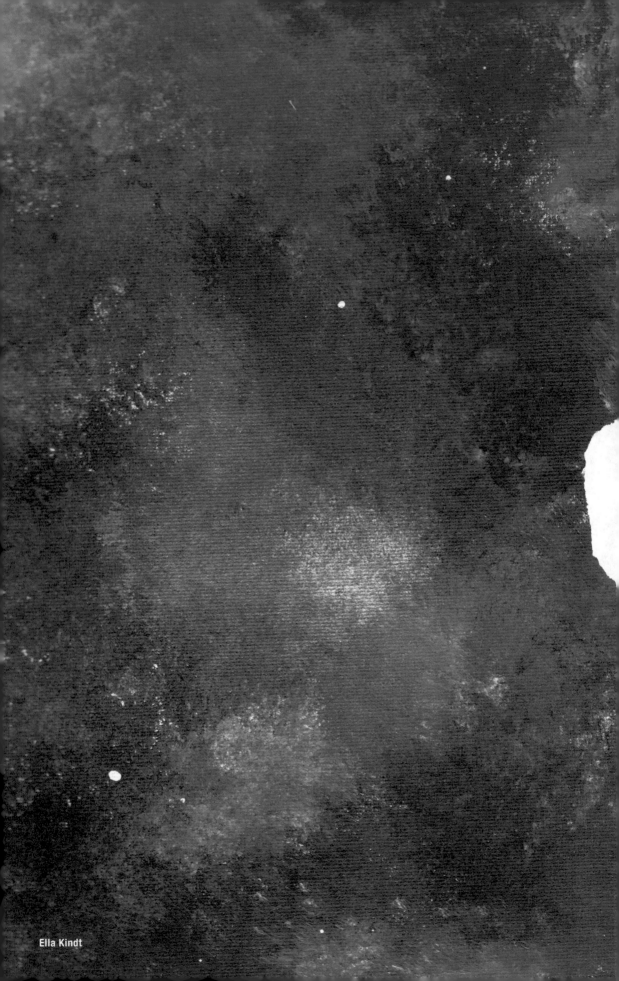

Ella Kindt